YANKELE

A Holocaust Survivor's Bittersweet Memoir

To Ellie my sisters best friend with pleasure and best wishes Yankele **Alex Gross** *Alex Gross*

University Press of America,® Inc.
Lanham · New York · Oxford

Copyright © 2001 by
University Press of America,® Inc.
4720 Boston Way
Lanham, Maryland 20706
UPA Acquisitions Department (301) 459-3366

12 Hid's Copse Rd.
Cumnor Hill, Oxford OX2 9JJ

Library of Congress Cataloging-in-Publication Data

Gross, Alex, 1928-
Yankele : a Holocaust survivor's bittersweet memoir / Alex Gross.
p. cm
1. Gross, Alex, 1928- 2. Jews—Ukraine—Mukacheve Metropolitan
Area—Biography. 3. Holocaust, Jewish (1939-1945)—Ukraine—
Mukacheve Metropolitan Area—Personal narratives. 4. Mukacheve
Metropolitan Area (Ukraine)—Biography. 5. Holocaust survivors—
Georgia—Biography. 6. Jews, Ukrainian—Georgia—Biography.
7. Georgia—Biography. I. Title.

DS135.U43 G774 2001   940.53'18'092—dc21   [B]   2001053075 CIP

ISBN 0-7618-2138-4 (pbk. : alk. paper)

"I try to master my grief; but my heart is in pain within me."
(Jeremiah 9:18)

To the memory of my beloved parents
Chayim Akiva and Etye Liebe

To the memory of my dear wife Linda

To the memory of my precious son Benjamin

"May their souls be bound up in the bond of eternal life."

CONTENTS

LIFE IN THE VALLEY OF THE
SHADOW OF DEATH

IMAGES

Following Page 107

Before the War
After the War
America
Family 2001

LIFE IN THE NEW WORLD

PREFACE

The photograph hangs in my study. It shows Alex Gross in a formal academic gown facing the president of Emory University, being hooded for his honorary degree by a dean. To the side stands the chairman of the Board of Trustees applauding. Alex's face shows the honor he feels as the degree of Doctor of Laws, *honoris causa,* is bestowed upon him and the citation is read out:

> Alex Gross, a survivor of Auschwitz and Buchenwald, teaches students about the depths of life as he tells the harrowing story of his stay in concentration camps during the Holocaust. Taken from his home in Hungary during the last years of World War II, he was confined in the ghettos, used as slave labor in Auschwitz, and then transported by open boxcar to Buchenwald, where he was liberated by the U. S. Army.... He became the first and foremost of the survivors in Atlanta to tell his story, including his own later tragedies. He regularly stuns classes at Emory with his narrative of faith, courage, and perseverance.... He teaches by example how to be a witness — to the horrors of humanity as well as to a deep faith in humankind.

Afterwards, we gathered for further pictures — of Alex and his daughters, of Alex and his brothers, of Alex and his wife, and of Alex and his friends. Who could have believed that this would happen — that one of the nation's most prestigious universities would confer an honorary degree on this survivor of the shoah,[1] on this man who never finished high school and never went to college? It was a great moment — for Alex and his family, for Emory University, for those of us who had worked to nominate him for this honorary degree, and indeed for all those who survived and for those who didn't.

I met Alex Gross shortly after I had come to Atlanta. My wife and I were at a performance in the local Jewish school which our children attended and our youngest son, Benjamin, who was three or four and very outgoing, was moving around the room talking to strangers and saying, "Hello. My name is Benjamin. What's yours?" One man, with a radiant smile on his face and a number on his arm, swept Benjamin up in his arms and said, "My name is Alex and I used to have a Benjamin like you." I did not know who this man was but later found out that it was Alex Gross, a survivor of the shoah who lived in town and who had lost his own son, Benjamin, in a construction accident a year or so before we came to Atlanta. Alex and our Benjamin struck up a long friendship; so much so that, when Benjamin as a teenager had trouble at home, we knew he would turn up on Alex's doorstep. They have loved each other ever since that day in Hebrew school over twenty years ago. How fitting, then, that Alex should receive his degree at the same time that Benjamin graduated from Emory College. And how fitting that Alex, still in academic robes, should mount the platform once again to be the one to hand Benjamin his diploma when the time came.

It was a Christian colleague, Jack Boozer — a professor of religion at Emory and a minister in the United Methodist Church — who persuaded me to teach the shoah. I did not want to do so. I thought the material was too raw, too difficult. But Jack was persuasive: "How can you as a young Jewish theologian, rabbi, and teacher, not teach the holocaust? Don't you owe it to the dead and the living to do so?" Jack was right and, after an appearance on campus of Simon Wiesenthal, I agreed to teach the course but only if Jack would teach it with me. For several years, we taught that class together. For most of our students, the highlight was when Alex Gross came to talk. Alex had been speaking about the shoah for a while. His story was narrated well. He was patient with questions. And he never hated anyone. He had (and has) no hatred in his heart. The students were left speechless, though often they would write moving letters to him after the class. The first time Alex came I introduced him. When the time came to thank him, I just couldn't. I was so moved by this man's pain and by the simplicity and goodness with which he told it that I couldn't talk. I motioned to Jack and he, always the warm colleague, thanked Alex for us and the class. The second year the same thing happened. And then again. The story and the man moved us all again and again including myself, who was an experienced teacher and rabbi, and who had heard the story before.

Alex Gross still comes to our classes as he does to dozens, perhaps hundreds, of other classrooms to tell his story. Jack Boozer has died and I no longer teach that course. But Alex's story remains. We videotaped it once. I'm glad we did that because I had noticed that he always tells it in the same sequence, with no notes, of course. This phenomenon turns out to be well known; it is called "the narratizing of trauma" and trauma victims in general do this. We also had the videotape transcribed and published, but the text did not get the wide circulation it deserved, nor was it the complete story.[2] I'm glad Alex decided to write his memoir so that we can now have more of the story though, as he indicates in the concluding interview, there are still parts he can't tell.

It was another Christian colleague, Fred Crawford — a professor of sociology at Emory — who persuaded me that we needed to take testimony from survivors but also from liberators of the camps. Fred had been an American aviator who had been shot down during the war. He was captured by the Hungarians who had been told by the nazis that all American pilots were Jews. His captors had put a noose around his neck and were about to hang him when they discovered the little gold cross Fred wore until his death. The discovery confused the mob and Fred was put into a prisoner-of-war camp not far from Dachau. When he was liberated by his fellow Americans, undernourished as he was, he demanded a jeep to go see Dachau, thus making himself one of the first to visit that camp. The experience never left him, and so Emory was among the first to interview liberators. Fred, as a former army person himself, could not be fooled. He also knew how to elicit the true stories from these men. Liberators, unlike survivors, had no community to rely upon. They had no one to talk to, no one to help them deal with the memories of opening up a boxcar and having emaciated corpses fall out. One of the most interesting artifacts to be revealed to us were booklets published by local army units right after the liberation with pictures and narratives. We republished them as fast as we received them.[3] We also acquired a file of pictures taken by soldiers, including one of the late General Eisenhower touring one of the camps.

It did not take long before we found one of the men who liberated Buchenwald, the camp in which Alex had last been interned. Mr. William Scott, an African-American solider and then editor of a prominent Atlanta African-American newspaper, agreed to be interviewed. Fred saw his chance and brought Alex and Mr. Scott together. I was present in the studio as a local television station taped the three-way interview for public broadcasting. It moved all of us in the control room to hear Alex talk about seeing men with black faces for the first time in his life — and as liberators from the hell of the concentration camps — "black angels" he called them, and we all wept. The tape still exists and is available to the public.[4] The Fred Roberts Crawford Witness to the Holocaust Project continued its work for many years and it is an honor to both men that the Project co-sponsors this book.

What is it about Alex's story that is so compelling? There are, after all, thousands of survivor stories. First, Alex's innate goodness and optimism, in spite of what he has experienced, radiate through his story. There is something so natural, so normal, so banal about Alex's goodness.[5] I doubt I would have been so positive about life if I had his experience, and I think this is true about almost all of us who hear and read this story. We stand in wonder at Alex's goodness, given his context. Second, there is the lack of finesse. Alex, who knew Elie Wiesel in the camps and continues to revere him, is no Elie Wiesel. There is no literary elegance to this narrative. It is simply life as lived by one man who went through so much.

Finally, as the reader will see, Alex's suffering did not stop with the horror of the shoah and the difficulties of reconstructing a life afterwards. His subsequent personal tragedies make his life sound like the story of the biblical Job — one deep tragedy after another. Do you know a Job? I do; I know Alex. But without Job's anger. And, again, how would I react in his place? Would I still believe in humankind? Would I still want to be Jewish? I doubt it, and yet Alex persists. His evolution from one who did not want to go to synagogue after the war to one who is active in his community, goes to synagogue regularly, and contributes time and money to dozens of Jewish and other organizations is itself a story of recovery from trauma that is remarkable. We who hear and read his story stand dumbfounded before Alex's courage in facing what he faced. We stand awestruck by his persistence in life, in goodness, and in community. This makes his story unusual.

There is another issue that haunts those of us who listen. Alex did not give up his faith in God. How is this possible? How can someone who has seen what he has seen still believe in God, especially in God's goodness? Like all modern Jews, I faced this question and it troubled me more than any other for decades. Finally, I wrote a book in which I argued that, since the Jews did not deserve the shoah and since God is ultimately responsible for what happens in history as well as in nature, God must be an abusing God.[6] I argued, as best I could, that we cannot get rid of God as committed Jews but that we must confront the truth — that the shoah constitutes abusive behavior by God — and that we must say this — to ourselves and to God, in theology and in prayer. Alex was not much impressed. The language was too strong for him. This issue was not his. And we continued to pray side by side in the orthodox synagogue we both attended in Atlanta. One Yom Kippur, it struck me fully and I wrote a poem in Hebrew and in English:[7]

Praying Next to a Survivor
Yom Kippur, 5747

We recited confession
I was astounded
What was he confessing, and why?
Who was asking forgiveness from whom?

We recited the penitential prayers
I saw
the shadow that crossed his face
memories welling up from the depths.

"Therefore, put fear of You into all Your creatures" —
an anger hidden in his body
Why were they not afraid?
Why did He not put fear into them?

We recited the Shma
I was ashamed
Who am I to recite Shma next to him?
What is my faith next to his?

"Our Father, our King" —
he has the advantage
Job, faithful servant
'How horrible are the terrible deeds You have set aside for those who fear
    You
An eye other than Yours has seen, O God.'

"Act for the sake of sucking infants who have not sinned" —
Were they my children?
Woe unto the eyes that saw such things.
I do not want to see; I cannot
He too does not want to see but he is compelled, and I am compelled in his
    compulsion.
My son ...... my daughter ......

"If as children, if as servants ..." —
Lord, we really and truly only wanted to be good children, loyal servants

Even now
    "we are Your children and You are our Father"
    "we are Your servants and You are our Sovereign"
Have mercy on us.
Have pity.
Heal us and we shall be healed.

A book like this requires the support of many people. First, I wish to thank Alex's family for their warm support of him and for their critique of his work. Without them, he could not do what he does for so many. All of us connected with shoah studies, especially those of us who have come to love and respect the survivors, owe a special debt of gratitude to Elie Wiesel for he, more than any other, has given them, and us, the courage to tell and to publish their stories. Without his example and his support, we would all abandon this work too quickly. Finally, special thanks also go to Ms. Colleen Goidel who edited the lion's share of the English manuscript; to Ms. Pat Ledford who typed and retyped the text; to Ms. Susan Peabody who prepared the camera-ready copy; and especially to colleagues who have offered advice, some of which is incorporated in the editorial notes written by me which are scattered through the text.

In gratitude for the witness of Alex Gross and in deep personal friendship, we are proud to offer to the public Alex Gross' autobiography. His story, while one of many, is unique and the example of his life is very special. This book is supported by a grant from the Fred R. Crawford Witness to the Holocaust Project. Fred and Alex were good friends and I am glad that the Project is involved in this undertaking.

David R. Blumenthal
Jay and Leslie Cohen Professor of Judaic Studies
Emory University
Atlanta, GA
Hanuka 5706 / December 1999

LIFE IN THE VALLEY OF THE SHADOW OF DEATH

CHAPTER ONE

MY LIFE IN PALANOK

I was born on September 18, 1928, to Chaim and Ettele Gross in the Carpathian Mountain region of democratic Czechoslovakia — a very diverse place where every nationality, religion and ethnic group enjoyed equal status. My Yiddish name was Yankele (Jacob), and I was the sixth son.[8] I had five older brothers, Fishi (Phillip), Benjumin (Ben), Bendi (Bernie), Beresh (Bill), and Smilku (Sam). We were blessed with a sister Rajziko (Rosalyn), who was born two years after me.

Our small village of Palanok, which adjoined the city of Munkach, was remote, poor, and very backward by American and even European standards. But despite our lack of material goods, my childhood was rich with the love of my family. I felt very blessed with loving parents and siblings, wonderful grandparents, many aunts, uncles, cousins, and good friends. We lived in a friendly neighborhood and our family got along with everyone.

Munkach had a majority of very religious Jews. Our village overflowed with true pride in "Yiddishkeit" — Jewish traditional life. We went to the city often for our needs and for social as well as religious reasons. We felt content with our neighbors of German, Russian, and other nationalities, and we were proud of our democratic Czech government and our freedom. We even had a few Gypsies who moved in and out of our area but never actually settled in. As children we had heard stories that the Gypsies kidnapped children, so we were a little afraid of them. Jews comprised ten to fifteen percent of Carpathia, and as much as 40 to 60 percent of nearby Munkach. We were treated equally and felt safe among this melting pot of ethnic and religious groups. Our daily life was very busy, and we felt secure and content.

My Father was born and raised in the Carpathian mountain village of Lavik, a farming and grape-growing area on the other side of Munkach where the Gross family resided. My Mother's parents, the Lebovitzes, were born in Palanok, as were my Mother and her siblings. Our village was also surrounded by mountains. For the most part, people grew their own fruits and vegetables, and raised chickens and other animals.

Our region was nestled between Hungary, Poland, and Romania, close to Russia. The Carpathian Mountain area was filled with streams, rivers, fruit trees, vegetables, and dense forests. It was rich in coal and other minerals. The weather was rainy in summer and icy cold in winter. Snow began falling in early autumn and stayed till late spring. The Latorca River, which ran adjacent to our village, froze about a foot thick in winter. As kids we would tie a bit of metal to the bottoms of our shoes to skate on the frozen river. Snowball fights, sledding down the hill in homemade sleds, and making snowmen were some of our favorite pastimes. In early spring we would cut the ice up, store it underground, and use it all summer to keep food from spoiling. Of course, in summertime the river was the only place to swim.

Our house, which was also my Father's tailor shop, fronted on the only main road in our village of Palanok. It was made by hand from blocks of mud, horse manure, and straw. We had no paved streets. The homes had earthen floors and no running water. We used outhouses and had a hand-dug water well. Of course, there were no bathtubs or showers and we had very few clothes.

When I was about six years old, my parents assigned my brother, Sam and me the task of supplying firewood to heat the house and water for cooking. We were also charged with lighting and keeping the coal fire going to heat the pressing iron in the tailor shop. I had to blow air at the coals by mouth to get them burning so that the irons would be hot enough to press garments when the tailors needed them. It was a difficult task, and not my favorite as we worked many hours inhaling coal soot.

Although we were young, we skillfully chopped wood and drew water from the well, then carried the heavy buckets to the house. Sometimes a goose or rooster would chase me and scare me, and I would spill the water. My older brothers thought this was funny; I would get angry at the goose for scaring me and at my brothers for laughing.

Electricity was scarce in our area at that time. Most people could not afford it; it was certainly too expensive for us. When I was eleven, we finally had electricity in the front of our home for use in my Father's shop. This is where Mother, Father, sister Rosalyn, and I slept. We had no electricity in the back of the shop, where we used foot-pedalled sewing machines, or in the building where the older boys and employees slept. Like most people, we used kerosene lamps or candles for lights.

My Father, Chayim Akiva (known as Hugo), was strict but very devoted to his family. His life centered on his work, religion, the synagogue, and his children. If he wasn't at work in his tailor shop, he was in the synagogue or with us. One thing he always taught us was to think for ourselves. For instance, he permitted us to grow our hair long and didn't force us to wear *payes* (long side locks) like most of the religious Jewish boys in Palanok. We felt very proud to be given this privilege. Nor did Father make us attend synagogue services every morning and evening, as many of our Orthodox Jewish friends were required to do. Of course, we had to work six days a week from early morning till very late. However, in other ways he was very insistent, especially regarding Sabbath observance. His employees, who were just like part of the family, were also expected to attend the holiday Sabbath services every Friday evening and Saturday morning, as well as on all Jewish holy days. He not only made sure that we kept the Sabbath holy, we also kept a very strict kosher home — using separate milk and meat dishes, pots and pans, silverware, etc. We had to wash hands and say the special prayers for fruit, water, bread, and so on every time we sat down to eat. All Jewish holidays were kept according to *halacha* (Jewish Law) just as it had been practiced for thousands of years.

My Father was known as the best tailor in the entire Carpathian region. He specialized in quality and personalized tailoring, and his suits were hand-sewn, stitch by stitch. In today's market these would be several thousands of dollars. He was trained in Vienna, Austria where, in that era, the world's best-tailored clothing was made. People came from far away to have him craft their clothing. I was very proud of his far-reaching reputation.

Father tried to train us in his trade. He dreamed that we would become famous tailors and eventually take over the business. Back then a tailor earned a good wage, even better than here and now. Although he had other dependable men working for him, he still dreamed of giving apprenticeship to his own "flesh and blood." As each son reached ten years of age, he had to help in the tailor shop. Father felt that this would give us a feel for the profession; plus he needed the help, with fifteen to twenty mouths to feed.

My parents showed all of their children at a young age the value of hard work, self-sufficiency, and living up to one's responsibilities. Our family's unity was of utmost importance. They also taught me to treat elders, friends and strangers respectfully. I was proud of how my Father never failed to help someone in need and never considered himself superior to anyone. When he met strangers or even beggars passing through our village after synagogue services, he made sure they would not go hungry — especially on the Sabbath. This was Father's way. Regardless of how little chicken there was, or how many cups of water *Mamika* (Mother) had to add to make enough soup to go around the table, Father invited them to our house without embarrassing them. He would say, "Are you Mr. So and So? No? Well sir, my wife, Ettele, was expecting out-of-town guests and it seems they did not show up. She has prepared far too much food for us, so would you please honor us at our home and help us eat the food?" They gladly accepted because there were no restaurants in our area, nor could people afford to eat out anyway.

Our Mother, Ettele, affectionately called Etuko, always had a smile. Like my Father, she was very proud of her large family. Our friends and the neighborhood kids loved to come over — especially on Sabbath — for her scrumptious desserts. Afterwards we would all sing *zmiros*, ritual Hebrew songs of appreciation for the food and blessings which the Almighty had bestowed on us. Every Sabbath I felt the joyous melodies lift me up and keep me going the whole week.

Most of the time we could not afford to purchase much food for our large family, so we grew carrots, cucumbers, corn, beans, cabbage, and other vegetables. We also had large apple, plum, cherry, peach, and walnut trees. We housed a few chickens, plus a few ducks and geese which mother fattened up, and we had our own cow for milk. Mother milked the cow and gathered eggs every day. Her hands were never idle — she was continuously canning vegetables and making preserves during the fall to help feed our family over the long, cold winter.

Even with well over a dozen people living at our house, I never felt crowded or hungry. There were no frills in our home, as only the very few rich people of our area had; yet I still felt our home was our castle. Mother was not only a wonderful cook, she also made quilts, pillows, bed covers, and other beautiful things. She even plucked the feathers from our geese to make the quilts and pillows thick and plump, and the few curtains we had were sewn by her. My Mother never complained about the extra long hours of work; in fact, she never appeared to be working at all. Her jovial disposition permeated the whole house.

Like most people in those days, Mother baked most of the bread we ate, especially the *challah* (Sabbath bread). She did her daily cooking on a wood-fired stove, using the largest pots and vessels to make enough to last for several days. The ice we saved from the river in early spring kept leftovers from spoiling. My Mother generally fed up to twenty people three times a day — seven children, six or more workers, parents, grandparents, plus guests or pure people. Breakfast and lunch, our heaviest meals, gave us energy for work. Supper was the lightest because we had finished work for the day and didn't need the sustenance. Potatoes and beans were the mainstay for each meal, with other in-season vegetables added for variety and taste. Mother canned most of the luscious fruits and vegetables that were so abundant in the fall and used some for her famous desserts. Her pastries — especially the fruit pies — were the envy of many.

My brothers, Filip and Bernie, the first and third sons, in certain ways were much like our Father. They liked to work in the tailor shop. Bernie learned to play the mandolin, and he provided music for us to sing and dance to in the evenings. He also played the balalaika, a Russian instrument much like a mandolin or banjo. Sometimes when Bernie played, we danced with Rosalyn or Mother. One of us would pick Rosalyn up and dance with her, then pass her on to another brother. Her face would light up and she would squeal with delight.

As the youngest child and only girl, Rosalyn was the apple of our eye. She was tall, good- looking, and very smart. Except for Filip, Rosalyn was the only one of us lucky enough — as we were not wealthy — to go to the famous Hebrew School (Polgary Gymnasium) in Munkach. Polgary Gymnasium had exceptionally fine teachers; children came from all over the region to attend this wonderful school.

I was too young to know my grandparents well. My Father's father passed away before I was born; his mother lived in Lavik on the other side of town. I used to visit her at least once a year, especially during grape-picking season. Our Mother's parents lived with us until my grandmother's death in 1933 when I was five. My grandfather died when I was eleven. They were a part of our daily life and I felt very fortunate to have them so close by. Grandmother was slender, beautiful, and jovial. Our grandfather, a true Jewish *Zaideh* (grandfather) had a long, gray beard. I remember him caring for his horse and buggy, which he used for his livelihood, and spending time with us. He was a very pious man who attended religious services every morning and evening. Every year I light a candle for my grandmother and grandfather. They are dead. They are gone and will not come back. It saddens me not to hear my precious grandfather sing again. He will not bless us again because God has called him and, when God calls, one must come immediately, even if one doesn't want to go.

My Mother's brother Yosef and his family also lived in our village. I was very close to my cousin, Bumi. He often came over to spend the night with me. Along with Yonchi, our schwabisch (German) buddy, we would sleep in the back building next to the hay shack, where the cow and horses were housed. Most of the sewing machines, ironing tables, and my Father's work place were there.

After the shop closed at the end of each day, the cutting tables (which were filled with straw) were opened up as beds — a very practical arrangement for our small home. I spent many happy hours in the back bungalow listening to my older brothers tell stories about girls and playing soccer. I was too young to tell stories myself, but I loved to listen. In the summer, Bumi and I slept on the haystacks.

Because life was so difficult, most of our relatives on both sides had emigrated to America right after World War I, when our area was part of Austria/Hungary before it became Czechoslovakia. America seemed like a golden land of opportunity, but we did not go. My Mother wanted to care for her parents, who were elderly, and my Father preferred to stay with his tailor shop. Mother had four brothers and a sister who emigrated and a brother and sister who remained. Father had two brothers who went to America and one brother and one sister who stayed in Lavik. Growing up in such a backward, rather poor village, we had no reason to believe we could ever leave.

We had American visitors in 1939, just before Czechoslovakia was divided — the Weis family from Chicago, who had owned a bakery and lived across the street from us before moving to the States. They made quite an impression on me. We were so glad to have visitors, especially from America. Our families had been close; I was named after their father who had passed away just before I was born. They came to visit their brother and mother, who still lived in our village, and brought their young daughter, Janet. The moment I laid eyes on Janet at the tender age of eleven, I fell in love with her. She was about ten, and had the most beautiful long braided hair I had ever seen. Her smile was so bright and enticing.

Janet and I were inseparable during her entire visit; there was nothing we didn't share. She ate frequently at our home and her parents took me with them everywhere. They told me that if I ever got to America, I was invited to stay with them. I felt I had a friend and true love for life.

My family was one of fifty or so Jewish families in our village. We were very close to everyone, although we were not as ultra-orthodox as most Jewish families in our area. We shared strong traditional family and neighborly ties through our synagogue and our strict kosher diet. Common languages also unified us: Yiddish, which we spoke at home, and Czech, which we learned in public school. We also spoke Schwabisch and Russki. We were all within walking distance of each other, the school, and the synagogue. We lived together, attended school together, worked together, and prayed together. Most of the Jewish people attended synagogue services every morning and evening. There was little time for anything else; our lives were very full and we enjoyed being together. Everyone learned to do things for themselves as well as help others.

Sabbath was the highlight of our week, and it entailed a lot of preparation — especially for Mother. The cooking, baking, and cleaning were done in advance so that she would not violate the "no work" restrictions on observing the Sabbath laws and rituals. The Sabbath was a very special time devoted to rest, prayers, and togetherness. As Rosalyn matured, Mother taught her to do all the things that were expected of Jewish women in preparation and observance of the Holy Sabbath.

On Friday afternoon, the boys had to get cleaned up and ready for the Sabbath. First we went to the *mikva* (ritual bath) next to the synagogue, then got dressed in our best clothing. I wore hand-me-downs from my brothers and did not get my first pair of new shoes until I was eight years old.

Many times we watched our Mother say the prayer and light the Sabbath candles Friday night. Then we boys left with Father for synagogue and returned home together for the festive Sabbath meal. Early Saturday morning the entire family again went to synagogue for morning prayers. This was followed by *kiddish* — a little vodka (*schnapps*) and sweet tidbits provided by celebrants of a special occasion, like a wedding or bar mitzvah.

After *kiddish* we came home for a festive Sabbath lunch — our main meal of the week, which we thought was a feast. There was sometimes real meat, like roast beef, ribs, or steak, before Czechoslovakia was divided and when we could afford it. Otherwise we had a duck, goose, or chicken. To this Mother added every vegetable and fruit she could get. Her desserts were the highlight of our fine meal. Often our neighbors' kids would drop by after their own Sabbath meal just for those wonderfully delicious desserts. After the Sabbath meal was finished, we sang the ritual *zimiros*. Then we ended with the *birkas hamozon,* a prayer thanking the Almighty for blessing us with the food from this earth.

In the afternoon we were supposed to rest. It was our special time together. Father, Mother, Rosalyn and I often went for walks. Sometimes my brothers sneaked away to play soccer at a nearby field. It was our only sport, and we all played fairly well. We had no soccer ball, so we tied rags with strings, winding them round and round to make a hard but light homemade soccer ball. For goals we placed caps or rocks at an appropriate distance.

After our "rest" most of us returned to the synagogue for the late afternoon service, which was followed by evening prayers. I could tell that Mother was happy and proud of how we looked and acted. That made me feel terrific. My Father's routine was predictable at the Sabbath's end. As soon as we returned, he reached for his pipes. Father usually had a lit pipe in his mouth all week, but come Friday afternoon he cleaned all his pipe, saving the unused tobacco (*bogoch*) for the gypsies, and put them away. He did not light a pipe until the Sabbath ended.

For many years, Father was the *Gabbai* (overseer) of the synagogue. He also frequently led the congregation in prayers and song because he had a good voice. Our Jewish community was so small that we could not afford to hire a cantor or full-time rabbi. Of all the children, Filip and Bernie had the best voices. I loved it when they sang the prayers with our Father. Later, Bernie was accepted in the famous Munkacher Cantorial school to study as a cantor. Some of the most famous cantors, like Yosele Rosenblat, studied there. Father was very proud that one of his sons might someday become a fine cantor.

Before 1937 our Czech leader was President Thomas Garik Masaryk. He was well-liked and respected by everyone because he showed concern for all segments of the population. His leadership was reflected in the attitudes of our village. Despite our economic, language, ethnic, and religious differences we were a small, friendly village. Everyone got along, even with those in the adjoining villages.

Most people in our region made their living by farming or mining. They worked hard six days a week and rested on the Sabbath or Sunday. They grew enough food on their property for their own consumption; the rest was sold, shared, or bartered to other villagers. Once or twice a week they would sell what they grew or made in the main market in Munkach. Food or craft gifts were given at weddings or when new babies arrived, and moral support was given when someone got sick or families lost loved ones. All the children gathered together to play games, especially soccer.

Public school consisted of several age groups bunched together in a small building, because there were just a few classrooms and teachers available. The school was in a run-down building with a very small backyard for a playing field. I remember it was a long walk to and from school. We also attended Hebrew school (*cheider*) in the late afternoon and on Sundays to learn the Hebrew alphabet and prayers (I tried but could not learn the meanings). We were taught to respect the religious laws and principles of Judaism.

Of all my siblings, I enjoyed going to Hebrew School the least. I was not a good student of the *Alef-Bet-Gimel* (the Hebrew ABCs) and I was not fond of the strict teacher (*le'rer*). I got my share of beatings from him, but I did not dare tell Father because he would have given me more of a thrashing for being a bad boy! One time I came home all bruised and marked up. My older brothers decided to teach the teacher a lesson, so they threw him down the stairs at a ritual bath. Another time they locked him in the woodshed with our maid and they were caught. This was considered extremely inappropriate behavior for a teacher and, as a consequence, the teacher was fired. Luckily, my brothers never were punished for this, thank God.

Our village adjoined a very large military base and a large man-made bastion that was a man-made mountain. This base brought many military people, especially officers, into Father's tailor shop. Many times I would sit and gaze at the "mountain." It had been hand-built during the Ottoman Empire and was supposedly used to defeat Napoleon and the French Imperial Army. The base had a huge castle-like military fortress on top, which was also used as a bastion by the Austro-Hungarian Army before World War I. As a result, my birthplace also became a training ground and military base for the Czech army, and eventually the Hungarian and German armies.

As children, our thoughts and dreams about this bastion were filled with ghostly stories. The center of the mountain contained the military headquarters; it also had a hollow core. It was rumored that in previous wars, enemy soldiers were beaten, tortured, then thrown to their deaths in the well, plummeting down several hundred feet to a stream and eventually ending up dead in the Latorca River. The age of the mountain alone kept us away. It was made before there was earth-moving equipment or other ways to compact the dirt. Our parents were afraid that if an earthquake, tornado, or torrential downpour occurred, the buildings on the mountain would collapse and create an avalanche.

To reach the base of the structure from the city, people had to travel through our village and then take a brick paved road that twisted and turned to the top. Fruit trees — and especially grapes for wine — were abundant not only along the path, but all around the mountain, which made it very hard for us kids to stay away. Some of the more daring youth would sneak up to pick the "forbidden fruit" late at night, but they had to be very careful because it was steep, privately owned, and guarded. Of course, some were caught and punished.

In 1939, when I was eleven years old, our democratic country of Czechoslovakia was divided. First, the Allies permitted Sudetenland to be annexed by Germany; then in 1939 Carpathia was annexed by Hungary when Hungary collaborated with Germany. The name of our region was changed by the Hungarians from Carpathia to Carpat-Alja, and our village became Va'r Pola'nko instead of Palanok (the Czech name).

This change brought out a new dimension of our countrymen. Many of our Hungarian, German, and schwabisch neighbors changed from being good playmates, friendly neighbors, and caring people into uncaring, inhumane, hateful killers. Later, many became SS men.

After that, Czechoslovakia and our lives would never be the same again. When Hungary took over our area, it was the beginning of the end for most of us. Within a few years things got very rough. Food was rationed, but Jews were not given ration coupons. Rumors about the arrest, starvation, and killing of

Jews began to reach us from Poland, Germany, Austria, Lithuania, Ukraine, Russia, and other countries. We simply could not believe those horrid tales — especially about the killing centers. We just wanted to get on with our lives and work hard to be able to eat and live normally.

In 1941 our part of Czechoslovakia was completely annexed and given to Hungary, as Hungary was part of Germany's axis. Some of the older villagers told us that our region had changed hands many times before. Before World War I, it was part of the Austro-Hungarian Empire. Since we had no choice, we tried not to worry about what the new changes would bring. After all, we lived in an area where everyone had gotten along for many generations and survived other governments before.

Our parents were very confused, and I, as a twelve-year-old, was dumb-founded by the horrific rumors spread by passing strangers fleeing Poland and other occupied areas. When I started noticing strange, hateful behavior from our neighbors — especially from my friends, boys my age and older — I became very scared of what might be in store for us. Even the trees and flowers did not bloom as before.

CHAPTER TWO

A CHANGING VILLAGE

As part of Czechoslovakia was taken over by Germany, the peaceful co-existence of our community began to disappear forever. Rumors circulated about Jews being persecuted and murdered in Germany and its occupied countries — especially in nearby Poland. We simply could not and did not believe these horrible stories. We thought that our neighbors and the decent people of the world — particularly our American relatives — would not let the Nazis harm us or stop us from leaving for America. Once our area was controlled by the Hungarian fascists, Jews in and near our village who were desperately trying to escape Hitler's wrath repeatedly had the door shut in their faces. Even Jews with visas and money to go to America were not allowed to cross over any of the fascist-controlled countries to board a ship, train, or any other transportation. Nor were we allowed to enter Britain, Palestine (Israel), Australia, or South America. It seemed no one wanted to help us.

Initially, most elders did not concern themselves with this transformation because they just did not believe it. But in our village — and in every region under fascist or Nazi control — Jews were becoming the scapegoats for past problems. Anti-Semitism rapidly grew out of hand. Once the Hungarian regime took over our area, we started being harassed openly — especially by our young neighbors, even though our ancestors lived among their families for centuries. The local Schwaben (people of German origin) became affiliated with the Nazi party; the young ones became Hitler Youth (*Hitlerjugend*). Palanok had become a vastly different place. Instead of caring or loving, it had become hateful and uncaring; even the weather was dismal.

Before World War II, the scariest thing that had ever happened to me was having neighborhood boys jump out and frighten my sister and me when we walked by the cemetery to or from the city at night. Once those boys joined the Hitler Youth, we had much more serious fears; they were like gangs, attacking us in broad daylight.

When our area was still part of Czechoslovakia, the building adjoining our backyard was first a meeting hall for the labor party; then it housed the communist party. Under fascist Hungary it became the headquarters and training center of the Hitler Youth and Nazi party. Having these hate mongers next door became more difficult for us each day.

To get on with our lives, somehow we had to devise new ways to eat and live. Trying to follow the Jewish customs and kashrut law was making the situation more dangerous. Ben and Uncle Yosef defied the new law against koshering or selling kosher meat. They slaughtered cattle at night in our barn next to the tailor shop and secretly prepared the meat according to kashrut law.

Supervised by a *shoichet*, a certified Jewish slaughterer who acted as a kashrut observer, Uncle Yosef and Ben would work till early morning skinning the cattle, cutting out the veins from the front, and weighing and cutting up the meat to fill the delivery orders. The secret deliveries went to Jews in Palanok, adjoining villages, and Munkach. While they did the butchering, other family members watched for the police. When Ben and Uncle Yosef were finished, the *shoichet* inspected the meat again and approved the front section as kosher. (Only the front of cattle is considered kosher.) This undercover arrangement greatly helped our village and Jewish communities in the surrounding area.

Father, who was very upset about the anti-kosher law, would say, "I cannot understand why the Hungarians, who used to be nice to Jews, won't allow us to kosher our meat!" It was really just another fascist ploy to make our lives more difficult.

The watchers continued to look out for police as Uncle Yosef and Ben placed the packages onto a covered horse-drawn wagon or bikes to be taken to waiting Jewish families. Although Uncle Yosef and Ben were scared, they were proud to provide kosher meat to the Jewish people for their Sabbath meal. They knew that the fascist police would arrest them if they were caught. But most Jewish families in our area kept strict kosher kitchens like ours — having kosher meat was important, especially for the Sabbath.

Because I was tall, strong and healthy, I was permitted to help Uncle Yosef and Ben with their deliveries. Usually very late Thursday night, I loaded my bike and my knapsack with meat and made the deliveries in time for the Jewish people to prepare for their Sabbath meal. In winter I would deliver meat on my homemade sled. Naturally, I too was frightened and anxious, but I wanted to help in any way I could. Generosity, compassion, and brotherliness were values I learned from my parents and grandparents. It was our tradition.

The Hungarian militia gave strict orders that all boys age eleven and up must report once a week for *Levente*, or paramilitary training. This meant different things, depending on whether you were Jewish or Christian,

Hungarian or German. The Jewish boys had to dig ditches, clean latrines, and do other hard, menial jobs that were considered degrading to Hungarians or Germans. The Hungarian Christian youth in our village were given wooden guns and taught how to use them, as well as how to march, wear swastikas, and salute their Nazi superiors with outstretched raised arms, enthusiastically shouting *"Heil Hitler."* In other words, they were taught how to become loyal Nazi soldiers and they screamed and laughed when they sowed terror in our village. Most of the Schwaben (German) boys were encouraged by their parents to join the elite Hitler Youth movement. They were convinced this would help them go up the Nazi ladder faster and eventually become leaders of the Third Reich. Most of the boys did, and very enthusiastically. Even one of my best friends from across the street joined and became a leader of sorts. They, too, received paramilitary training.

Although we had very close schwabisch Christian friends and neighbors for many years, when the Nazis took over completely they stopped visiting us regularly. They also stopped patronizing my Father's shop. What hurt me most of all was that those who weren't Schwaben or part of the fascist organization did nothing to protest the anti-Jewish acts — injustices that were happening right before their very eyes. Apathy prevailed. I was shocked to see that some were even smiling, enthusiastic participants.

It is hard to describe the pain I felt. Our neighbors and friends turned their backs on us when we needed them most. When my best friend joined the Hitler Youth, I was crushed. Not too long ago we had eaten and spent the night together, played together, worked together, and helped each other. Our parents, too, no doubt, cried because of us, fearful of what might be in store for us from such neighbors.

Those well-meaning, respectable, God-fearing Christian people just sat back and let others think and act for them. Surely they were not too busy with their own lives to sift through the propaganda against Jews. We hoped that the decent people, especially our neighbors, would stand up for their neighbors and friends and not let the Nazis get away with this.

Soon the Hungarians started drafting both Jews and non-Jews into the military. Jews of military age were shipped to labor camps (*munko tabor*). Father received notice to report for military labor immediately. One of the soldiers who came for him had been a patron of his shop. Father had tailored his army suits for him which, no doubt, made it painful for that soldier to take him away, but he did it anyway. We cried and begged Father not to go. We begged the soldier not to take him away from us, but it did no good. I still remember seeing my angelic Mother cry at the train station when they took our father away. She was scared and did not want to let him go. If I had understood,

I would have cried too but I was too young, petrified, and dumbfounded to understand.

One by one, my older brothers were drafted and taken to labor camp. First Filip, then Ben, who had been living in Budapest came home because he was afraid of being arrested there. He was drafted a week after his return. Bernie, who was not as strong as the rest of us, was taken away next. Our hearts were broken.

Fortunately, Father was permitted to come home after six months because his sons were in the labor camps and his health was questionable. We were delighted to have him back, but we were concerned because he had become weak, sickly, and pale. The hard slave work at the Russian front had taken its toll on him.

Father spoke of the labor camps very reluctantly, giving only a sketchy account of his experience. He told us of very hard work from sun-up to sun-down; of beatings, abuse, and very little food; of dogs that attacked if you moved away from the work area or tried to escape. He said the Hungarian guards would shoot to kill for the slightest infraction or misdeed by a Jew. We were not worldly; we were politically naive and completely stunned by the situation.

Our parents were convinced that the wonderful, pious rabbis would perform miracles and save us. After all, the revered chief rabbi of Munkach said that the *Moshiach* (Messiah) would protect us and would soon deliver us to our promised land of Israel.

In late 1943, the Nazis decided they were unsatisfied with how the Hungarians were handling their part of former Czechoslovakia, especially not eliminating the Jews. Without warning they replaced the Hungarian leaders and military officers in charge of our area overnight. Now, to our dismay, German control had tightened. This tore Mother up. First she cried silently, then she began going into the barn to cry because she did not want to upset us.

It seemed that all the schwabisch people in our village had become bigots. Even neighbors not of German descent were openly anti-Semitic. They even strove to disturb our holy Sabbath. What was so extraordinary were their cocky, proud, resonant, and often raucous voices. Our first thought was that they were crazy, showing off; but we were wrong and, as time passed, it only got worse. Our Mother was terribly upset to hear neighborhood kids using hateful curse words or shouting obscenities, especially when she was getting ready to light the Sabbath candles Friday evening.

The Germans[9] promoted anti-Semitism by saying how lazy the Jews were. I don't remember even one lazy Jew in our area. Most were farmers, shoemakers, tailors, cabinet makers — hard working people who sustained themselves.

Soon there were all kinds of shortages for us. Food and clothing were rationed, but Jews did not get ration coupons. When non-Jewish people had to stand in line for these items they soon began to grumble, like Hitler and his Nazis, blaming the Jews for everything that was bad. There seemed to be no end to the hate epidemic.

Every day new anti-Jewish measures were instituted. Through the Jewish grapevine, we realized that German clubs and professional organizations had been closed for membership to Jews. Schools refused to teach Jews. Many Munkach restaurants suddenly refused to serve Jews because we were considered unclean. Eventually, most of our Christian neighbors wanted nothing to do with us. Our stores were boycotted and we were driven out of business.

Jews were not allowed to purchase newspapers and were barred from every form of communication; even radios were confiscated. Everything had become censored and forbidden to us. Only the fascists, government employees, and the military were allowed to use the few telephones in our village. Our only way of communicating was by word of mouth. We wanted to know what was going on, but the only news we received was from passersby and it was bad.

There were so many different languages and dialects spoken in our region that often one group could hardly understand another. It was easier to believe that it was all a miscommunication, rather than believe the terrible rumors. We began hearing about Jews being massacred by the thousands in Poland, Germany, Ukraine, Lithuania, and other countries. We were told that our people were being wiped out all through Europe. These rumors spread like wild fire, but we desperately did not want to believe them.

As the Nazi youth groups became more popular in our village, they increasingly vented their hatred on non-Germans. This hatred was initially targeted toward Jewish youth. With my blond hair, I looked more Aryan German than most Christian kids, but it did not help. The fascist youth traveled in groups, especially after they left school, church, or meetings at the Hitler Youth hall. Now, anytime they saw us, they would attack us with stones or hit us with sticks. The Nazi youths liked to attack people who were unable to stand up to large groups, like elderly Jews or young people. They liked to impress each other with how mean they could be.

We were astounded at how proud our neighbors had become of their own children's vicious behavior; the parents of these Nazi youth even gloated. In good weather they would come outside and watch approvingly as their children threw rocks and mud at passing Jews. There is no doubt that the children were encouraged by their parents, either verbally or by their silent acquiescence.

If the area fascists wanted to get rid of a neighbor, they would tell the Germans that the accused was a communist, Jew, Jew-lover, or other "undesirable." This person was then arrested by the Hungarians and often never heard from again. But it seemed they were not quite ready to eliminate all of us. First they had to eliminate the three million or more Jews in nearby Poland, then Russia, Ukraine, Galitzia, Lithuania, Romania, Czechoslovakia and other countries. Hungary was still an ally of Germany; a few neighbors and even some fascists were still somewhat decent to us.

Our parents became more fearful and worried for us because each time we left home we were accosted by young fascists and the Hitler Youth. Our parents were petrified if we were late coming home from school or synagogue. Rumors of arrests, deportation, confiscation, and murder were no longer troublesome events that only occurred in other countries. Soldiers were reportedly responsible for muggings, rapes, and robberies, especially against Jews. We were urged to stay away from the military mountain, the nearby military base, and other places where the soldiers congregated. When they were drunk, the German and Hungarian soldiers came to Jewish homes demanding money, gold, and other valuables. They told us it would eventually be taken from us anyway.

We truly began to fear for our lives. Even going to the synagogue or visiting a neighbor was an ordeal. To go to school, we had to walk past a Catholic church where the schwabisch Catholic boys would attack us and accuse us of killing their Christ. The priest — a friend of Father's — sometimes tried to stop them, but to no avail. We could not even take our cow to pasture or try to locate some food without fear for our lives.

Amid this growing alarm, our family tried to keep a sense of normalcy. We worked very hard six days a week, and on Friday we would prepare for the holy Sabbath, offering extra food whenever possible for travelers. We especially tried to be hospitable to Jews who had escaped persecution in Poland or other nearby countries.

Before they were drafted into the labor camps, my older brothers and my Father's employees were the most daring Jewish boys in our village. They tried to fight back, no matter how they were outnumbered. Even with bare hands they would stand their ground against the fascist attackers, who had the military fascist government on their side. I was proud of them for fighting the Nazis, but it made matters that much worse by drawing unwanted attention our way.

Father urged us not to react to the attacks, even when the attackers didn't outnumber us. Father taught us that if the Hitler Youth or military men lifted their hands to attack us, we should lift our legs to run away as fast as we could.

Our parents not only worried about us, they worried for our relatives — even those in America whom we had not heard from in a while. We did not know what was really happening in America because we were forbidden to communicate with anyone anywhere. According to fascist publicity, Americans were starving, jobless, and homeless, and many were committing suicide. Americans were reportedly fighting among themselves and did not care what happened to us. Also rumored was the possibility that the U.S. would soon join or surrender to Germany. Meanwhile, we were hearing more and more about Hitler's killing centers in Poland and Lithuania.

I heard that when Hitler began occupying most of Europe, almost every Jewish family in Germany and occupied Europe was trying to get papers to exit Europe. It was every Jew's dream, especially ours, to get out of Nazi-dominated Eastern Europe as quickly as possible. Rumors circulated that many Jews tried to enter Palestine (now Israel), which was under British control at that time. The British occupiers would not allow most fleeing Jews to enter, supposedly because they were trying to appease the neighboring Arab states. But if we were not permitted to enter our own homeland, where could we expect to go?

My three oldest brothers would have been happy to join the Allied armies to fight against Nazi Germany, but no army would accept us Jews — even though most of them knew it was certain death for us once they took us away. The Germans had us trapped.

I wondered if the Allies hated us, too. I could not imagine decent people throughout the world not caring about our fate. Young innocent children, elderly women and men — every one of us had a face. We were each a person with a life story and a future. We did not hurt anyone. Surely our family in America cared about us. And what about Janet, the American girl whom I met when she visited our village? Surely she cared.

Our only "crime" was being Jewish. It was a crime that we had no control over. We were born to Jewish parents and were of Jewish faith. We just could not believe that when all of the political changes were made, we would end up being punished simply for being Jewish.

Before World War II began, a very few rich or lucky Jews managed to gain passage to Cuba, America, or England. At first, we'd heard they were reaching those hallowed shores safely and were permitted entry. After the War we learned that the ships they sailed on were forced to return to Europe and extermination. We also learned that some ships carrying people fleeing Nazi Germany were torpedoed at sea by the Germans and everyone on board was killed.

My oldest brother, Filip, probably could have gotten an American visa in the early war years. Our uncles sent him the papers just before the borders were shut down, but he decided to stay because our parents had so many mouths to feed. To forfeit the opportunity to leave for the golden land of America must have been life's hardest decision for him. Perhaps he could have lived safely in America, even if it was without the family; nevertheless he decided to stay, despite the terrible situation and frightening rumors. (Ironically he was trapped in Russia for twenty-five years and was the last one of us to come to America.)

We were hard-working, decent people and good citizens. How could things suddenly change so much? Rumors were rampant that the Russian army was very close; I hoped we would be liberated at any moment. We watched thousands of German soldiers move toward the Russian front with heavy equipment, night and day. In my imagination I heard heavy guns exploding.

One early morning in 1942 there was a knock on our door. Some military men came with a local Nazi who was not pleasant and had designs on Father's tailor shop. They wanted to take our Father away — we had no idea where — but Rosalyn and I hung onto his legs and refused to let them take him. She was crying and screaming, and so was I. I ran to get our brothers. They arrived with a few of Father's other employees, and fortunately the "gendarme" (Hungarian militia) left without Father. It was quite a relief to have him stay home with us. He was very strict, but a good hard-working Father.

Toward the end of 1942 it was becoming very difficult for us to make a decent living. Anyone caught dealing with a *persona non grata,* meaning a Jew, was frowned upon by neighbors, and the fascists would most certainly boycott their livelihood. Food was in very short supply all over Europe, and our area was no exception. Since most men eighteen or older were taken to the military or labor camps, there were very few able-bodied men to work the farms, fields, factories, or mines.

Just obtaining basic necessities to keep us alive was difficult. Food-ration coupons became a dire necessity, even for the non-Jewish citizens of our area. Since Jewish people were not given ration coupons, we were forced to buy food on the black market. This meant we paid several times more than the normal price. Some Christian former friends and Russian-speaking farmers from the surrounding village liked Father's tailoring, so we were lucky because Father could sometimes barter tailoring for a few potatoes, a little flour for Mother to make bread, or — miracle of miracles — a chicken for the Sabbath. Sometimes my brothers and Father's employees would search the fields at night for vegetables left behind by farmers. Somehow we managed to secure enough food to keep us going.

We had heard stories that the Germans accidentally bombed a church in Poland, and that the Christians vowed revenge. But when the Germans destroyed hundreds of synagogues and Jewish homes, no one said a word. The

Nazi youth even destroyed Jewish cemeteries just for kicks. Actions like those caused me much anger and frustration, but I had no means to express it. What frightened me most was the Germans' air of invincibility and cockiness. I kept hoping that the Russians or other Allies would free us at any moment, but the Germans seemed completely confident of their success.

Because of my fear of constant attacks, I once ran away from Palanok. I left one early afternoon on foot and met a farmer with a buggy and cows who let me travel with him. During our journey we ran into a pack of wolves. Luckily the farmer had matches, which we lit to frighten them off. We arrived the next morning in Lavik, where Father's mother, brother and sister lived. I came home after just a few days because I missed my family so much.

Upon my return, I learned from my brothers that the Nazis were looking for me because I had defended myself and was liked by the German neighbors, young and old. I decided to leave again. I went to the village of Vari, near Beregsaz where Mother's affectionate sister, Leichu and Uncle Weiss lived with their three children. (Unfortunately she, her husband, and their children were later killed in Auschwitz). Once again, I very much longed for my family so I returned home. But life there was no better. I found that the persecution — which had been intolerable — had become even worse. I felt I had no choice but to run away again — this time to Budapest, the capital of Hungary.

In Budapest I somehow managed to get a job as a plumber's apprentice, and lived in a large shelter for a while. Luckily, I also got a position in the Boy's Choir in the famous Dohány Synagogue; we were apprentices, "paid" with cookies and milk. But soon the Hungarian fascists started arresting Jewish boys like me because we were not registered with the police in Budapest. Although I was saved temporarily with a Swiss paper, soon I had no choice but to leave. Somehow I made it back home.

I arrived home in March 1944, just before Passover. The local Germans had been organized into an army unit and were in charge of the sector.[10] We were told by these soldiers that if we cooperated, we would be relocated away from our hateful neighbors, many of whom had become openly and ferociously anti-Semitic. They promised that we could live tranquilly at our new location with decent housing, proper food, and good jobs because they needed good workers.

It seemed too good to be true. And what choice did we have? Where could we go? Certainly not to Poland, which was rumored to be a graveyard for all Jews. We had also heard that there were hardly any Jews left in any of the adjoining countries. We asked ourselves whether Jews would be welcome anywhere in this world now. After all, even our own schwabisch acquaintances and other neighbors and friends had turned against us. They were happy in our sorrow.

Soon posters appeared on walls and trees warning that Jews who opposed or did not follow orders would be shot. It was hard to believe, and it scared the hell out of us.

The Germans informed us that we were to be relocated and that we should take all our money, jewelry, and valuables. However, the Hungarian soldiers, local Nazis leaders, and our friends and neighbors had said that they would take care of things for us, so we should take only the minimum — a change of clothing, a small amount of food, and essential items. The Germans said to take everything — they would keep it safe for us until we returned or asked them to send it to us. We did not know whom to trust or what to believe; we were befuddled and scared.

Why didn't the Americans and other allies warn or inform us of the danger we were in? Had we known the truth about what was in store for us in Auschwitz, most of us would have tried to hide or escape.

While we worried for ourselves, the welfare of Filip, Ben, and Bernie in the Hungarian labor camps was also a constant concern. My parents anxiously awaited news of them. Word-of-mouth information came to us only when people were discharged from the labor camps because of sickness, or if they escaped or came home on leave. Sometimes the information we got was months old, but we were desperate to receive any information about our family.

We eventually learned through rumors that they were okay. We guessed they were somewhere along the Russian front, digging ditches on the front line or performing other dangerous slave labor.

Now it seemed that even time was our enemy. The constant harassment and attacks were beginning to take their toll on us.

Passover 1944 was the most dismal I have ever known. Even as we celebrated Jewish freedom of enslavement from Egypt, we were petrified about our future. On the last day of Passover, new posters appeared in the center of our village stating that all Jews were to assemble the next morning with whatever possessions they could carry. We did not even have time to put the Passover dishes and utensils away when the Nazis came to our door early the next morning. The day was very cold and bleak. Mother and Father tried to console us and stay calm, but we all cried hysterically as the Hungarian gendarme under German[11] command pounded on our door. They told Father they needed good tailors in Germany. We were ordered to quickly pack our bags and assemble in the center of Palanok within a few minutes.

We did not know what to pack, what to take, what to try and hide. We took only money, jewelry, and what little food, clothing, and heirlooms each of us could fit in a knapsack or suitcase. Father insisted on taking his *tefillin* (phylacteries) prayer book, and *talis* (prayer shawl). Mother, of course, took her Sabbath candles and some quilts to cover us in cold weather, but we had no time to think rationally. To pack took only a few minutes, but it felt like a lifetime. After all, we were leaving our hearts, our home, most of our belongings, and especially several generations of roots and history.

The Germans, the Hungarian gendarme, and the local Nazis lined us up, ready to shoot if we disobeyed. Then they ordered us to march forward to the center of our village. Our neighbors — some of whom had identified to the Germans which families were Jewish — stood watching as we were gathered together. After the Nazis made sure all the Jews from Palanok were accounted for, we were marched around the corner, past the church, and out of our village.

It was indescribably painful to bid goodbye to our land, our possessions, our past, our childhood, our home where we had family get-togethers under one roof. My heart was shattered and my legs trembled as the guards meanly forced us to march away from our home on a bleak road to the unknown.

We were frightened beyond words. The memory of our last Passover — the family together, the joy, and the anguish — would be only a memory, reminding me that many times enemies would rise up against us with guns, and whips, threatening annihilation. As I watched our neighbors snicker gleefully, seeing us chased brutally from our homes and glad to get rid of us, I realized that life as we knew it was forever changed.

Chapter Three

Two Weeks in the Ghetto

I shall never forget the gray April clouds hanging low on the bitter cold day the Nazis led us away. Nor shall I forget the terror in my parents' eyes. I also worried about our little dog and cat we left behind, and the friends and neighbors we loved so dearly.

We had witnessed many frightening changes over the past four years since Hungary had taken over our area. But nothing was like being forced from our home by armed guards, and being prodded by guns and bayonets.

As we marched, my mind raced. In spite of my misery, I hoped that we would be able to stay near our village. Would I ever see our home again? Rumors abounded that Russian and other allied armies were defeating the Germans on all fronts and drawing ever closer to us, so my hopes for being liberated imminently by the Allies were high. I needed those hopes to cling to. Most of our elders were crying and praying for the Messiah to come and save us — they still believed in a miracle. Perhaps the church would break its silence and speak out against the Germans murdering our people.

The Nazis led us to a temporary stopover where we were without a roof over our heads and had nothing to keep us warm. My thoughts ran rampant. Was there any truth to what the SS told us? They promised us honest work, sufficient food and good shelter. Or were the horrible rumors we heard really true? Were Jews indeed dying of starvation in the ghettos, being shot in the forests, and slaughtered in mass killing centers around Europe? I wanted to think that everything would be okay, that we would be safe, but I didn't believe it. The rumors sounded more realistic now that we were enroute to a ghetto with the Germans[12] screaming, *"Farshtukene Juden"* ("stinking Jews"). I was frightened so badly by their guns, whips and cursing that I could hardly think.

Father, who was a strong man, suddenly became weak. My dear Mother, who had always loved everyone and smiled constantly, suddenly had a frown on her face and looked so sad. My brothers Bill and Sam suddenly could not express themselves. Rosalyn was as petrified as I was.

As we approached the ghetto, I was horrified to see our Christian neighbors watching our deportation without even a trace of caring or pity in their faces. No one voiced any opposition to what was happening. I was so bitterly disappointed. I did not know whom to trust or what to believe anymore. Our old neighbors could have at least thrown us some bread or potatoes. That would have lifted my spirits immeasurably.

Eventually we reached the old brick factory near Munkach, previously owned by a prominent Jewish family, which the Nazis had confiscated and converted into a ghetto. The factory was somewhat isolated even though it was close to our village and Munkach. Since railroad tracks passed through it, it was a convenient location for the local Germans and the Hungarians to assemble Jews and move them in and out.

As soon as we arrived, I knew we had been deceived. The ghetto was surrounded by watch towers and barbed wire. They were not bringing us to a better, safer place as they had said. It appeared that their first objective was to deceive us, degrade us and make our lives miserable.

There was absolutely no way to practice our Jewish faith or traditions. Not being able to live out our faith was very difficult, especially for my parents. No words could comfort their pain and anguish. Even worse, there were no food, toilets, or even sanitary water except what little we brought with us.

I became afraid beyond comprehension. I had no doubt that the worst was yet to come. Our nightmare was just beginning.

My parents, Bill, Sam, Rosalyn, and I — along with several of our uncles, aunts, cousins, and our Jewish friends and neighbors — were all cramped together. There were absolutely no accommodations for the hundreds of Jews arriving daily from the surrounding villages and towns. There were no bedrooms, or kitchens. There was not even a roof to protect us from inclement weather. Although it was early spring, the night air was still very cold, and icy rain at night was not uncommon.

It was humiliating not to be able to wash ourselves or our clothes. Sanitary items for the women were nonexistent. Worst of all, there was no place to sleep and we were running out of food. It was so painful to see my parents, the many little babies, and the elderly being exposed to extreme temperatures without food or water. Although the Nazis tried to set up a Jewish council, called the *Judenrat*, to run the internal affairs of the ghetto, it was mostly a pretense to get us to cooperate and to make sure their instructions were carried out promptly by everyone.

I was still a young boy, but I suddenly and painfully felt the loss of my childhood. I just wanted to get back home, play soccer with my friends, and live a normal life with my family. We all just wanted to be good humans, good citizens, good neighbors, and be able to practice our faith. Apparently, for the Nazis that was asking too much.

My family and the other Jews of our village were among the first to arrive in the ghetto, so we were lucky enough to claim a filthy brick baking oven as shelter at night. We removed the bricks and tried to clean out the ashes and soot. We squeezed in to accommodate about fifteen families — almost a hundred people. In this miserable oven we were fortunate to be able to lie down on ashes, which cushioned our bodies, although it was difficult to sleep while breathing in the ashes and soot. But our meager shelter was better than nothing — at least we now had a roof over our heads, unlike the new arrivals.

After the first few days of ghetto confinement, the food shortage became a real problem — especially for the babies, children, and elderly. Only a short time ago, many ghetto prisoners had money, connections, prestige, and more food than they could consume. Now they were paupers in desperation, just like the rest of us.

Our pleading and cries for food went unheeded. Even if a person had money or other valuables hidden in his shoes or clothing, there was no food for purchase. We prayed that someone would bring us some food, but no one was allowed near the ghetto. Occasionally, people were able to bribe the guards and arrange for someone outside to throw clothing or food over the wall at night, but not often. We prayed for the war to be over. We hoped for a miracle. But almost immediately we realized that we had to become tough and learn to expect nothing.

Even though we were desperate for food and living in squalor, I was relieved to be among Jews rather than Jew-haters. We could not take our ritual bath and get ready for the Sabbath on Friday afternoon, and we had no Sabbath candles for Mother to light because they were taken away. But Father and a few others found a corner, then began the Friday evening Sabbath prayer with mumbling and tears. Afterwards we quietly wished each other a good Sabbath.

To add to our pain, we found ourselves being guarded by former friends and neighbors; they were helping the local German soldiers! Now that Hitler and fascism was popular, they not only volunteered to join the Nazis, they participated enthusiastically. As one of our people was whipped, I heard someone shout, "Take lessons, you Jews."

The Germans were masters in concealing the true purpose of what they were trying to do with us. Even in the ghetto, they still wanted us to believe that we were just being relocated away from the local Jew-haters. They also said that we would be taken as soon as possible to Germany, where we would be farther away from the fighting. We were assured that we would be able to use our work skills to better ourselves. They said they needed good tailors, construction workers, and other tradespeople because most German workers were in the military. They promised us much better conditions than what we had, which was surely something we wanted to hear.

The Germans thought that if they lied to us about looking out for our best interests, we would believe them — even if they were behaving abominably. I suppose they considered this insurance against uprisings. Although their guns and attack dogs were better insurance, their lies did generate confusion. Their other statements were less comforting, however. They boasted that soon they would soundly defeat the communist Russians and their evil empire, as well as Britain's royalty. They bragged that it would not be long before they eliminated the capitalist Americans and any others standing in their way of complete world dominance. They were so confident and persuasive, it all sounded almost believable.

On the other hand, we knew enough German to understand the meaning of the comments we overheard from the local German guards. When they thought that they were not being heard or understood, they discussed where we might be going next and the dangers we would face there. In some cases, the guards actually wanted to be heard as they talked among themselves.

I wondered when my other uncles, aunts, and cousins would be taken to a ghetto. Once all Jews were gathered, I thought the Nazis would probably dispose of most — if not all — of us. It looked like the dreadful rumors we had heard of what they did to the Jews in Poland, Ukraine, and other places could be true, based on the way they treated us when we had "outlived our usefulness" to them. I feared they would kill us all, one by one, to be rid of us.

I was miserable each hour in the ghetto. The cursing, threats, beatings, and malicious mistreatment were unbearable. Time seemed to drag on and on, with each day seeming longer, dimmer, and darker than the previous one. Yet because I had no choice, I tolerated it.

We were so afraid that nobody spoke to each other — it was as if we were at a funeral. We stopped crying and even greeting each other. But at least we were still together as a family, I reasoned. At least we could see with our own eyes that we were all still alive and in relatively good health. My three older brothers were missing, toiling away somewhere in the Hungarian labor camps, but it was a blessing to be with the rest of my family.

Even in this unspeakable misery, I was sure that the world was still populated with decent people like the ones we used to know. I clung to that belief, but I worried what the future held for us, or — for that matter — for others in the world. How could any of us — Jews or Gentiles — survive in a world filled with hate?

No doubt the Nazis wanted to weaken us physically and spiritually. The guards, and especially the Germans, created "jobs" for us. I don't know if it was out of meanness and spite, to keep us from becoming restless, or just because they could do anything they wanted with us. They had us move, by hand, piles of large, industrial bricks that were stacked up on one side of the factory. We had to throw these heavy, rough bricks to the nearest person in line, eight to ten feet away, and catch them with our bare hands. This way, the large piles of bricks were moved from one side of the ghetto to the other. When the bricks were all stacked up at one end, the guards ordered us to move them back to the other.

And so it went on all day, moving bricks from one end to the other. Because we had to throw and catch the bricks without gloves, after just a few hours the palms of our hands had very little skin left. They became raw, bloodied, and swollen. As a result, our hands dripped blood onto the frozen ground in the morning, then the blood would thaw and smell awful during the day. And of course, it continued to hurt. But if we dared to slow down or stop, the guards flogged us with sticks or rifle butts. This went on day after day, hour after hour, over and over again. Often our hands were too tender or too slick with blood to catch the bricks, but the guards were always ready to flog us, so we did not dare slow down or drop the bricks.

The brick-throwing continued for the duration of our stay in the ghetto, which was over two weeks. Sadly, our misery was the guards' entertainment. No wonder Father, who had previously been strong and healthy after recovering from labor camp, began to look old and weary after only a few days in the ghetto. We hoped that the frail look on his face was only temporary — not, God forbid, because he might be physically ill or that his worry for us was getting the best of him. He was exhausted, but as a caring Father he was mostly concerned and very fearful for our future. Uncle Yosef tried to calm us all; he was especially unable to soothe his wife, our Aunt Pimchu, who was obviously scared out of her wits for her family.

CHAPTER FOUR

THE CATTLE RIDE TO HELL

My family and I were among the first to be shipped out of the Munkach ghetto. On our fourteenth day there, we learned that cattle cars apparently designated to transport us had been brought in by railroad during the night. We were told that we were being sent east to work for the Fatherland. By now we knew not to believe the Nazis, but what choice did we have? Overwork, exposure to threats and the elements, and lack of food had made many people exhausted, hopeless, sick, and vulnerable to influenza.

The next morning before daybreak, the guards woke us with screams and curses, shouting *"Schnell, Jude, Raus"* ("Quick, Jew, out"). We were ordered to assemble promptly for counting. After everyone was accounted for, they started jamming us into the cattle cars. I heard a German officer[12] scream to one of my friends that he would make him crawl on his hands and knees, then shoot him if he did not carry out the order quickly. I was petrified. The guards continued to scream for us to move quickly as they laughed and whipped us, forcing us with bayonets into the cattle cars.

We took everything we had brought to the ghetto. But we were not prepared for this miserable mystery trip, no matter how much hardship we had already been through. For now we were without food or water for what we were afraid might be a long journey. From eighty to 120 people, including young babies, elderly, sick, fat, and skinny, were jammed in the little cars with no room to breathe, turn or sit, let alone lie down to sleep. We tried to help the elderly, handicapped, and mothers with babies sit down. Many times I held on to the head of some child or elderly person to make sure no one fell or stepped on it.

Once we were crammed in, the sliding doors were locked and bolted from the outside to ensure that no one escaped. The worst part was not knowing where we were going or how long the trip would take. After a few weary hours standing on our feet, the train finally began to move slowly. My heart pounded out of my chest from fear of the unknown (I thought everyone could hear it).

The train stopped first at the main railroad terminal, then stopped and started again many times, switching tracks to make room for other trains to pass — especially military trains headed for the Russian front lines. Sometimes it seemed we were heading in the opposite direction. I hadn't the slightest clue that our destination was Auschwitz II (Birkenau).

During that ride to hell, Father pleaded with me repeatedly, "Yankele, no matter what, I want that you should live." He made me promised to find a way to stay alive. I am sure he did the same to Bill, Sam, and Rosalyn. It was very strange and frightening to me — our strict Father had never repeated himself before, but now he begged us over and over to hold on to our lives, no matter what we must face. I was overwhelmed to see him this way, and it made my promises all the more important to me. My angelic Mother just looked at me, petrified; her demeanor said it all. She told me to please listen to Father and do what he says.

We were packed so tightly that there was not even room for young mothers to breast-feed their babies. It was very disturbing and agitating to hear the babies' plaintive cries as they waited to be fed. When their mothers found a way to nurse, we tried to turn our heads away so they wouldn't be embarrassed as they breast-fed their infants. Their suffering made me want to vomit.

After a few hours the elderly could no longer stand, and we could not hold onto them, so they just collapsed. People shoved and pushed, trying to stay warm and protect the heads of elders and children. After dark it was even worse — the people near the outside of the car had no protection from the cold, howling wind. Those in the center were a little warmer because they were shielded by other bodies. We were at the back, closest to the door and the open, airy exterior. At night we froze to the bone.

Whenever the train stopped at a railroad station or bridge, we screamed, cried, and pleaded for help to the people outside through the openings in the boards. But there was no help to be gotten. The people who saw us through the little windows and slats covered with barbed wire simply didn't respond. Surely, they must have felt our anxiety, our fear, our helplessness, but they did not even give us sympathetic looks, much less food or water.

Things became worse as time passed. There was no bathroom. The younger boys and girls needed to relieve themselves first, and since there was no way to move and nowhere to go, they had to urinate in their pants or on the people next to them. People threw up on each other; vomit was all over the car. This brought on outcries and created more pandemonium. The stench grew increasingly putrid, especially during the day.

Those few days in the cattle car felt like an eternity. The trip no doubt transformed me; my emotions went haywire. I tried to rationalize between reality and the possibility of what was in store. Most of us silently cried; some could not help but cry out loud. I felt like I was suspended over the ocean by a thin thread, with sharks awaiting my fall.

Near the disembarkation point, when someone said that this was Auschwitz, I felt a sick feeling in the pit of my stomach. We had heard unspeakable, unbelievable rumors of this place. I feared that the rumors might be true and that this was indeed the hell on earth we had heard about. The thought of never seeing my parents again or never emerging from this place was unimaginable.

After five or six tortuous days and nights, the train reached its final destination sometime after midnight. We stood in the car all night, freezing, waiting for daybreak. During the entire journey we had received no food, water, or the use of bathroom facilities. The terrible stench penetrated my nostrils.

CHAPTER FIVE

A9018
SURVIVING THE FLAMES

Our inhumane trip ended in Auschwitz with armed guards opening the locked railroad car doors and once again shouting, *"Jude, Raus, Schnell!"* My imagination was running wild. Would they treat us humanly as promised — or viciously, as they had proved they could? I was too hungry, scared, and exhausted to focus on what was occurring around me. The horrible smell of human waste and vomit, the guards' screams, seeing the skinny, half-dead people in gray-striped uniforms, the confusion and fear in the air — all combined to make me feel as if this whole nightmarish place was a horrible hallucination, a delirium brought on by hunger and fright.

First we were ordered to jump off the cars and stack our belongings to one side. The guards told us not to worry because we had our names on them, as though we might retrieve them later. Each of us had some precious valuables that went back several generations, which we stacked nearby. I remember that my parents brought our precious silver candlesticks, cups, gold, rings, and some hand-crocheted things. We were ordered to line up; anyone who did not move fast enough got kicked or hit with a *cajale* (club) or rifle butt. We attempted to comply with the guards' orders as we surrendered the last things we owned in the world. They told us our belongings would probably be taken to our new living quarters. (We never saw our valuables again.)

The SS men and the collaborator kapos[13] in striped uniforms screamed maliciously at us to move faster. Suddenly, out of nowhere, I was hit hard with a *cajale*! An SS man shoved me with his foot and hit me with his whip straps, making me fall to my knees. Although I thought I was moving quickly, it apparently wasn't fast enough for him.

The prisoners who had been there awhile looked more dead than alive. They whispered very scary things to us in Yiddish. In the adjoining line, an SS man kept smashing a little baby on the ground till it stopped crying and breathing. Then he beat up the mother. I tried not to look. It made me feel sick and very guilty that I was not able to help.

I felt so betrayed and powerless. How gut-wrenching it was to watch babies crying for their mothers, being snatched from their shocked and horrified parents! Some parents tried to resist, but it was useless. They were told they would be reunited with their children soon, but that lie did not lessen their trauma. Auschwitz was more frightening than the worst nightmare I could ever imagine.

As the guards divided us into lines, a frightening man referred to by other prisoners as the "angel of death" waited for us. They quickly separated us by gender, age, and physical condition. We were told we would see each other on weekends (or in heaven, some kapos mumbled). The young and strong were quickly separated and assigned — without realizing it — to nearby labor camps to perform work that we soon learned would exceed human ability. The men and women were led in different directions; they would be sent to separate camps. We were so scared and rushed that we did not get a chance to hug, kiss, say farewell, or wish our parents or each other good luck. Oh, how I have wished a million times since then that I could have hugged and kissed my precious Mother, Father, sister, and brothers goodbye. The Nazis denied me that opportunity.

A skeletal man in a thin, ragged *katzetnik* (prisoner uniform) muttered to me in Yiddish that I was eighteen years old. I didn't understand what he was talking about or why he had to hide the fact that he was whispering. But when the angel of death — whom I later learned had been Dr. Joseph Mengele,[14] who had the power of the Almighty to decide who would live and who would die — asked me how old I was, I impulsively said I was eighteen. Thank God I was tall for my age. I was sent to the line of healthy-looking young men.

Since I was separated from my family, I could not see where they were headed. The young, strong women were sent to a line on the far right. Most of the others — the children, elderly, retarded, and people with visible illnesses or disabilities — were lined up in the middle. They were marched straight toward what the Nazis portrayed as a bathhouse. I thought I saw someone very familiar in that line — from the back he resembled Father. I ached to hug and kiss him, and especially my precious Mother, brothers and sister, goodbye. I couldn't even bid my cousins, uncles, or aunts farewell. We saw the machine guns, the whips, and the black uniforms with revolvers in their holsters and we knew that, if anyone disobeyed an order, his fate was predictable; disobedience would cost one dearly.

I had no idea why we were in this particular line or where anyone was going. It was so painful to be separated from my family. My mind was totally numb from not knowing what would become of us. As we were forced to march to the left in cadence, the guards watched with loaded rifles pointed at us, ready to shoot. I couldn't tell what the awful smell was or where it emanated from. The powerful, penetrating stench assaulted my senses. I was far beyond tired after the long cattle-car trip. I lost my ability to think, let alone speak. I felt terribly deserted, lonely, and empty.

After surviving the initial selection, I was hurriedly marched through the processing center, being screamed at and cursed along the way. We stood outside in the cold as the Nazis ordered us to remove our clothing and drop it on the ground. I learned quickly not to think, act, or try to do anything I was not specifically ordered to do. While we stood at attention, totally nude — like animals or criminals — the guards inspected us to see who was strong enough for the hard slave labor awaiting us and to make sure that we had nothing hidden on our bodies.

I could not help noticing the tall double row of electrified fencing and watch towers, with even more guards pointing machine guns down at us. The SS guards and killer dogs patrolling inside the double fences made it impossible to even think about escaping. Although I had been guarded in the ghetto, these sights sent chills through me. Dear God, I wondered, why are we here? Why are we being handled so brutally? What on earth could I have done wrong at my young age to deserve this shameless treatment?

Still naked, we entered another line to have our hair sheared brutally and quickly with blunt hand shears. It felt like my hair was being torn right out of my scalp. Afterwards I reached up to feel my head and saw that it was bleeding. That was painful and humiliating. After all, I was a lively young boy, and in my humble opinion, fairly handsome. Losing my attractive blond hair made me feel very low because I had always taken such pride in it.

After the shearing we were ordered into the showers. Given neither soap to wash with nor towels to dry ourselves, we stood momentarily under ice-cold water before quickly lining up again to be branded. The number "A-9018" was tattooed slowly and painfully into my left arm with the same unsanitary, dull needle used on others before me. (Of course, my tattoo soon became infected and full of pus.)

After the shearing and branding, I was thrown a funny-looking striped cap (*Mutze*) and a striped cotton uniform, and told to sew my number on it. This uniform and number would be my constant and only identity. Now I was no longer Yankele (Alex) Gross — I was merely A-9018.

It was becoming crystal-clear to me that our lives did not matter to the Nazis — only our labor was important. We were simply numbers to be kept track of.

In yet another line, I was thrown wooden clogs for my feet. I was to wear those clogs, that thin uniform, and the hat in all kinds of weather. We had no underwear, socks, or warm clothes to protect us from the cold. In contrast, we were surrounded by soldiers wearing sharp-looking, warm uniforms — comfortable, stylish, and weather-appropriate. Looking and feeling good no doubt supported their image of being invincible task masters. And it only made them more cocky and mean.

As dehumanizing and skimpy as our uniforms were, they were the only clothes we had. And we would wear them through hell every day and every night, for the rest of our stay in the camp.

Last but not least, we received a canteen and spoon for when they fed us meager rations of soup. These items were attached to the back waist of my pants by a string. Ironically, that string kept my pants up as I began to lose weight. My canteen and spoon were my only valuable possessions — and they would ultimately save my life.

As I put on my uniform, I kept looking for someone in my family. Miraculously, I saw my brother, Sam, as I was marched away — he was marched away in a different group. I was so overjoyed to find a familiar face that I wanted to rush over and say "Hello, Shmilku." Oh how I wanted to join him, hug him and tell him that we would have to stay together — and most of all, be careful if we wanted to live. As I started walking towards him, I got a good whipping from the kapos, so I fell quickly back in line and continued to march. But I was able to wave to him and shout, *"Geit gezunterhait, mein tajerer brider"* ("Go in good health, my dear brother") as they pushed me back in line. I could only hope he heard me.

I was heartbroken that I could not join Sam or be with any of my family, even for a moment. The Nazis made it clear that orders and rules had to be obeyed unquestioningly and we were not allowed to do anything unless specifically ordered to. I quickly realized that here hatred replaced love, and inhumanity replaced caring. Human feelings were nonexistent. Only loathing, cussing, screaming, beatings, torture, and hunger would surround us, day and night, from then on.

We were taken to a barrack to sleep on rough boards three tiers high with no mattress, straw or blankets. Of course, I could not sleep under those conditions so I stayed awake, traumatized and worried for my family. (To this day I have a difficult time sleeping.)

The next day the whistle blew at 5 a.m. and the guards started screaming, *"Jude, Raus!"* Shivering, we hurried to assemble for roll call in the freezing cold. They counted and checked us by our tattoos, gave us a meager ration of bread and what they called "coffee," then ordered us to march.

As we marched past the women's section to Auschwitz I, the main camp, I heard someone call "Yankele, Yankele!" For a few moments, I could not believe I had heard that wonderful, familiar voice. Then I remembered the beating I had gotten when I tried to communicate with Sam.

I heard the call again. I searched longingly for a familiar face through the barbed-wire fence that separated the men from the women. I looked at the women's faces. They too had had their hair cut off and wore the striped uniforms with frock-like jackets, and their heads were covered with striped kerchiefs. They all looked frail and very frightened.

Then I spotted my Mother and my sister. My Mother held her head high as usual, in the proud Jewish mother's tradition. She held Rosalyn's hand and they waved to me. Again, I heard her call to me *"Yankele, miner, vi-bis ti, Yankele? Geit gezunt."* ("How are you, my Yankele? Go in good health.") Those words have remained with me every waking moment for more than 55 years. They were the last words I would ever hear my precious Mother speak.

In my joy at hearing her voice, I longed to tell her how much I appreciated and loved her. I started to walk toward the fence so I could touch her. But as I stepped out of line, the kapos beat me with sticks, then a guard grabbed me, knocked me down on the rocky street, and beat me almost senseless to remind me again what would happen if I broke their rules. Once more, the Nazis made it absolutely clear that we were not allowed to do anything unless specifically ordered to. We were just Jews, considered subhuman. We would live only if, and as long as, they wanted us to.

It must have devastated Mother to see me, her youngest son, brutally beaten. Unfortunately it was the last time I saw her beautiful face. I shall never forget the look of worry in her eyes. Although she looked petrified, her love and concern poured out to me, even under those unspeakable circumstances.

I was terribly frightened of what the guards would do to her and Rosalyn simply because they had called for me and I had responded. Rosalyn was only fourteen, but she was tall and mature for her age. That probably saved her life, as it had mine. After that I worried about them every waking moment. I was afraid they would not be able to keep pace with the slave work day and night that I assumed was also required of women.

Cattle cars overflowing with human Jewish cargo continued to arrive at Birkenau around the clock from Hungary, Poland, Romania, Lithuania, Ukraine, Galitzia, and other parts of Europe. Like us, they were processed quickly so that they could be immediately exterminated or assigned to work in the nearby factories, forests, or coal mines.

From Auschwitz II (Birkenau), I was transfered to Auschwitz I and I read with dread the sign over the entrance: *"Arbeit macht frei"* ("Work Makes One Free"). I wondered if that sign — like the Germans' empty promises — was indeed the ultimate deception.

From the first day and throughout my internment in the camps, a profound horror remained in my heart. Time seemed to stop. Each day lasted a lifetime. I knew that unless we were liberated soon by the Allied armies, I would have to do hard labor until I died — or be killed for not working even harder.

To survive, I trained myself to answer only to A-9018. I quickly learned that hard work and absolute obedience — minute by minute, hour by hour, day after endless day — were the only tools I had to stay alive. To stay sane, I thought of our past family life which now seemed like a fairy tale. But I held onto it dearly and hoped for a better future soon.

I started losing weight immediately and had to tighten the string around my waist more and more to keep my pants up. As time went on, my physical exhaustion grew to levels I could not have imagined. But even more painful and difficult to handle was the constant mental stress. To communicate anything, the SS or kapos would scream and curse. They were vicious simply for the sake of viciousness. Many of the kapos, who were prisoners and convicted murderers, were as bad as the SS. They never talked to us calmly or addressed us as fellow humans. They liked venting their anger and frustration on us.

Witnessing such cruelty by the guards, the SS, and the kapos petrified me. I was especially dismayed to learn that some kapos and *blockaeltesters* (senior prisoners)[15] were actually Jewish people, assigned to oversee the barracks and work detail. Some of our people were even handpicked by the SS to work in the crematoria and gas chambers. They had to perform horrible tasks, such as removing gold fillings and crowns from the thousands of Jews who were burned to ashes. Often they had to carry the dead bodies of family or friends from the gas chambers or barracks to the ovens, remove any valuables, then remove the ashes after cremation. They even had to sift through the ashes for valuables, in case anyone swallowed their own gold, rubies, diamonds, or other precious belongings before they perished.

I felt completely cut off from humanity. It was difficult to comprehend that there were absolutely no moral principles where we Jews were concerned. It occurred to me that while most wars include some recognition of basic human rights, ethics or international law, here in Auschwitz, having Jewish blood in our veins meant that we unquestionably had no rights. We were not even permitted to notice if an SS man tortured or killed one of our people right in front of us. If he saw someone watching, it would be the end for that poor soul, too.

How painful it was to have to hide my compassion! When the guards were not around, I acted on my compassion and cared deeply for my fellow prisoners, regardless of the nonstop danger facing us.

We knew we were in the constant shadow of death. The SS and their cohorts carried out the mighty Nazi genocide program with such vengeance and enthusiasm, I felt that they were stalking us just as packs of wild beasts stalk weaker animals. They enjoyed every excuse to torture or kill us. Because I had lived in a village where German was spoken, I understood what the SS guards said to each other as they exclaimed how proud they were of their perverted inhumanities.

I heard, after liberation, that the Nazis had the very important goal of killing twenty-thousand Jewish people in Auschwitz every day. If for some reason they failed to meet their quota on a given day, the commandant would make sure it was made up the next day. If not, everyone would be in deep trouble. The officers were even given incentives for meeting their daily Jew-killing quota, so they sped up the killings by sending healthy young or middle-aged prisoners to their immediate deaths.[16]

I also heard, after liberation, that the shower spigots spewed deadly *Zyklon B* gas into the huge bathhouse instead of water, killing thousands of people upon arrival. If the bodies could not be burned fast enough in the many crematoria which operated 24 hours a day, they were piled high, thrown into dump trucks, and taken into the nearby forest. There they were dumped in huge pits, covered with gasoline, and burned. Sometimes even living people were dumped into those pits. The ashes of the dead were often used by the ultra-efficient Germans for fertilizer on their farms. Any telltale bones were thrown into mass graves and covered with lime and dirt to hide the evidence of the Germans' heinous crimes.

Fellow inmates told me of savage medical experiments. One involved deliberately infecting Jewish people with typhoid, diphtheria, and other diseases to see how long it would take to succumb to death. I was probably experimented on too, although I don't know for certain.

In Auschwitz there was no way to avoid these atrocities. We had to do what they ordered or face immediate death. We were sure that death would catch up with us eventually, anyway — either from starvation, overwork, disease, illness, or exhaustion.

Each morning and evening we had to stand at attention on the *Appelplatz* (parade ground) so they could check us by our tattoos. Sometimes we stood at attention for hours, during which, of course, I focused on missing my family and friends. I also remembered what I learned in Hebrew school — that we are first commanded to survive as Jews, lest we as a people shall perish. If we deny the existence of God our Creator, Who is above us and everyone else, then we deny the existence of humanity. No matter what horrors I endured, I tried to maintain some hope that we would soon be liberated because the Russians and Allies were getting close to us and, I surmised, starting to win the war.

The Nazis tried to dehumanize us in every possible way, but with me they failed. I certainly could not — and would not — stop caring for other humans or ignore the compassion I was brought up with. It would be like giving up my own life. Of course, that is exactly what the SS wanted us to do. Somehow we managed to encourage one other to get through the ordeals we endured, even if it was just one minute at a time. We desperately hoped that the camp would be liberated soon.

Although I hadn't seen it myself, new Auschwitz arrivals spoke of righteous Gentiles who were rescuing and protecting Jews. A fellow prisoner also told me that some non-Jews who were appalled by the Nazi atrocities actually shared food with Jewish friends in the ghettos. It was reassuring to hear that not all Gentiles were behaving unethically and brutally.

As uplifting as these stories were, they could not heal the cavernous wound in my heart. Unfortunately, the Germans were not doing this alone; there were many enthusiastic collaborators. The SS and other guards at Auschwitz consisted of Ukrainians, Lithuanians, Poles, Slavs, ethnic Germans from Romania and Hungary, and more. And these soldiers had the tacit support of local citizens all over Eastern Europe who saw and smelled the ghettos and death camps — who witnessed the cattle cars full of starving, sickly people and the cruelties we endured — and said nothing. The positive stories could not erase the reality that most Europeans condoned Hitler's fascist ideals and enthusiastically supported his agenda to take over the world and rid it of Jews. It proved to me that evil triumphs when good people stand by and do nothing to stop it.

After standing at attention all morning in the cold, we were checked once again by our tattoos, then ordered into the open trucks waiting to take us to Buna (Auschwitz III). I felt lucky, in a way, to be leaving the killing center's death headquarters — I thought my chances for survival might be better somewhere else. To go anywhere and work held such positive connotations for me that I even saw the SS and kapos in a better light. The SS were dressed very primly and properly. In fact, some of them were handsome. I saw them momentarily as soldiers and patriots performing their duty.

Our ride was short. When I arrived in Buna (Auschwitz III), I was glad to be away from the killing centers of Auschwitz I and Birkenau (Auschwitz II), but the grim looks of the inmates there scared the wits out of me. As I took in the double row of electrified twelve-foot fence, the screaming SS guards, their venomous German shepherds, and the machine guns pointing down at us from the floodlit watch towers, my feeble hope of a better chance for survival subsided quickly.

Chapter Six

Buna: Part I

Upon arriving in Buna (Auschwitz III) we were ordered to jump down from the trucks quickly, as SS guards and kapos savagely screamed at us and beat those who did not move fast enough to suit them. When we lined up to be accounted for by our tattoos, I noticed that we were surrounded by kapos wearing different-colored triangles. We learned that most of them were convicted criminals; not Jews. These "privileged" people were assigned by the SS to oversee us. Their presence was absolute assurance that anyone who stepped out of line would be killed; or would wish they were dead. My emotions vacillated between defiance, hope, fear, utter disgust and total despair as I awaited my next order. My hopes for better treatment disintegrated.

We were assigned immediately to a barrack and work detail. What seemed like a thousand prisoners were crammed into each small, wooden barrack, which was originally designed to house approximately fifty people. These barracks were uninsulated, windowless, and poorly made, with rough bunks three to four tiers high. Our beds were rough, wooden boards with no cushioning or covers. Sleeping on cold, splintery wood made my bed of hay back home seem like pure luxury.

I began my horrific slave work at the adjoining I.G. Farben factory very early the next morning. The I.G. Farben Industry was one of Germany's major producers of military hardware.[17] They kept the German army supplied with the best war machinery, electronics, and armor available in Europe at that time. When I first saw the massive military equipment they produced, I thought the German forces might indeed be invincible.

One of my tasks was to help construct several thirty-foot-high fire walls in the warehouses, which would serve as buffers to protect the highly sophisticated equipment stored there from bombing or fire damage. We had to haul large industrial concrete blocks with our bare hands or on our shoulders into the building, then lift them up to a platform to build the walls. We were to make several of these walls inside each of the huge warehouses we worked in. We would constantly be pushed to work harder and faster, sometimes sixteen to eighteen hours a day.

I soon discovered that our work assignments would change by the day, or even each hour. Such unpredictability — along with the Nazis' rude demands for instant, unquestioning obedience — made me feel they were forcing us to become robots or revert to childhood in order to survive.

As meager as our meals were, eating was always a joyous ritual. When — and if — we got some watered-down soup or bread mixed with sawdust, these "treats" helped warm our insides and gave us courage to stick it out — with God's help — until we would be liberated.

Time and the hard work dragged painfully on and on. We hoped and prayed for liberation. To help defeat the fascists and shorten the war, we sabotaged some of the anti-aircraft gun gauges by knocking out their quicksilver, which rendered them useless against Allied bomber planes. When the SS found some quicksilver in a garbage can and realized what we had been doing, they picked a few boys for hanging in the *Appelplatz* as a warning. We were forced to watch as our friends and bunkmates were hanged. The guards did not even cover the boys' heads; they wanted us to learn from their deaths that we could be next. How painful it was to be marched so close to those friends and see them dangling by the neck from a rope. Although I pitied them, I felt glad that at least they would not suffer any more. We had no pity for anything but life itself. Chance ruled our lives because of the extreme conditions, yet we tried to keep some moral sense and dignity.

Our work often included digging ditches with shovels or picks and working on roads and railroad tracks. We also had to hand-load railroad cars and trucks with heavy military equipment or confiscated goods to be shipped to the battlefields or the German interior.

To I.G. Farben, Mercedes Benz, Krupp, and other German industrialists, we represented nothing more than free slave labor. The leaders of these corporate giants did not care what the guards did to us to make us work. They totally ignored the fact that we were driven by beatings and punishments, that we had hardly any food to sustain us, and that many prisoners lived only a short time under such horrific conditions. I suppose they were confident that they could get more Jews and other slave laborers when we were gone. As a result, we were subjected to cruelties beyond comprehension. But no matter how difficult things were, we managed to rise above the evil surrounding us. We watched out for each other and encouraged each other whenever possible.

The trucks that had brought us here commuted between Buna and Auschwitz I and II probably a dozen times a day; some Jews were marched on foot from Auschwitz I and II to Buna. Between 1,500 and 2,000 healthy young men arrived daily, and approximately the same number of near-dead and dead bodies were transported back to Auschwitz I every day for cremation.[18] Many of my fellow inmates disappeared as a result of frequent selection for the gas chambers and crematories, or for starvation, exhaustion, and disease. The task of loading dead bodies onto the trucks was usually assigned to a special group, but once I had to do it. It was very torturous, to say the least. These people had been our bunkmates, fellow workers with whom we suffered. This abominable assignment tested our faith in humankind. The inhumane behavior of these hard-hearted people was totally unbelievable. Unfortunately, it was happening before our very eyes.

I had hoped the whippings, shouting and cursing would subside when we came to Buna, but it only got worse. The guards vented constant rage and hate at us, with their guns aimed and their whips ready to unleash their incessant anger at a moment's notice. Many times I wondered if the people in charge were really monsters in human bodies. Even though I was beyond petrified, emotionally lost, and told constantly that my life meant nothing, I knew that I did not deserve this horrible treatment.

Most of the time, the *blockaeltesters*, who oversaw the barracks and kapos, woke us before dawn, screaming *"Jude, Raus!"* The kapos lived in our barracks, but they had better quarters, straw and blankets to sleep with, a little more food, extra clothing, and a few other perks. To maintain these privileges, the kapos and *blockaeltesters* threatened us and traumatized us regularly. Although some kapos were less vicious, they were mostly all greedy, cruel people who wanted some extra food and took their hate and frustration out on us. They also wanted to prove to the SS that they were meaner to us than the Nazis were.

More than anything, we craved more food. Although we needed at least 3,000 calories each day for the heavy work we did, I doubt we received even 1,000 calories daily. I was constantly haunted by excruciating hunger pains. In my delusions I recalled my Mother's hearty breakfasts, with homemade bread and a tall glass of fresh milk from our cow.

Breakfast at Buna was a cup of so-called "coffee," although I don't think it actually contained much coffee. The main noon meal was supposedly a liter of meat soup four times a week and vegetable soup three times a week. Unfortunately, the soup contained very little meat or vegetables, if any. My weak body ached as I stood in line to receive a little sustenance. I fervently hoped the server would dip deeper into the large pot and give me something solid from the bottom that contained a little nourishment, such as a piece of potato. Or maybe I would be lucky enough to be served from that pot last and get a larger piece of potato — or even a sliver of meat. Everyone hoped for that; almost no one ever got it.

Being first in line was also desirable, as there might be a sliver of fat or spoiled meat floating on top of the soup. But very rarely were any of us fortunate enough to get this wonderful delight — it was usually slipped to the kapos, *blockaeltesters*, their favorite buddies, or boys they might want to have sex with. We knew that asking the server for more would mean additional punishment by the brutal ever-vigilant kapos. So we gladly accepted whatever we got — the watery soup or the bread mixed with sawdust. We were just happy to have something to put into our mouths. To get a fuller feeling, we would let the bread dissolve slowly in our mouths or drink water soon after eating it, which made the sawdust swell up in our stomachs. But later we would become sick from it with intestinal cramps.

In spite of the sawdust bread's unpleasant taste and texture, we were very careful to savor and protect our meager rations. I usually broke off a small piece at a time and let it dissolve slowly in my mouth, then stored the rest inside my jacket which was tucked in my pants.

I was afraid to fall asleep at night and lose my cherished bread to a bunkmate who thought I might be dead, instead of asleep. As I lay there, listless, I remained alert to the goings on around me and held tight to my bread, canteen, and spoon at all times. Those possessions were my only link to survival.

We even had to fight rodents for our precious fare. The mice and rats had a feast at night, nibbling on dead peoples' bread or their bodies. One night I was awakened by a large rat trying to nibble at my bread. I caught it by its tail, but it got away with part of the tail remaining in my hand.

The winter weather was especially harsh on us in this mountainous, swampy area, with strong winds and temperatures dipping way below zero. My miserable, weak condition made it feel like 100 degrees below zero. Indoors was not much better because there was no insulation or heat in either the barracks or the warehouses. But working outdoors was the worst. Even the SS men and their collaborators stayed indoors in bad weather; the kapos and *blockaeltesters* did their dirty work for them.

Although the cold weather produced ice, which we could sometimes break up and eat to quench our parched throats, unfortunately it only worsened my hunger, thirst, and injuries. I did not realize it, but I had many bruises, cuts, boils and even broken bones. Going to the bathroom added to my misery. We had to sit on ice-cold toilets made of rough stone mixed with concrete, 50 people to a row on two sides. Thanks to our terrible diet, my digestive system was a mess. In a short time, I became just like the *Muselmänner*.[19] We were zombies, moving about in silence. I actually had many near-death experiences, but somehow I kept listening to my Mother's precious voice inside my head, inspiring me to go on despite my pain. If I could somehow keep my emotional control, I could stay alive, I reasoned. I sometimes worried about my sanity in the camps. I felt alone, yet I heard the voices of my parents urging me to stay alive.

At Buna, death was commonplace. Many mornings I awoke to find that the man bunking next to me had died, his shriveling *Muselman's* body had given out and his troubled heart had stopped beating. Sadly, there was never time to say *Kaddish* (the Jewish prayer for the dead) because we were expected to line up for counting on the *Appelplatz* immediately after awakening. Some inmates just stopped trying to stay alive because they simply could not take the suffering anymore. For many it was easier to give up — especially when your son, father, bunkmate, or close friend had just died in your arms or next to you in the bunk. Some tried to take themselves out of their misery. Of the many attempts, a few men succeeded by hanging themselves with the string that held their pants up. Some tried knocking their heads against the wooden bunk posts. Along with my other bunkmates, I managed to talk some people out of giving up on life. I remember talking to a man around forty years old who had seen his son die. He wanted to end his life, but we saved him. After having suffered so long, I said, please do not give up now that we are so close to liberation. I secretly hoped I was right. It was a constant struggle to sustain ourselves, mentally and physically.

I was especially terrified about my family's fate. More and more people around me looked half-dead; I realized that I probably did not look much better. My family members were perhaps just as frail, I feared, wherever they were. I began to grasp exactly what my wise Father meant when he made me promise that no matter what, I must stay alive. This was the moment he had been afraid of for, in the camps, some people gave up and killed themselves out of despair because they could not tolerate any more pain, abuse, and hunger.

I made every possible effort to keep my promise to Father. I mustered all my energy to remain visibly human and keep my dignity intact. I especially tried to walk erect, look healthy and alive, properly salute the SS men with my *Mutze* (cap) off, and at least give the appearance that I was fit so that I would not be selected for the next group to be shipped to the gas chambers and burned to ashes.

I tried to ignore my constant hunger and other pains, even when I overheard the SS men take pleasure in our sufferings. I pretended not to hear as they assured us that we would never get out alive, and that the rest of the world would never believe their evil actions for lack of evidence. I vowed not to let them destroy my spirit; it was my only tie to survival.

The Nazis worked us very hard for up to eighteen hours per day, seven days a week. When we returned to the camp at night, they made us stand at attention once again to be counted. It was so hard to stand at attention when I desperately wanted some food or to lie down and rest. (Unfortunately, lice and disease made it impossible to actually rest; even the SS worried about their health and avoided getting too close to us.)

For entertainment the SS arranged more "hanging parades," picking their victims at random for hanging on the *Appelplatz*. These horrific events typically took place on Jewish holy days or the Sabbath. We stood at attention for hours, watching our friends being tortured and hanged; then we were forced to march past and look at them dangling from the gallows. They announced that these people had planned to escape, did not salute properly or obey commands. Their excuses for these murders were designed to keep us scared and worried. It was fun for the Nazis, but painful beyond comprehension for me. I asked myself, if they were going to kill us anyway, why did we have to endure such humiliation and cruelty? I also wondered how much longer I could hang on to my fragile life.

When the SS grew bored with the hangings, they invented new ways to amuse themselves at our expense. They did not need a reason to punish or hurt us; they knew we were in constant agony. But sometimes they randomly chose a few prisoners to beat and chase, forcing them to run into the electrified fence. The Germans watched with interest to see how high 1,500 watts would throw a boy. No one survived that game, of course.

The SS were also known to occasionally bring in specially trained German shepherds to attack prisoners between the legs and rip out their genitals. What sport for the Nazis! Once I had the misfortune of seeing a guard order some prisoners to pick up a young boy about my age and toss him into the air. The SS took bets among themselves regarding which one could shoot out the boy's right or left eye before he hit the ground. The SS even made some prisoners throw a young teen into the air so that an officer could impale him with his bayonet. When I saw this, I wanted to be taken out of my misery quickly. Death was becoming more and more appealing.

I remember seeing an officer get his jollies by removing a boy's ears because he claimed the boy did not hear him. The SS even cut the ears off of living people just to see whose were the largest — in full view of us prisoners and the SS comrades. Those who dared to hide their eyes became victims, too.

At times like that, the future looked beyond bleak. I felt as helpless as an animal in a cage.

Once a big Ukrainian SS man knocked my bunkmate down and stepped on his head, crushing his skull. He lasted only a couple days after that. Then I watched with sorrow as he was thrown onto a pile with other dead bodies to be shipped to Auschwitz I for cremation. It seemed we were condemned to die, whether from hunger, torture, pain, or abasement. The Nazis sought to annihilate all vestiges of humanity, reducing us to below the lowest wild animals. Maybe they wanted to make us as hateful as they themselves were.

An SS woman known as "The Bitch of Auschwitz" would come into the camp and make us stand for hours on the *Appelplatz* (parade ground) with our bare arms straight out. She selected young boys to step forward so she could see their skin color. The hands or arms of those with the "right" skin tone were hacked off with a large knife and the skin removed so that she could have lampshades, handbags and other goods made with it. Those victims literally bled to death. All that mattered to her was that the skin colors blended properly. Once she picked boys in front of me, to my side, and behind me. Somehow I was spared; I'll never know why.[20]

We occasionally saw the Nazi hierarchy and visitors. The guards would take photographs inside the camp for them and I overheard them brag to each other that these photographs would be used to show future generations about an extinct race — and to threaten others about what would happen if they did not fully cooperate with Nazi Germany. I imagined them boasting to their kids about how they had abolished the inferior Jewish race. I was sure that once they had disposed of us Jews, it was only a matter of time that other races would follow. Maybe the Russians, Czechs, French, British, Muslims, Gypsies, Slavic, or other people. After all, the Nazis had the power to decide which people were desirable and which weren't.

I asked myself many times, "Why has God embittered our lives so cruelly?" I thought, "He took our Jewish ancestors out of Egypt from slavery, but now we are suffering horribly, much worse than our ancestors did. Had we Jewish people sinned so much more than others? Do others not sin?" I felt there was no escaping Buna. To maintain my sanity and to cope with my hunger and so many other pains, I had to set aside these questions and hold onto the slim hope of liberation. I had promised my parents that, no matter what, I would try to stay alive. I wanted to survive and be reunited with my family, be able to love again, to get the chance to live like a human being. I wanted very much to believe that there were good people left in this world, even though I had not seen any for a very long time.

I felt that my continued survival was a fluke and nothing short of a miracle. Once I was kicked very hard in the leg by an SS man with big boots. It became excruciatingly painful to walk, but I did not dare show the kapos or SS that I was hurt or that my leg was broken. On another occasion, I was punched by a kapo so hard that he knocked me down. Then he kicked me until he wore himself out. There was nothing I could do but get up, look healthy and go on as though nothing had happened. They certainly wouldn't have cared — they probably would have just finished me off completely.

The camp had some sort of nursing center which they called a hospital, with a red cross on it. But I saw very few people ever come out of there alive. We learned that some of those who went there were used for medical experiments, then shipped with the other bodies to the crematoria.

Whenever I managed to gather the mental strength, I was able to take an objective look at the SS men in charge of us. In spite of their stylish dress uniforms, boots, and robust health, I actually felt a little pity for them. They had lost all trace of humanity, empathy, dignity, and compassion, which I thought must leave them feeling very hollow inside. I was also angry that I — the victim — looked and felt less than human, and those who acted like monsters looked well and civilized. We had to salute those savages with our caps (*Mutzen*) off every time we saw them. What an irony to have to pay servile tribute to such barbarians.

After a short time in Buna, the smell of the barrack at night was overpowering — not only from the dead and dying, but from our filthy, lice-infested bodies. Unfortunately there was no air circulation or any way to cleanse ourselves, and we had no clean clothing to change into. Keeping clean and healthy was impossible. After wearing the same dirty clothing every day, day in and day out for weeks and months, it felt like the dirt was glued to me. If I live forever, I will never forget the oppressive, overwhelming stench that was all around me.

CHAPTER SEVEN

BUNA: PART II

Lying on my crude wooden bunk at night, wanting but fearing sleep, and struggling with sores and lice, I often thought of my wonderful grandfather, Moishe Aaron, and his never-ending smile, as well as my two grandmothers. On one hand, I hoped that my grandparents were in heaven looking after us; on the other hand, I was relieved that they had not lived to see the horrifying fate of their children and grandchildren. It would have been sheer torture for such righteous people to see our good name replaced with a number tattooed on our arms, just because we were born and raised as decent Jews. They had such unbending faith in God and immeasurable pride in being decent and Jewish. Thank goodness they knew nothing of this hell.

Most of us stayed awake at night thinking about our families, wondering if we would ever see them again. I hoped with all my being that my parents, brothers, sister, and other relatives were okay. My greatest wish was that they had all been liberated by now. I reassured myself that they were young, strong, and healthy, surely they would be assigned to work, instead of the unthinkable alternative. I wondered about Filip, Ben, and frail, Bernie — who were all in Hungarian work camps — and Bill, who was brought to Auschwitz with Sam, Rosalyn and me. I asked if there was news of them whenever new prisoners arrived.

I was especially concerned for Rosalyn, who was tall and mature-looking but only 14. I was afraid that she would not survive the brutality the Nazis were dishing out. Sometimes I even worried about our American relatives whom I had never met. Were they still alive? Did they know what was happening to us? I wondered if fascism had taken over America. My greatest hope was that my wonderful American uncles and aunts were alive and, by now, well-informed of our plight. I fantasized that they would soon arouse the American people to defeat the Nazi Axis powers (Germany, Italy, and Japan). I pinned all my dreams and hopes on them.

In a way, I was glad that Filip, Ben, and Bernie had been taken away to the labor camp because I thought perhaps they would not suffer as much there under the fascist Hungarians. I hoped that they might have already been liberated by the Allied Armies.

Each morning as I marched off to work, I was always on the lookout for my Father, brothers, uncles, cousins, or friends. One day as I was on my way back from work, indeed a miracle occurred. A voice startled me as we marched past another group in the camp. I recognized it as the voice of my brother, Sam. What a relief for my aching eyes and shattered heart! I was absolutely elated when I saw him. He was the best medicine for my impoverished soul and shattered heart.

Despite how terrible he looked, just knowing that "Smilku" was alive and in the same camp gave my broken life new purpose. That purpose was to see him again and again — if not today, then tomorrow. If not tomorrow, then the following day, even if only to glance at him. I now had something to look forward to, especially while being marched to or from work. Whenever I did see him, I could hardly believe my eyes. My brother was alive!

Even though we were close physically, talking or socializing was forbidden in the camp, so we could never really spend any meaningful time together. The entire camp was only a few city blocks square, but it contained 20-22,000 inmates. We were literally crammed next to and on top of each other, yet it felt like Sam was miles away because I could not be with him.

I had to be content with just seeing Sam alive on occasion; I knew better than to publicly communicate or try to be with him. Not only could both of us be in trouble for being together, but as punishment for such a "crime," our bunkmates could have their food withheld, be assigned additional clean up detail at night, get beaten up or worse. As badly as I wanted to be with Sam, I refused to bring that wrath down on my fellow prisoners. I did not want to give the Nazis more excuses or opportunities to make it worse for us.

Regardless of my renewed hope, sometimes I felt I did not have the strength to go on living. Even getting in and out of my upper bunk took more strength than I had. But I reminded myself that giving up now would mean letting fascism and evil triumph. It would destroy the love and faith that my Mother and Father had in me. I still had faith — even though at times it wavered — that the spirit they instilled in me would help me survive. No matter what happened or what I had to endure, I knew with every ounce of my being that I must keep my promise to my parents to survive.

After having to endure so much suffering just because we were Jews, some inmates began to doubt their tradition, their faith, and even the existence of a God. Some felt He had turned away from them. Yet many of our "elders" — some of whom were in their thirties — had such a deep, abiding faith in God that they continued praying silently through the torture, beatings, and killings. I did not blame God for our misfortune. I realized that it was not God, but the uncaring fascists, the apathetic do-nothings and bad people, who were making us suffer so.

My heart ached and I pleaded with the Almighty, please do something to stop our suffering! Enough is enough! I prayed for myself, for my inmates, for my race, my family and for humanity. I tried to adhere to the traditions we learned as children at home and in Hebrew school, and to place my faith in our elders and the Almighty. I kept telling myself that Buna is just a bad dream. I hoped someone would wake me up any moment and tell me it's not true — that this incessant suffering, pain, and hunger was not real. I have no idea where we found the courage and strength to survive.

Like all the other prisoners, my body was shrunken to that of a little child, my legs were thin as rails, my mouth was pinched and my face puckered. No matter how a man appeared when he arrived at the camp, whether he had dark or light hair, small or large features, whether he was tall or short, fat or thin, joyous or sad, he lost his distinguishing characteristics in just a few weeks. The stronger-looking arrivals were given even less food than the others. Our pitiful condition pleased the SS men, kapos, guards — even the German civilian plant foremen and I.G. Farben executives — because it proved that they worked the life out of us and that they needed and deserved more healthy, young slaves.

I soon began to realize how starvation can make you crazy. Minute after minute, hour after hour, day in and day out, our sanity was tested — especially about lack of food. Everyone wanted to get in front of the soup or bread line before the food ran out. Our next breath often depended on the next bowl of soup or piece of bread. In our emaciated condition, to be denied even one meal was perilous. I wanted all of us to survive so I tried very hard to maintain some consideration for my fellow men and waited as patiently as possible for that next meager but precious meal.

The Nazis made it so very hard to keep our dwindling wits about us. If one of us lost his mind, caused a problem, complained, forgot to walk straight, or to salute properly, fainted, or lost his composure, the guards took it out by killing, beating, or shooting not only on that person, but on any number of us. If the guards felt like making life even worse, they would withhold food and water for several days from a person or group. Their theory was, "Why waste food or water on condemned Jews?" If they picked a reason to randomly single someone out, that sorry soul would soon be dead anyway.

The cold spring ended in Buna. Spending the summer in a low-lying wetland meant very muggy and hot weather, and an increase in insects and rodents. All kinds of bugs feasted on us, especially lice. They came by the thousands to gorge themselves on our heads, underarms, and groin, weakening us even more so and spreading all kinds of illnesses and disease among us. I remember running my hands over my head and picking up hundreds of them.

At midday, when it was hottest, we prayed for rain to cool and cleanse us a little bit — especially while we worked outside digging ditches, lifting heavy building blocks, and hauling rock and steel. When we did receive the gift of rain, we stayed outside. It felt so good and I was so grateful just to be able to catch the rain in my hands to drink it, and splash some fresh water on my parched, filthy body. Even the all-powerful guards couldn't control the weather, nor could they diminish that wonderful feeling we got from the rain. When they fled temporarily for shelter from the rain, we revelled in washing our faces, hands, and heads. It felt like manna from heaven.

Sometimes during the heat of the day, the guards would have water delivered to us, rather than lunch. They would give it to a just few people, then they would look at the rest of us who were madly, expectantly craving it and they would pour that liquid gold onto the ground. The guards laughed at our misery as the hot sun soaked up the wasted water. I will never forget the horror of seeing people lying dead with their tongues hanging out, their bodies empty yet swollen from lack of fluid. How sad to see someone whom I had suffered with, befriended, worked with or bunked next to with no strength left to stay alive.

As exhausted as we were, even blessed sleep was dangerous. There was no relaxation for us because sleep could mean death. As time dragged on we became foggy, like in limbo. But strangely enough, our instinct, vigilance, and reaction quickened when we needed it most. Somehow we all managed to adapt ourselves to those horrid conditions, even if we had become like infants in diapers, without completely surrendering to our fate.

As the Allies got closer to liberating our area, they began bombing our factory more often. Whenever the sirens sounded, the SS, German civilians and executives ran for the air raid shelters we were forced to build for them. One time, as the bombs fell all around us, a young rabbi created a sensation by mustering his courage and strength to climb upon a mound of dirt and proclaim loudly in Hebrew that it was a holy day for us. "The way to truth and justice is often filled with affliction and pain," he proclaimed. "Let us ignore the atrocities and our sufferings; please come close. Let us pray to the Almighty for deliverance." He led us in prayer and, of course, we had no prayer books or the energy to pray. No doubt most of us had trouble believing there is a God; some thought He might be Satan. After all, who else could make us suffer so much?

One day, in the midst of an air raid when the guards were in their shelters, another rabbi got up and, paraphrasing the Yom Kippur liturgy, declared: "The decree is signed above. The fate of man and nations has been determined: who shall win and who shall lose, who shall eat and who shall go hungry, who shall die of the plague and who of hunger or suffocation." Later he said that our fate was proof that God had chosen to remain deaf to their prayers because of their sins and those of their forefathers.

We had prayed so hard and waited so long for deliverance, but the Messiah did not come. Our slavery, hunger, and suffering continued. How could we have faith under such ungodly conditions? Unfortunately, salvation did not come quickly enough for many of us.

The summer was thankfully short-lived; soon fall weather set in. At first I enjoyed the cooler weather. I thought maybe the lice would stop feasting on us. My sixteenth birthday was September 18. Even though 1944 was the most painful, traumatic year yet of my young life, I considered myself fortunate to be alive and to know that at least one brother was still alive, too. But with an early winter on the way, I worried that survival would become even more torturous and difficult. The wind and cold would whip right through us; we had no body fat to keep us warm.

Every day and every night we were covered with nothing but the same thin, striped uniform that we were issued when we arrived. As the cold worsened to ten to fifteen degrees below zero, the wind cut mercilessly through the threadbare cloth like a knife through my weak body. I felt I would not be able to stand the driving gusts of frigid wind much longer. Of course, seeing the SS guards, and civilians wearing high leather boots with thick socks, warm uniforms and overcoats, underwear, ear muffs and hats made my suffering more acute. I desperately craved a warm outfit, some long, toasty underwear, and especially the thick socks that my Mother used to knit. I thought of the many woolen scarves and blankets that my Mother and grandmother had made by hand for us, and the thick covers on our beds at home. These warm thoughts helped keep my wavering hopes alive at night as I lay in pain on my hard, wooden bunk in the drafty barrack.

The Allied air attacks were becoming more frequent, which fed our hope for imminent liberation. As the bombs exploded only a few feet from us, we watched the Germans shoot at the Allies and miss, thanks to the gauges we had managed to sabotage. Almost daily we heard warning sirens and anti-aircraft guns going off. Rumors spread that the Russian troops were nearby and even surrounding us. As time progressed, it seemed that the war really was going against the Germans. This was very encouraging, although we were getting less food — only a small slice of bread every day or two. Hunger and suffering continued to pierce our hearts and bodies, forcing us to cry silently, yet we refused to give up life and hope. I held tightly to my dream of salvation, liberation, sufficient food, and a better, safer life to come.

The increased bombings seemed to feed the Nazis' fear. Every day the guards pressured us to work harder and accomplish more for the greedy German companies. We had no choice. We did work hard, especially outside, which helped keep the cold at bay. Some days we had to break through the thick ice just to be able to repair the buildings, streets, railroad tracks and other areas damaged by military vehicles or Allied air attacks.

When snow fell during the day, we caught the flakes in our hands and wet our thirsty lips as if it were ice cream. Surprisingly, the SS started giving us a little more drinking water, and we were even allocated an occasional shower. Even though the water was cold, I felt relieved to remove some of the lice that covered much of my body.

By November 1944, the roads and the ground water were frozen up to a foot deep, but we had to work on them just the same. We had no way to keep our feet and hands warm. Many people lost toes, feet, and lives because their sockless feet froze to the ground as they stood for hours on the *Appelplatz*. One late afternoon when I was working with ice-coated concrete blocks, my fingers stuck to the ice. I was afraid I would lose my fingers, but somehow I managed to pry them loose. It is a wonder that all my digits remained intact.

We dreamed of spring and its promise of new life. Perhaps by some miracle we would see spring as free humans. Perhaps we would live to see the green grass grow again, see the budding of flowers, smell the fresh air, and maybe return to vibrant life among other humans.

The downside of the coming spring was, once again, the smell. Even in the cold weather we could detect the stench not only from our own bodies, but especially from the corpses piled outside the barracks. They were supposed to be picked up early each morning to be taken to the crematoria for burning. Otherwise, they would rot and stink when the sun came out. Although we were several miles from the crematoria, when the wind blew in our direction we could smell the smoke from the burning flesh. It is an odor that I will never forget as long as I live.

As I lay in my bunk, sometimes I thought regrettably of the heartaches I had caused my parents — especially when I refused out of sheer stubbornness to eat the good, hearty food made by my Mother's loving hands. Or when I grumbled about being forced to wear hand-me-downs from my older brothers, or failing to learn in Hebrew school, or not doing my work because I would rather play soccer with my friends. Oh, how I would like to be asked by my family members now to do something for them! I would gladly do anything they asked, seven times over.

I recall the day when a fresh bunch of healthy, young people arrived from Alsace-Lorraine, France, along with a new group of Jews from Hungary, Holland and other countries. They were very robust-looking, as most newcomers were. Several were assigned to our barrack. I shared a bunk with a celebrated Frenchman who vehemently denied being a Jew or having any first- or second- generation Jewish ancestors but somebody turned him in as a Jew. Another bunkmate was a famous Jewish physician from Germany who somehow managed to hide his Jewish identity for a few years, thereby avoiding arrest. Later a very nice former Dutch aristocrat was assigned to a bunk above me.

These once-elite people experienced true culture shock when they were arrested, taken to Auschwitz, processed, and given a skimpy striped uniform. They were immediately assigned to our camp for heavy manual slave labor, just like the rest of us. They did not expect this harsh treatment and certainly were not used to the lack of food. For the most part, they had a harder time coping with life in Buna than I. Perhaps it was the comfortable lifestyle they had led. To the Nazis, they were just as undesirable as other Jews, regardless of their stature.

It was only a matter of time before these newcomers would be reduced to skin and bones. We tried to give them courage — even if it was only whispering to each other a few minutes at night on the *Appelplatz* or in the barracks. We were determined to retain our human traits — and help others retain theirs — in spite of the traumas, impossible obstacles, and grave dangers we faced.

I felt very inept among those well-spoken, sophisticated aristocrats. I was one of the youngest and definitely the least educated in our barrack. I was unable to communicate in French, Dutch, Greek, Italian and some of the other languages they spoke. But I looked forward to my rare, short conversations with such fine men — somehow it made life a little more bearable in that hell hole. I respected their former status and splendor, but most important was that they were nice. I felt sorry for them because while they tried to retain their good manners, they could not do it for long. Most of the time they spoke a broken Yiddish to no one except me; for some reason they liked me and I was pleased. Maybe they felt sorry for me; they tried to teach me more about the world and I tried to give them courage.

Eventually they told me about the wonderful lives that had been taken away from them. Some had been raised as Christians and had continued to practice

Christianity; some had even joined the fascist movement. They spoke of their confusion of living as Christians in a Christian world that had turned on them. Their Christian friends — and even worse, their Christian relatives — betrayed them. All the security they had felt earlier was suddenly gone. Now they were just numbers, condemned like the rest of us, eventually becoming sickly and infested, forced to perform slave labor and stand with us in the cold for hours for some paltry food and water.

They were in terrible agony. Often they cried with their heart and eyes open, seeming to hear and see nothing of the horrible reality going on around them. There was something very pathetic in their muteness.

The Allies (mostly British military planes) were now bombing our factory almost every day.[21] Although the Nazis were obviously suffering losses, things did not get easier for us. Our hard slave work increased with the bombing damage. One time a bomb fell very close, knocking me down. Other bombs hit the building we were working in, setting it on fire. After the fire was put out, we had to clear the rubble and repair the damage to the buildings, roads, and railroad tracks. Many prisoners were killed by the bombs and shrapnel or were buried alive under the dirt. Sometimes I felt envious of them because their suffering was over.

One day when we were clearing the rubble away after a bombing attack in the warehouse where I worked, we discovered a big, unexploded bomb in the pile. We were ordered to clear the rubble around the bomb, then tie ropes around it and slowly pull it out from the building. Just as we lowered the bomb into a crater where another bomb had fallen only a few hours ago, the bomb exploded and killed several of our boys. It had been set with a timer. Had it exploded one second earlier, I also would have perished.

As time went on, we expected the British or other bombers to target the factory and warehouses constantly, but they only came one or twice a day. Sometimes the bombers even skipped several days. I prayed that they would bomb the railroad tracks leading to Birkenau (Auschwitz II) to stop the killings of our people, or that they would bomb our camp — especially the watch towers and electrified fences — so that maybe we could escape. But no such luck. Life and misery continued as usual in Buna. Our barrack was continually filled to capacity with new people brought into camp almost to the last days.

Finally the Germans began to get serious about the Allied attacks. They forced us to work night and day, loading the warehoused equipment into large trucks and filling the railroad cars to capacity. They wanted the valuables shipped out away from Poland and the Russians, into the interior of Germany. I guess they still felt they could take over the world.

It was a race against time for the liberators to arrive. After we emptied the warehouses and loaded all the merchandise, we learned that we were next on the evacuation list. I hoped the SS and guards would be forced to flee and abandon us so that we could finally be liberated by the Allies. I didn't care who liberated us for the chance to get some food and feel human again — even the Russians would have been okay with me. But the SS would not let us alone for even a moment. The sinister clouds of suffering and death continued to surround us as those cold-blooded murderers constantly confronted and suppressed us.

My eight interminable months in Buna ended abruptly one evening just after work. It was one of the coldest, snowiest evenings I can ever remember. As we entered the barracks there was a loud, *"Raus!"* from the *Blockaeltester*, who ordered us to assemble on the *Appelplatz* to be counted and checked out by our tattoos once again.

Tonight it seemed something wasn't going right for the SS. They seemed in a panicky mood, although they still managed to be hateful and cocky.

We were lined up in ranks of five, with guards on both sides, and ordered to march out of the camp. I wondered where we were going; it was too late to be going back to work. The cadence started *"einz-zwei-drei"* ("one-two-three") as we were forced to move quickly into the dark oblivion and freezing weather, with no idea where we were bound.

CHAPTER EIGHT

THE MARCH FROM BUNA

As I marched out of the camp along with about eleven-thousand others, I kept looking for Sam. Anguish enveloped me as I considered the possibility of being separated again from the only brother I knew was alive. Each night I felt alone. My heart was heavy as I clung to my flimsy existence. I considered trying to stay behind, but that would surely mean death because I believed the Germans intended to eliminate every trace of evidence of their crimes. I assumed that the Russian Army was advancing fast and that the German guards realized there was too little time to exterminate all the prisoners and dispose of our bodies — plus they needed us to load the railroad cars and trucks up until the last minute to move their equipment, confiscated bounty, and military hardware into the German interior. I quietly asked the people on either side of me what they thought was in store for us. I had a constant need for personal reassurance that we were to be rescued soon, before it was too late. Fear squeezed me breathless.

Our barrack was one of the first to leave. The cruel wind howled and snow blew in our faces, making it difficult to walk. We could not possibly have been prepared for this. Marching quickly in my weakened condition stretched the limits of my determination. I did not know how we would survive even a few minutes of this journey, let alone hours. Guards were positioned on all sides of us, and anyone who slowed down was whipped, hit with a rifle butt, trampled on, beaten, or shot on the spot. Once again, I was jealous of my dead comrades. I was ready to give up; I did not want to suffer anymore.

As darkness set in, the bitter cold passing through my body felt like sharp knives carving my insides. My wooden clogs were as heavy as lead as I pulled them painfully through the snow and slush. Ice formed around my toes. My feet were frozen through and through. I thought of those thick socks Mother used to make which would have helped cushion my blistered feet and given my shivering body some relief.

I worried continually about Sam and the rest of my family. I desperately wanted him to survive because I did not think I could go on without him. Just knowing he was alive had kept me going in Buna. I watched for Sam, but there was no way to track him among the weary mass of people. We were not allowed to stop or slow down, let alone step out of line to go to the bathroom. We marched as fast as they could force us, and I thought longingly about my childhood. I may have been hallucinating, but dreaming of the good home I had been taken from helped me find the strength to keep moving.

We marched through populated Polish villages and communities. The faces of those healthy, strong onlookers were ugly to me because they lacked all compassion. How could they look at us and not care? We were obviously so hungry and weak, barely able to drag our feet. They could have thrown us some clothing or food — or at least given us some encouragement — but they did not. Perhaps I should have been used to the overwhelming presence of inhumanity by then, but it never stopped depressing me to see the absence of mercy in my fellow human beings.

As we slogged through the snow, the officers and guards often relieved each other from the weather. Sometimes they rode in comfortable, heated jeeps or trucks, still guarding us fiercely on all sides to make sure everyone continued marching straight ahead.

They vented their anger at us when they had to be out of the warm vehicles that transported them. Some beat us with whips as we struggled to walk; others used their bare hands — either out of frustration or just to exercise their limbs and ward off the cold. Anyone who got out of line or slowed down was kicked or hit. When that didn't work, they shot to kill — sometimes at random. Over and over, I saw guards shoot people who strayed from the group or could not march fast enough to suit them. They didn't care that we had no strength left to go on. Many times I heard my fellow campmates pray for death, but death was not an option for me.

It had been quite awhile since we had received even a halfway-decent portion of bread; the past few weeks in the camp we had been given mostly watered-down soup. After the first full day and night of marching we had still not been given any food. The guards got extra rations and threw the leftovers in the ditches, just to watch us scramble for it. Then, for additional entertainment, they would stop us from reaching it.

By now, we had absolutely no meat on our bones. The sight of my fellow prisoners was beyond frightening. I realized that I too must have looked like a walking skeleton.

Prisoners marching in the center of the long, wide lines were slightly more protected from the fierce wind that those in the front, back, and sides. We huddled together whenever possible to ward off the blustery winds and tried to keep each other going, even if for just a little while longer. When someone was completely spent, the others marching nearby (who still had enough energy) would try to support him so that he might gain enough strength to continue. When they could no longer hold him up, he crumpled to the ground and was trampled over or left behind.

Prisoners who died or were too slow to keep up were thrown like rotting garbage onto the military trucks. When the trucks were fully loaded, the guards used machinery to dig ditches in the woods, then dumped the bodies in unceremoniously. When the graves were full, they poured gasoline over them and threw in a lit match. After that, they tried to hide their crimes by bulldozing dirt over the remains.

Amazingly, civilians watched, emotionless, while the dead were discarded like trash and the nearly dead were forced at gunpoint to continue walking.

The guards and kapos continued to hound us and we dared not stop or slow down. As time went on, more people on the edges fell over, frozen. Soon we were no longer in lines — we were bunched as close together as possible. Our numbers dwindled as we continued on for miles. Every excruciating minute was an hour. It seemed like months, not days, since we had left Buna. I thought we would never reach our destination.

I stumbled on resolutely. I felt that we had endured too much suffering to give up now. I was also encouraged to see for the first time an SS man's fear of being captured by the Russians. He stopped prodding us, turned to the guard next to him and said in Hungarian, "I am tired of the killings. It looks like we are losing the war. If we are going to be captured by the Russians, they will surely torture and kill us." Then he put his gun barrel in his mouth, pulled the trigger, and killed himself. It was horrible to watch, but it made me think that perhaps we would be liberated any moment, bringing an end to our interminable suffering.

Military vehicles whizzed by us in all directions, and gunfire grew louder. It was sweet music to my ears. I imagined that the Nazis would be defeated by morning. Perhaps we might even be liberated by nightfall, then reunited with our families. I was afraid to get my hopes up because they were often dashed, leaving me feeling more despondent each time.

The cold night dragged painfully on as the Nazis forced us to continue. We urged each other to keep moving, no matter how painful it was — that bit of encouragement helped me greatly.

In my stronger moments I helped several boys my age. I literally carried a young boy on my back as I crawled on all fours, knee-deep in snow. He paddled the snow with his feet to help us keep moving. As we struggled together to keep up the fast pace, we both miraculously survived the ordeal and finally arrived at our destination: Gleiwitz, another Auschwitz sub-camp. Although it was still a prison camp, Gleiwitz offered at least a roof over our heads, a piece of bread, and a bowl of warm "soup." I was grateful for that.

Always uppermost in my mind was some food and my family. After I ate and gained a little strength, I wandered around looking for family members. Amazingly, I found Sam who was in almost as bad shape as I was. What a relief to know he was still alive! We somehow communicated in Yiddish with tears in our eyes and heart. This was more important to my remaining alive than even nourishment.

The next day, the Nazis woke us with their usual screams and ordered us to assemble outside. (Even after all those months I never adjusted to being screamed at continually — it always jolted me — which I suppose was what they wanted.) After checking us by our tattoos, they forced us into roofless coal-carrying boxcars constructed of icy steel not only on the bottom, but on all sides. A hundred or more of us prisoners were stuffed into each small car in our smelly, weak condition, more dead than alive — again with no food, water, or protection from the biting below zero cold and wind. The Nazis separated me from Sam once again, but at least I knew he was alive.

The thought of escaping crossed my mind, but I did not have the strength to lift myself or anyone else up and over the side of the car. Even if I had gotten over the top, how far could I go in the sorry shape I was in? No one was in any condition to resist or try to flee. We were drained of real life. It seemed the end of all ends.

I guessed we were headed into the German interior, but I didn't really know. As I wondered where we were going and what to do about it, the guards bolted the locks from the outside. I was doomed to continue my torturous trip.

CHAPTER NINE

FROM GLEIWITZ TO BUCHENWALD

The next days and nights in the coal car were like a tormenting dream. I could barely think; the overwhelming cold numbed my senses. During the day the harsh weather was terribly painful; at night it was incomprehensible. Despite all I had already endured, I had great difficulty believing this nightmarish trip was happening to me. Being separated again from Sam was even more difficult to accept; this time I felt there was no way either of us would survive. I did not know who would be the first to go, but I did not expect that we could last long enough to see each other again.

At this point I no longer expected the Nazis to give us food, water, blankets, or warm clothes — and they didn't. I felt like a sardine in a topless tin can, crammed in so tightly that my body sores ached when I pressed up against my fellow sufferers. The sores on the bottom and sides of my feet from the march were the worst, but I couldn't relieve them because there was no room to sit. It felt like we were crumpled stand-up wooden soldiers — somehow still upright, but shaking terribly at the knees. One push and we would collapse in a heap.

After many hours of waiting for the military and booty trains to pass, we finally started moving. For a while the cars only jerked back and forth, then they were finally put on the right track. The train began chugging along slowly, then it soon reached speeds of up to 50 miles an hour, which created a below zero blistering wind in our faces. But in spite of the unbearable cold and terrible hunger pain, the sensation of extreme thirst was more tormenting than anything I had ever experienced.

We passed through many towns and villages, stopping often to allow trains and military transports to pass or because of Allied attack planes overhead. I heard frequent air raid sirens in action. When the train stopped — under a bridge if we were lucky — sometimes a piece of sleet or ice would fall on us from above. Most of us — including myself — were too weak or could not free our frozen hands to catch the precious ice or snow as it came down. It was so tragic to miss this gift from heaven. I imagined it tasted wonderful.

Once again, the witnesses to our fate along this barbarous journey were indifferent. We pleaded weakly with them for food and water — or even for a snowball or an icicle — but not one person responded. It was very sad to see such appallingly apathetic behavior. I could not believe how they stared through us as though we did not exist. It was the ultimate proof that we had been totally abandoned by the world, that humanity was surely dominated by evil.

Each day in the coal car stretched into a stagnant lifetime. By the second day of this death ride, many people in our car succumbed to the bitter cold, hunger, and especially the excruciating thirst. We survivors were helpless to stop their deaths. Those who were not dead were definitely close to it. The hours upon hours I had spent pleading with my fellow prisoners not to give up, holding onto them, trying to keep them alive, will remain in my memory forever. I tried desperately to retain my humanity when all remnants of normalcy had been stripped away.

We tried in vain to draw warmth from each other; in desperation we crawled under the dead bodies to fend off the raging wind. For a little while their bodies retained some warmth, but eventually they turned into clumps of awful-smelling ice.

After a few days in the coal car, the stench of death and excrement became utterly unbearable. Those of us who managed to stay alive were forced to urinate and defecate in our clothing — there was no place else to go. Our waste froze on our bodies, which of course were covered only by our thin, ragged uniforms. Some prisoners managed to remove the clothes from the dead bodies and wore them to keep from freezing to death. Our clothes were torn and rotted through from filth, mud, urine, sweat, and blood, so the extra jacket or pants were sorely needed. I was fortunate to get a pair of regular shoes that were a few sizes too large for me, so I discarded my wooden clogs.

At one of our many stops I overheard the guards discussing our destination: Buchenwald. They boasted that if any Jews arrived alive — which they doubted — it would be the last stop on our life's journey.

The coal car ride was undoubtedly the most painful, heartbreaking journey any of us had ever endured. I saw one of our people actually tear his own guts out with his hands, he was so overwrought with suffering. Some banged their heads violently against the steel wall to end the pain. Those harrowing images will remain in my memory forever.

The train finally stopped inside the electrified fences of the camp called Buchenwald, near Weimar. The guards unlocked the steel door from the outside, screaming their usual *"Jude, Raus!"* But this time most of the passengers could not obey. Of the approximately 120 in our car who began the merciless journey from Gleiwitz, only eight arrived alive. God alone knows how we survived. We were too weak to remove the dead bodies to be burned or buried, so we were spared that additional anguish. The Germans ordered the inmates of the camp to begin piling up the dead bodies to be taken to the crematorium.

Once again I saw the familiar electrified barbed-wire, the watch towers looming over the camp, and the iron sign at the entrance stating *"Arbeit macht frei"* ("Work Makes One Free") — just as in all the other camps that had imprisoned me.[22] I wondered how many more times I would have to pass through those gates and experience the irony of that message before "freedom" became completely meaningless.

We were assembled in the center of the camp and identified by our tattoos. As we were marched to the camp interior, I recognized the unforgettable stench from the crematoria. It was the same smell as Auschwitz-Birkenau where the ovens burned human flesh twenty-four hours a day.[23] I realized that I was on unholy ground yet again.

In spite of the odor and my profound fatigue, I had no trouble eating the amazing feast we were given after roll call — a full ladle of warm "soup" and two slices of real bread. I looked up to Heaven and thanked the Almighty as tears of gladness rolled down my sunken cheeks because they treated us like political prisoners, not condemned people.

As we marched to our assigned barracks after dinner, I heard the anguished cries from inmates around me who survived the coal car ride, only to expire after arriving in Buchenwald. Although I was weaker than ever, at least I was still alive. For that I was thankful.

I hoped that after a few days of rest and better meals I would get stronger. As soon as possible I started to look for my family — especially Sam — among the recent arrivals. When I could not find him, I shook with the petrifying fear that I might never see him again. I heard similar stories from others about the fates of their families after they were separated at Auschwitz. We wanted to survive, but what kind of future would we have if everyone we loved was killed? I tried to quell my fright as I vowed never to stop looking and hoping.

CHAPTER TEN

BUCHENWALD

When I arrived in Buchenwald in early January of 1945, I was extremely weak, physically and mentally. I could not think clearly. I was too frail to walk and too sore to lie down. Yet, in my imagination, an angel called to me gently. I heard my Mother calling, her cries tearing me apart.

Although Buchenwald looked just as dreary and frightening as Auschwitz, I soon realized it was different. It was not designed specifically to be an extermination camp like Auschwitz I. The food was scant but more equitably distributed. The hospital seemed less of a death sentence. I discovered that children were not automatically exterminated when they arrived, but placed in a designated children's section. Regardless of these "improvements," the darkest months of my incarceration would occur here.

As usual, my new "house" consisted of long wooden barracks. We slept on rough planks, three tiers high, with no mattresses, pillows, straw or blankets. The earthen floors were covered in human feces. The now-familiar stench in the barrack was dreadful, from both excrement and death.

I was assigned a third-row upper bunk, and the climb up to it each night was agony. My frozen feet continued to feel like blocks of ice. They were so sore that I couldn't stand to touch them, much less put my weight on them. It was a struggle just to move one aching foot in front of the other. Standing for roll call, which occurred several times a day, and waiting in food or drink lines, which formed once or twice a day, took every ounce of strength I possessed. But I was not alone. Most of the new arrivals were true *Musulmänner,* teetering on the brink of death.

My mind drifted in an endless stupor. I would often stare blankly into nothingness, pitifully hoping for food, water, or a shower, yet expecting to expire at any moment. In my daze I dreamed mostly of food and of seeing my family again. But the lice that feasted on my head, between my legs, and under my arms abruptly brought my reveries to an end. My striped and torn uniform was covered with sweat and filth. I was frighteningly pale. Even when I was allowed to speak, my voice was slow and faltering. I remember thinking many times that I could not go on, that I had reached the end of my strength. I often felt too weak to make it even for another minute, let alone another day. I was a small, helpless child in a shrivelled-up old man's body. But I kept trying to hold on to the thin thread of resolve that was left in me. I expected to die and was ready for death, but I wanted very much to live. I refused to give up.

After a few days of food and rest, I began feeling a bit better. I soon learned that the camp, although hidden far off the main routes, was located close to the center of the Third Reich, near the city of Erfurt in what had been the Weimar Republic of Germany. In the past Erfurt had been known for its art, music, and literature. How far it had fallen.

I felt certain that the Russian Army had already liberated Auschwitz. If only the Germans had left us there, we would be free by now. When would the Allies reach this God-forsaken place?

Whenever I thought I had suffered the worst-possible beatings or overcome the most tormenting pain, there was always something worse in store. Every miserable minute, hour, and day was a repeat of the preceding one.

There was not a large factory here, as at Buna, but there was a stone quarry. Sometimes they took us out of the camp to work on roads, farms, or high German officials' properties. As the Allies moved closer and bombed some of the surrounding cities, they brought us out to work less often — mostly just to repair railroad tracks, roads, buildings and such.

The Nazis began taking prisoners out for other reasons, however. The guards gathered us every day on the parade ground and chose nearly a thousand prisoners each day to be marched or shipped out. The people they chose were supposedly taken to other camps, but more often than not we heard machine gun fire in the forest shortly after they left. I could imagine the mass graves the Nazis were creating, even though I could not see them. The threat of arbitrary disposal that hung over us all each and every moment became more intense whenever the camp became crowded with new arrivals. The Nazis proudly stated many times that they were doing Hitler's work for the Third German Reich. Their barbarism never ceased to amaze me.

I also found out that there were all kinds of political prisoners, as well as prisoners of war, in the camp. Czech, French, Dutch, Russian, and even American prisoners of war were in another section, and lately it seemed as though they were running things, not the SS. These relatively healthy-looking prisoners kept us informed of current events. They said that soon we would be liberated.

Jews had been brought to Buchenwald only the last few years, towards the end of the war. Like me, most were from other camps. Although Buchenwald at first seemed less brutally run, once the SS began realizing that Germany might lose the war, their fear fed their malice. More and more frequently they came to our barracks and removed prisoners at their whim to be tortured and beaten to death.

One day it seemed as if everything had switched into high gear. The lightning pace of the killings and disposal no longer satisfied the guards and their SS. The barracks were being emptied faster and faster; no doubt those "lucky" people were bound for yet another camp or a fatal "walk" in the forest.

Even Ilsa Koch, the Commander's wife — also known as the "Bitch of Buchenwald" — no longer made her macabre visits.[24] I had heard that, like the "Bitch of Auschwitz," Koch would come into the camp to select boys with the "right" skin tone for her lamp shades, handbags and other leather goods. We were relieved to hear that she would not be coming.

We prayed fervently for quick liberation from our misery. Even in my state of near-death, I felt glad that the end of the war seemed imminent. Something was about to change for the better. Unfortunately, liberation did not come in time for most of the prisoners. Within a few weeks of my arrival, we stopped getting food twice a day. Many mornings, when I reached over in the bunk to touch the hand of the fellow next to me, he had died. Dead bodies continued to multiply outside our barrack, stacked as high as the eaves in some places. The crematorium continued to operate around the clock, but it still couldn't keep pace with the daily massacres. The crematorium's noxious odor and the smell of rotting bodies piled outside filled my lungs so intensely that I often could hardly breathe.

The constant presence of death — and the rate at which we were being exterminated like a bunch of rodents — was humiliating. As I drifted in and out of delirium, my frail jaundiced body totally exhausted, it felt impossible to maintain a connection to humanity any longer.

After that miserable winter, spring brought the sunshine and warmth we had prayed for. But like the spring before, the warmer weather increased the presence of lice. It also intensified the blood-curdling stench, as did our acute dysentery and diarrhea. Oh, how I prayed for some fresh, clean air to breathe! I doubted that the odor would ever clear out of my lungs.

Once again, just as I was ready to give up, my utter despair was abated. I was incredibly fortunate to find Sam again, this time in the children's section of Buchenwald. Although Sam was more than two years older than me, he was shorter and looked younger — which I assume is why he was lucky enough to be placed there. I was happy to learn that the kapo in charge of his group was a kind Czech political prisoner. Mercifully, the SS and other guards kept away from the children's section and the relatively gentle kapos and *blockaeltesters* did not club the children or force them to work as hard. (No doubt this section was used by the German Red Cross for propaganda purposes to make other countries think that Germany treated people decently.)

Even though I was frightened to be caught outside the barracks, I was more desperate than ever to be with Sam. The guards were still shooting at will, especially at anyone making unauthorized movements — yet I knew it was worth the risk. When I finally got with Sam, we were elated. We talked and cried awhile, encouraging each other to hold on until help arrived.

As we watched the guards react to the nearby explosions, Sam and I were encouraged. We probably would have laughed if we hadn't been so weak. The guards scurried around in fear and confusion, forcing our people to gather all the prisoners' files — and especially the valuables — and load them on anything that was mobile: trucks, railroad cars, jeeps, horses, or automobiles. Even the kapos and *blockaeltesters'* confidence faltered. Fearing revenge, some actually became a little gentler while doing the Nazi's dirty work.

Rediscovering Sam helped build my strength and confidence. I began sneaking out of the barracks in the very early mornings and evenings to visit the new arrivals in a fenced-off area to ask if they had seen *any* of my family or friends. One morning I questioned a fellow prisoner for about twenty minutes before I realized in utter amazement that I was talking to my brother, Bill! We were *so* elated to have found each other — it felt like heaven; but we could only talk for a short time, as I was so weak and we feared being caught. I told him about seeing Sam in the children's section. We decided that somehow we three would try to get together as soon as possible.

That night Bill dug a hole under the barbed fence to get to Sam and me, and we were finally able to hug and kiss each other. We were anxious to see Sam, so we crept around to reach him. Once the three of us were together, we vowed never to be separated again — no matter what! If we were to perish, we decided it would be together.

Despite their fright, the Nazis continued their screaming and mean-spiritedness. Each morning we were ordered out of the barracks to be assembled on the parade ground. Their plans were the same — to march us out of the camp, but this time we stuck together. We began trying different tactics. Some days we would run and hide in the barracks or lie among the dead as though we were dead, too. Or we would lie flat on the ground and refuse to leave, regardless of the consequences, until finally the guards left. Bill, Sam, and I would lie on the ground, listening to the explosions as they came ever closer, feeling the earth shake and listening to the barracks creak. We knew the Allies were gaining ground; their actions would keep us alive for one more day.

Although the Nazis were becoming less organized, we couldn't escape them completely. They continued to work us, either with camp details such as carrying out dead bodies from the bunks, or repairing buildings. Even in our exceedingly weak condition, the guards continued to extract free labor for themselves, their friends, Nazi officials, and their families. Sometimes they took us out to surrounding villages or estates to work for fascist leaders. Local Germans would come to the camp to pick out their allotted slave laborers. They clearly knew what was going on at Buchenwald.

At one point I was taken out with other prisoners to work at the Burgermeister's (mayor's) property. His son, who was about twelve years old, would beat us with sticks, throw stones at us, and kick us, all the while screaming *"Farshtunkene Juden"* ("filthy Jews"). Regardless of our run-down health, we had to dig ditches and haul stones as fast as we could, wash their pigs, and clean up their property. One day his mother came out to watch her son debase us. Maybe she was not satisfied with how her pigs were washed, or perhaps she thought her son had been too gentle. She went back into her house, brought out a large pot of boiling water, and poured it over us to show her son what the "filthy Jews" really deserved. My bruised skin felt as though it was engulfed in fire; the burning sensation seemed to last forever.

Shortly thereafter, our sojourns outside the camp ceased. The war — along with the Allies — was coming ever closer to Buchenwald, and the guards no longer felt safe accompanying us. It was increasingly evident in the Nazis' faces and actions that they were seriously concerned for themselves. They now seemed to be focused on eliminating and disposing of us even quicker so that they could disappear into the countryside or leave the country. By now we were getting no food at all. We were clinging to life by the tips of our fingernails. Death was everywhere. Corpses lay scattered on the ground, intermingled with the dying and with us.

Just before and during liberation, I could hear painful inhuman sounds rise from the depths of my comrades, their moans and pain rising along with the shouts of hate from the SS. Screams of the wounded and sighs from the dying. The killers groaned together with the victims.

Seeing the Nazis scared was a treat for me. The sounds of heavy gunfire and the explosions that seemed to grow nearer and nearer were music to my ears. The Allied airplanes flying overhead were sometimes so close that I could see their markings and hear their engines. One time they even dropped leaflets and some bread into the camp. When the earth shook from nearby bombs, we prayed quietly with both fear and rejuvenated hope. The promise of renewed life and the possibility of immediate death walked hand in hand. I only want to live long enough to be able to lift myself up and ask God why He had let our parents be taken away from us, and why He has let these mean people torture us so much.

Now the guards were almost totally preoccupied with preserving their own lives. There was a constant rumor that they had dynamite ready to blow up the entire camp. Those SS who had not already fled were frantically trying to destroy the tons and tons of incriminating records as quickly as possible or transport them further into the interior of Germany to be destroyed later. No one wanted their names tied in any way to such criminal acts, nor did they want us to point fingers at them. The Nazis committed their heinous acts against not only Jews, but also against Gentiles — especially Russians, Czechs, and other prisoners of war — and even against some anti-Nazi Germans. And it was all written down. Their ultra-efficient record-keeping was coming back to haunt them in the end. Those records would prove their unjust killings, medical experiments, mutilations, torture and much more if the Allies found them before they were destroyed.

We began noticing that increasing numbers of SS officers were wearing civilian clothes. They also started disappearing, one or two at a time. I wondered what they were taking with them. When our people arrived in the camps, especially Auschwitz-Birkenau, the Nazis confiscated enormous quantities of our precious valuables and heirlooms. I was sure we would never see the huge quantities of valuables and heirlooms which the Nazis had confiscated from us when we entered the camps. No doubt even the gold from the teeth of my dead comrades had probably already been melted down and made its way into their hiding places.

The guards' preoccupation with their own escape gave me an opportunity to sneak into the kitchen and take some food for myself and my fellow barrack mates, many of whom were too famished to move. I looked for bread, water, potato peels — anything I could easily take back without being noticed. It was absolutely vital that I not get caught in a round-up and be shipped out now. Liberation seemed imminent and luckily I had found two of my brothers. I had a new sense of faith in life, even though I was weak as a baby and terribly worried about the rest of my family.

Those of us who were able to crawl, walk, or talk were trying to keep up the spirits of those who couldn't. We urged each and every one to hang on for just a little while longer, assuring them that help was definitely on the way. We somehow maintained some spirit, pleading with God to help us.

I remember a man about thirty years old lying next to me, mumbling with a peaceful smile on his face as though he knew his suffering was about to end.

We just could not save him; the next morning he was thrown on the pile outside for cremation.

One day, some prisoners who were in relatively good shape — including Bill — somehow managed to get some weapons, and through shear guts they started to attack the guards that were in the watch towers at the gate and between the electrified fences. How wonderful to see our own people chasing the guards and those SS killers!

On the 9th and 10th of April, 1944, the Nazis attempted to assemble us for evacuation. We were told the camp had to be emptied by nightfall, but the sound of air-raid sirens interrupted those plans. The guards and the SS men disappeared into air raid shelters and underground tunnels. We tried to find refuge as well, but most of us were barely able to shuffle one foot in front of the other. We could find no safe place to rest our weary souls. We wandered or crawled aimlessly, wondering what could possibly happen next.

CHAPTER ELEVEN

ANGELS IN BUCHENWALD

Around April 10 or 11, 1945, my brother Bill participated in the liberation of Buchenwald by the Allies. He and several other prisoners mustered their energy and courage and stormed some of the watch towers, overpowering the guards on duty and taking their machine guns. They used insulated wire cutters to cut the double row of electrified fences, to stop the electric current. They made a hole just large enough to crawl through, then Bill and the stronger prisoners ran into the forest, toward the sound of the large guns firing in the distance. Their plan was to find Allied soldiers and bring them back to Buchenwald. I don't know just how long it took them; I was comatose, too weak to grasp what was going on.

Because of my semi-conscious state, many of the details of that day and the next remain a blur. But as long as I live I will never forget the feeling I experienced at the first glimpse of those armored American vehicles and tanks rolling into Buchenwald. It was one of the most beautiful sights that my mind, heart, and soul will ever remember. As the April sun broke through the clouds I could almost hear the Almighty answering my prayers, saying, "On this day I will bless you with a miracle and deliver you to freedom." I wanted to scream with elation but I could not move, think, or cry; I had no tears left in me. My lips moved but no words came out. I raised my hands in gratitude. Unfortunately, liberation came too late for most of our people.

Even though the vehicles were covered with mud, they looked to me like magnificent carriages built for the highest royalty. The world's finest jewels could not have looked more splendid. I was certain they were driven by angels. When the top of one of the turrets opened, I saw a helmet and then a black soldier's face. I had never in my life seen a black man before. I felt that he was surely an angel sent by the Almighty to save us. I therefore concluded that all angels were black.

As more Allied tanks came closer to our section of the camp, their turrets opened, allowing the gunners a better view. The U.S. soldiers looked well-fed, handsome, and confident. They saw us and immediately started shooting at the electrified fence in anger, as if they wanted to destroy that hell hole even before they got out of their vehicles. Sparks and explosions went off like fireworks, brighter than the mid-morning sun.

The handful of German guards remaining in the camp tried to fire back, but they were sorely outnumbered and retreated quickly. Those of us who were able to stand up could actually go outside and look around with no fear of being shot. Again I wanted to jump up, shout with joy, and run to the Allied vehicles, but I had no strength left. So I prayed, "God Bless America and its people for finally saving us."

Following the American tanks and armored vehicles was a contingent of ground forces with machine guns and other automatic weaponry. As they entered what remained of the German guards' headquarters, they darted around, looking for remaining enemy soldiers. When they were certain that all the SS and other guards had been killed, captured, or had left, they entered the adjoining forest to round up any others trying to escape. They must have destroyed several munitions dumps nearby, because the explosives were going off with enough force to shake the ground for miles around. Any military equipment that had been left behind by the Germans was destroyed; even their military automobiles were blown apart. Soon there was nothing left for the German guards to escape in.

As the Americans progressed into our section of "hell on Earth," they stared at us in disbelief. Once they had secured the camp and began looking around, many started to cry. Obviously most of them had not heard about the concentration camps; they had simply been following orders to defeat the enemy. They were shocked and dumbfounded to see what Buchenwald was really about. Even those who may have been warned about the condition of the prisoners were not prepared for what they saw: zombie-like, emaciated creatures, so sickly that we appeared alien. As the prisoners who still had a little strength left slowly staggered or crawled from the barracks, it didn't take long for the Allied soldiers to realize the magnitude of what the Germans had done to us. The Jewish GIs were struck personally by our condition and the realization that the Nazis had almost annihilated the entire Jewish population of Europe. They saw that we were yellowed by jaundice and malaria, sickened from disease, weakened from starvation, and injured from abuse.

As additional U.S. soldiers entered the camp, they too stopped dead in their tracks. I saw them open, close, and reopen their tearful eyes. Many became angry; some vomited. If our appearance and odor did not turn their stomachs, then the putrid smell from the hundreds of rotting corpses stacked up against the buildings and lying dead in the barracks did the trick. Clearly, nothing they had ever seen or smelled compared to what they discovered at Buchenwald. Although we couldn't understand their words, the shock and disgust on their faces was palpable.

Despite the language barrier and our repellent appearance, the U.S. soldiers quickly repressed their reactions and began to comfort us. We begged them for food, and they reached into their knapsacks or pockets for anything they might have to eat. They gave us water from their canteens. A few actually tried to hug us, even though we smelled so badly and were only skin and bone. They just wanted to show us that they cared about us and that we were still part of the human race, regardless of the mistreatment we'd experienced. Their compassion was more important to me than food. We tried to show appreciation to our heroes, but we didn't have the strength — or the language skills. I believe they sensed our gratitude.

While most of the mighty tanks continued their mission to defeat the German Army, some of the ground soldiers — especially medics — stayed with us until they received orders to move on. We feared that somehow a few German guards might still be hiding in the camp or nearby and would return to kill the rest of us to keep us from talking. Rumors also surfaced again that the Nazis had planted explosives around and under the camp to blow the entire place up.

The U.S. forces that stayed on were very generous. For the first time in over a year we were given good, clean water to drink and canned food with bread, made from real flour, as much as we wanted. Initially we ate and ate and ate, not realizing how sick we would become because our systems simply could not digest decent, normal food at first. In fact, some of our comrades died in our arms from eating too much too soon, which just tore me up. I could not deal with the fact that I was alive and the others were not.

When the medical teams arrived, they told us not to eat anything else until they decided what and how much we should eat for a slow, safe recovery.

The medics also disinfected our pestilent bodies. What a relief to be rid of the lice! Our hair was once again sheared off — this time with good shears, kind consideration, and gentle hands. We were then permitted to take a real shower with proper soap and hot water — the first decent shower I had had in over a year, and it felt wonderful.

Even after the disinfectant and many more soapy, hot showers it would take years before I felt totally clean again. The months of psychological torment by the German guards and their collaborators, constantly screaming and berating us with profanities, never being allowed to bathe or change clothes, and the ceaseless death and disease left me feeling perpetually unclean long after I became a free man.

The Americans' kindness also included toothbrushes and toothpaste. I had forgotten how to use these — as a kid I did not own a toothbrush, and I did not use one until I lived in Budapest. I was fortunate to have teeth left to brush — many prisoners lost teeth due to lack of proper nutrition and hygiene or because they had been hit or kicked in the mouth. For those people, the toothbrushes were useless.

Once we were cleaned up, the soldiers passed out clean clothing which was way too big for our skinny, shrunken bodies. Then the American medical staff evaluated our physical condition. They determined that we suffered not only from malnutrition but also from smallpox, diphtheria, malaria, typhoid, and other assorted diseases. (Of course, some of those illnesses were inflicted on us purposely by the German doctors in Auschwitz to see how long we could survive without proper medication.) Tuberculosis was especially rampant. Many men had to be quarantined as quickly as possible to avoid spreading the disease. Many were sick beyond recovery, some were still bleeding internally from gunshot wounds or beatings, and many had broken bones that had never been set. Untreated rat bites, dog bites, and gangrene were common. Everyone had open sores, blisters, and skin problems. Most of us had stomach ulcers.

The doctors could hardly believe any of us had survived in our terribly weakened state. The causes of the various diseases or pains had to be analyzed, but most could not be treated by the U.S. Army medical staff. They, along with the Red Cross (who finally — if reluctantly — emerged), were sorely understaffed and had their hands full just trying to diagnose our many illnesses. Typhoid was rampant.

A few days after liberation I fell into a coma again. I do not know how long I was comatose, but I awoke to a German woman's voice screaming, "It's a lie! It's a lie!" and cursing at the American Army officers. She denied that her people had inflicted such atrocities upon us, and she accused the Americans of having brought these near-dead bodies from Russia to make the nice Germans look bad. I recognized her voice: She was the woman who had poured boiling water on me while I was working on her property. A GI helped me stand and I communicated to him in Yiddish, "It's not a lie. It's the truth, and I recognize her." The doctor who was treating me was Jewish — fortunately he understood a little Yiddish. He held me up, listening as I recounted what had happened at that wicked woman's house. I didn't want revenge; I felt that those criminals should be brought to justice. I doubt if she was ever brought to trial for her crimes against humanity, but at least someone else knew what had happened.

Soon I collapsed again. I became delirious. I was told later that I was crying for my Mother. When I came to, all I cared about was regaining my strength and finding the rest of my family. An American officer asked me what I wanted to do or where I wanted to go, but I felt too weak to do or say anything.

The next day Bill, Sam, and I got together to make plans. We decided to ask the American soldiers to return us to Czechoslovakia as soon as possible so that we could look for the rest of our family. We had mixed feelings though, because we were afraid that the people of our village would still be hostile to Jews. Also, we were afraid to learn the fate of our other family members. But if we three brothers survived, there was a chance that our parents and siblings were still alive, too. We hoped that we would all be reunited soon. But I had been disappointed so many times, I didn't know if I could expect anything good from life ever again.

After an American doctor and nurse finished checking me over, I was urged to rest at least a few weeks. A day or two later I asked for a mirror — I had not seen myself for a long time and wondered what I looked like. When they brought one, I was horrified by what I saw. I looked worse than I had ever imagined. I said to myself, "This could not be me!" No wonder Bill and I had not recognized each other. When I was taken from my home over a year ago, I was a tall fifteen-year-old in great physical shape. I stood at least 5 feet, 9 inches tall and weighed about 130 solid pounds. I had a full head of light blond hair and nice white teeth. I guess I was considered handsome.

What I saw in the mirror a year later was sickening to me (and probably to others). I looked like a 90-year-old man. My yellowed skin sagged from my face, legs, hands, and all over my body. I had lost more than half my weight and had shrunk by about three inches. My hair had been short and full of lice for so long that I did not know if it would ever grow back — or what color it would be. My teeth were as yellow as my skin.

I don't know why I was shocked at my appearance. I should have expected it because all my other liberated comrades looked that way. My vanity made me not want to believe that at my young age I looked like a worn-out, sick, old man. I was reassured by the fact that the more decent food and water I consumed, the better I would look.

The food we got from the American army tasted almost as good as my Mother's cooking. Being free to move around, eat real food, and speak to anyone I wanted was refreshing. However, I had difficulty believing it was real. Taking advantage of all the opportunities that freedom provided had become completely foreign to me. I'd prayed and hoped for it for so many long, agonizing days and nights that when liberation finally happened, it seemed too good to be true.

Over the next few days many things happened on our behalf. The doctors started us on small amounts of very bland food, rather than letting us gobble down everything we could lay our hands on. That diet gave me a little more strength and I felt a little better right away. They told us that after our stomachs stabilized, we could have more food (and a greater variety) each day.

Soon child-sized clothing arrived for us. Although still a little too big and too short, it was a big improvement over our old striped, torn uniforms or the other borrowed clothing. It definitely boosted morale.

I was happy to see my hair starting to grow back. There were no lice pestering me now, and the medicines and food were healing my jaundice and other diseases. I was slowly becoming less zombie-like.

Some survivors — including my brothers and I — weren't seriously ill or dying, so we were able to be treated at the camp. But it was tragically too late for most others. So many died after liberation. Hundreds were taken to nearby hospitals. Those who could travel were shipped back to their homeland or to other countries that would accept them. France took some of the children from our camp.

All the hospitals in Europe were filled beyond capacity. Many had to be evacuated completely then filled only with patients who had contagious diseases. The medical teams were afraid our illnesses would be spread not only to military personnel, but also among the civilians — and perhaps even infect the entire continent. A shortage of sulfa drugs, penicillin, and many other antibiotics added to the doctors' worries. Blood plasma, also in very short supply, was saved for surgeries that needed to be performed on the wounded Allied soldiers. None was allocated to us.

In early May we received the wonderful news that Germany and then Japan had surrendered — the war was finally over. At last Germany and the fascist collaborators in Europe were defeated! What a boost for my mental and physical well-being. I longed for a peaceful life, surrounded by my family. I wanted to see people acting sanely, humanely. Was it finally possible? Could now be the time? Am I really free and part of the human race once again? I was flabbergasted by the possibility of complete freedom and the chance to live normally.

As I became stronger, I began taking walks outside the camp. Walking tall as a free man in the sunshine was glorious. No more scurrying around, hunched over, constantly afraid of being cursed at, beaten, or shot. But even so, the nightmare was not quite over for me — nor would it be for many years. The stench of death that hung in the air also clung relentlessly to my heart.

Because I spoke German and Ukrainian,[25] a Russian-Jewish prisoner of war invited me and a Romanian boy to accompany him into the nearby town one day — he needed a German-speaking person to help him obtain food and clothes. I noticed as we walked towards the village that he carried a hand gun. He said that beneath his coat were a couple of hand grenades which he had acquired "Russian style," meaning that he just took what he wanted. He felt that now the shoe was on the other foot — the Germans had taken the Russians for everything they had, but now the Russians had the upper hand.

After we made our acquisitions we began walking back along the forest towards Buchenwald. My newfound Russian friend noticed two well-dressed, healthy men walking quickly away from the camp towards the forest, carrying two large suitcases that looked very heavy. As we moved closer, my companion called to them in Russian, asking them to halt. They ignored him and continued toward the forest as fast as they could. Again my friend yelled for them to halt, but they increased their speed.

When they refused to stop, the Russian took the grenade from his belt, removed the pin, and threw it without hesitation towards the men. They were killed instantly. The contents of their suitcases flew everywhere: watches, gold rings, bracelets, and other fine jewelry; currency from several countries, including Swiss kronen, English pounds, American dollars, and French francs; gold bars, loose diamonds, and other precious gemstones. After looking the dead men over, we determined that they were former SS. Only moments ago they were on their way to freedom and wealth with their victims' belongings. I wondered how many people they had killed to obtain so much booty.

We stood and talked for a minute about what we had found. We did not have material gains on our minds. We looked around to see why the men were running in that direction. The grenade had blown a hole in the ground along a passage connecting the camp and the forest. It opened a passage into a tunnel. We followed that and ended up at a stone quarry where many of our people had been forced to work. and from which most had never returned.

The Romanian lowered himself into a hole in the quarry. Once he saw what was there, he yelled for us to follow. When we joined him, we found a massive cache of valuables: thousands more watches, gold rings, gold eyeglasses, gold fillings, and precious gems. Also stashed there were waterproof boxes filled with stocks, bonds, and currency from many different countries. Apparently, the Nazis did not have enough time to remove all their ill-gotten loot. The Russian immediately put on as many watches as his arms would hold, then we ran back to the camp to report to the American authorities what we had found.

When an American officer heard our story and saw the watches, he sent a few trucks to bring the booty to the camp warehouse. It ultimately took sixteen full 2.5-ton truckloads to remove all the valuables from the quarry. There is no telling the value of what we found, but it had to have been in the hundreds of millions of dollars — not to mention the millions in stocks, bonds, and currency. I'm sure that was just the tip of the iceberg; the vast majority of our possessions had been taken away by the Nazis before the Allies liberated the camps.

I wondered how many similar caches were found in or near the other liberated camps — especially the Auschwitz camps. I was proud of what we had found because it was hard evidence of the Nazis' crimes. In retrospect, I wished it could have been used to medically treat, rehabilitate, or resettle camp survivors. Later, I heard that those valuables were later turned over to the German people, with no effort to find the rightful owners.[26] Back then, however, I had only one thing on my mind — to leave that hellish place forever and find the remainder of my family.

CHAPTER TWELVE

PICKING UP THE PIECES IN PRAGUE

With very little sentiment, Bill, Sam, and I got on the first military truck bound for Prague, Czechoslovakia. The ride took only a few hours. Along the way we totally ignored Germany's people and what appeared to be well-tended farms and beautiful homes. Everything German looked very prosperous but bleak. All we wanted was to leave that country and its hateful inhabitants as fast as possible.

Outside Germany we found everything in ruin or semi-ruin. Most of the towns and villages we passed were bombed, pilfered, and ravaged by the German Army before they evacuated them. Yet despite the ruin, I could feel the warmth of the Czech people as we stepped onto friendly Prague soil. Although it was devastated, Prague was still beautiful. I got down on my knees and kissed the earth. It was comforting to see friendly, decent Czech people, and be able to talk and relate to them.

But things were not so rosy that cool spring. My brothers and I were broken-hearted because we were too scared to go back to our village and reclaim our possessions and our home, even though the war was over. We overheard that some of our former Schwabish neighbors wondered why the SS didn't turn us into soap and ashes, too. Once again I felt that I had been denied, at my young age, the opportunity for a decent life.

Czechoslovakia was still occupied by Russian troops, who were supposed to help our people reclaim their health and freedom. But it seemed that some of them had forgotten how to be friendly after years under communism and the war against Germany. Czech President Benes and Vice President Massaryk were trying to rebuild a democracy, but it took time, energy and cooperation — especially from the new occupying power — to accomplish such a feat.

Somehow the Russians had disposed of all our capable, caring, staunch democratic Czech leaders of yore. Massaryk had supposedly "fallen" to his death from a window several stories high; the Russians claimed it was suicide. President Benes was deposed by the communist coup of 1948.

Communism, even before the coup, was no different to me from any other enslaving dictatorship. We seemed to have escaped from one prison to another. Russia was spreading its communist bear hug all over Eastern Europe, trying to control Latvia, Galicia, Ukraine, Poland, Czechoslovakia, Hungary, Romania, and Yugoslavia. Perhaps they would eventually try to communize the entire world.

After the war it was hard for refugees to find housing in Czechoslovakia — not only because of the destruction of homes, but because much of our property was confiscated by Nazi collaborators who were afraid of being exposed with their ill-gotten property, so they would not rent to us. As a result, Prague was literally overrun with homeless refugees from many surrounding countries. Several survivor families and friends lived in crowded one-room apartments. Some families shared their sparse accommodations with former neighbors; even strangers took refuge with one another.

To me, any accommodation was better than being cooped up in a refugee center or hostel. Those makeshift temporary quarters consisted of tents or former military barracks that were terribly crowded and unclean. Yet, even those were better for many homeless Jews than going back to try and reclaim their homes and risk being killed by a former neighbor or friend. Some refugees who returned to Poland or other eastern countries came back with horror stories: They could not reclaim their homes or the possessions they had hidden with their former friends or neighbors. It seemed there was no help for Jews trying to return home to put their lives back together.

Jobs were even harder to find than housing. Good jobs were nonexistent, especially for newcomers. We all wanted to recover our health, to work, and to feel useful like other ordinary people. Unfortunately, the post-war economy and the ill health of most refugees made this feat extremely difficult.

The ability to work and support ourselves was important, but more important was finding our loved ones. Bill, Sam, and I searched refugee camps, hostels, hotels, the Red Cross, the United Nations Relief Organization — even the black market — in hopes of finding our relatives. Within weeks we were lucky to learn that Filip and Bernie were alive and Ben was living in Prague. They had initially been taken by the Hungarians to a forced labor camp, which was later liberated by the Russians. What a blessed gift!

We also located my sister, Rosalyn. She had been shipped out of Auschwitz to Bergen-Belsen, which was later liberated by the British Army. She had also found our half-brother just before liberation, who was our Father's son from an annulled short marriage. (Sadly, he died of typhoid the day of liberation.) Unfortunately, we assumed that our loving parents had been sent straight to the gas chambers at Auschwitz. While this assumption was beyond devastating, we siblings were grateful to have found each other. It was nothing short of a miracle.

Ben got a wonderful job with the American Jewish Joint Distribution Committee, helping reunite families by driving people around during their searches. For Ben it was most rewarding to bring lost relatives together. Just to be able to say, "Here is a member of your family alive, take them home and love them for the rest of your lives" must have felt very gratifying. Ben had such a big heart, and he was very proud of his job. I was proud of him, too.

Ben's job enabled him to live in an efficiency apartment in a decent area of Prague. Since he was the first of our family to arrive there, he was glad to have a place where we could stay when we were reunited. Although it was tiny, it seemed like a palace to me. It was "home" to all our siblings — and to Ruthie, Bernie's intended spouse, who had escaped from Russia with him — plus several cousins and a few close friends from Palanok. We slept on the floor, in the hallway, on tables pushed together — wherever there was room. One of my second cousins even slept in the bathtub.

We felt very fortunate to have such a nice place to stay. The apartment felt palatial compared to the camps and the cramped refugee centers. There was carpet on the floor to sleep on, instead of rough wooden bunks. We had solid walls that kept out the wind and blankets to keep us warm. There was a real bathroom where we could shower and keep our bodies clean. The place was free of rats, lice, and other vermin. Most of the time there was decent food on the table. Best of all, there was no danger, no horrible stench, and no constant reminder of death.

Post-war Prague was a sea of lost people. Children and adults wandered aimlessly. Many survivors were too young even to remember their parents' full names or where they came from. Some kids had been hidden in the forests by righteous Gentile neighbors or in Christian orphanages by nuns. Many had to accept the realization that it would take months or years, if ever, to find family members. During the war, many families had been split up and sent to several different camps in several different countries, as we were. Every reunion was miraculous.

Filip remained in our hometown area. He found his old girlfriend, Feigi, from Munkach, who had also survived the concentration camps. When she returned home, they immediately decided to get married.

Even with no money, we all managed to attend their wedding in June of 1945. The wedding was in our old home. It was beautiful, very traditional. We danced, sang traditional Yiddish songs, and drank vodka. All that was missing were our dear parents.

Somehow some Russian officers came uninvited to the wedding, got drunk, and started a terrible fight among themselves. That fight was an omen. Little did we realize that in the next few days the Russians would annex our area, close all borders, and trap whoever was still there. Although it became almost impossible to get back to Czechoslovakia, most of us siblings managed to get out. I hid in a train boxcar, under a Russian female soldier's skirt — unfortunately she did not bathe, so the smell was horrible. Sadly, Filip, his wife, and his family were trapped there and remained so for many years. We would not be allowed to visit him until twenty years later.

A few weeks went by when suddenly I broke out in boils that spread all over my body, as though my blood had turned into gangrene. I guess my system simply could not digest decent food yet, and rejected it. I went to the hospital and was immediately put in an isolated room. The doctors thought I had an infectious disease; they did not know what to do with me. After a few days of ignoring me, the doctors suspended me by ropes. I overheard them say that they did not have enough penicillin or other medication to go around, and not to waste it on me. They said they did not expect me to live because I was very skinny, sickly, and nowhere near recovered. But I had come too far to succumb. A few nights later I tore up the hospital bed sheets, tied them into a rope, lowered myself from the third floor window, and managed to find my way back to Ben's apartment.

I soon started to feel better, so I joined the ongoing search for survivors and tried to find a job — any job. I called on manufacturers, plumbers, electricians, and all kinds of stores. I wanted very much to make some money, learn a trade, and contribute to society. After all, I was over sixteen years old; I did not want even to consider having anyone support me.

I was fortunate to find work almost immediately with the Dosedel Company, which manufactured transformers. Mr. Dosedel, a good, religious Catholic from an old Czech family, took a liking to me and saw that I was a hard worker. He and his people taught me a lot. Presently I befriended one of the shop workers who invited me to his home in Zlicine, outside of Prague, to meet his family. His parents were very nice. His mother, who was of Yugoslav origin and his father, who hailed from the older order of Bohemian Czech, owned and operated a small grocery store. After a few more visits they invited me to move in with them, as they knew how crowded Ben's apartment was. I eagerly accepted their kind offer, although I soon began to miss my siblings very much. I went back to Ben's for frequent visits after work and on weekends to enjoy my family, look for other survivors, as well as enjoy my freedom, the food, and the camaraderie we had been deprived of for a long time.

When we weren't working, Mr. Dosedel and I would often go to the Catholic convent nearby to do repairs in the cannery. I enjoyed doing things for the nuns. They were very sweet to me, always giving me food. They wanted to adopt me, but I graciously declined. I told them that I was fortunate to have found most of my family, which must be God's way of making sure we kept our religious faith and stayed together.

Donating my time and labor to make life a little better for the nuns was very gratifying. I had seen the opposite of giving from your heart, which was hate — I felt that helping others was the right thing to do. Even though that was a short time in my life, I fondly remember those wonderful Czech people, Mr. Dosedel, the nuns, and the people in Zlicine who treated me like kin.

One day at work I was busily operating the heavy machinery to cut the metal for the transformers. In my eagerness to work faster, I almost cut off the finger of the friend who had taken me home to his family. I was very mad at myself and frightened that he and his family would never understand how sorry I was about the accident. Surely they would hate me and Mr. Dosedel would fire me. Instead, they were all very understanding and realized just how badly I felt for accidentally hurting my friend. They advised me to slow down and be more careful in the future, a lesson which has stayed with me all my life.

Soon thereafter, Bill became ill with tuberculosis and was quarantined in a sanitarium outside Prague for several weeks. It was difficult to visit him — the hospital was way out of town and we had no car. We had to take a trolley, then buses, then walk a long way to see him, so we could only go on special occasions — but we went whenever we could.

In late 1945 my Aunt Rose and Uncles Gene, Adolph, and Ben (my Mother's sister and brothers in America) learned through the Jewish Refugee Centers that my siblings and I were the only members of their formerly large European family to survive the Holocaust. They started sending us letters and occasional packages containing canned food, clothing, and toilet articles. Of course, our skinny, undernourished bodies thrived on the food more than anything else they sent. Food was prohibitively expensive in Europe at that time, and we had very little money or valuable possessions to trade or sell, so our American relatives sometimes sent money as well.

Although we all shared their gifts, there were so many of us that occasionally some were left out. But that was all right — we were just happy that our American loved ones were thinking about us and wanted to help. We realized that maybe they were doing without things they might have wanted or needed, just to help us. As a result, our love, admiration, and respect for them and their family grew. We never forgot their kindnesses.

Along with sending care packages, our American relatives were working on obtaining visas for us to come to America. They were willing to sponsor as many of us as possible — which would guarantee the United States government that our aunts and uncles would help us find jobs and a place to live, and assume responsibility for us for a certain time period. This also ensured that we would not be a burden on the U.S. government. We wanted to do everything possible to help them bring us to America but the quota was limited, and we were warned that the special legislation required to get visas might take several years. So we continued trying to straighten out our lives as best we could, and kept in close touch with our stateside family. All we could do was wait and see.

I could not accept the fact that my Mother and Father were not alive. Who could kill such wonderful people just because of their religion? There was no way to get real proof that they were dead or alive. Maybe someone had made a mistake. I kept hoping that they might still be alive, somewhere. I had to try, or to hope to not die trying, to find out.

CHAPTER THIRTEEN

SCOTLAND

As we continued our frantic search for lost friends and relatives, my concern about Russian communism taking over Czechoslovakia grew. There was no doubt in my mind that Russia would gladly enforce its own brand of ruthless communist control over all countries, including the people they liberated from Hitler's dictatorial Germany. This saddened me. Czechoslovakia had been a bastion of democracy before the war — now it seemed that would soon be history.

We were happy to learn that the British Jewish Welfare Agency had arranged to fly some of the younger surviving orphans to the British Isles to regain physical and mental strength, and hopefully deprogram them from the abuse and suffering they had endured. This effort began with the youngest surviving kids from Prague, which fortunately included my sister, Rosalyn, who was liberated in Bergen-Belsen concentration camp. She was still very weak, and I hated the idea of being separated again from her. We eventually learned that her plane — a former British Air Force bomber — was bound for Edinburgh, Scotland, where she could recover.

I envied Rosalyn and was happy for her. I hoped she would receive the protection, care, and education that she desperately needed. At the same time we all feared for her being without her brothers again. It was very difficult to trust other humans after all we had gone through.

The welfare volunteers who met us at the airport seemed sincere and caring, but my concern grew as her plane slowly disappeared from view. I could not stop crying for several days — I worried constantly if she was all right.

As time dragged on, nothing was as important to me as being with my sister. I decided to apply to go wherever Rosalyn was taken. I wanted to look after her and be there if she needed anything — after all, she was my one and only sister. She had suffered enough for her tender age, or for any age, a hundred times over.

When I visited the refugee center a few weeks later, I was elated to see my name on a roster of Holocaust survivors to be taken to an orphanage in Laswaile near Edinburgh.

I will never forget the day of my departure. Obviously I was heartbroken to leave my brothers — especially Bill, who was by now out of the sanatorium and nearly recovered from TB — and my wonderful friends and coworkers, including the family I lived with in Zlicine. I also thought longingly of Filip and his wife, who were trapped in Communist Russia and could not even communicate with us. I wondered if and when we would all be reunited in a free country — I hoped it would eventually be America. But as I focused on joining Rosalyn, my cares temporarily abated. Being with her was more crucial and exciting to me than anything.

With mixed emotions I boarded the plane for Britain that bright, early morning, with the few articles of clothing I owned in my small knapsack and my precious, recently acquired mandolin in my hand. As the plane prepared for takeoff, the loud engines were sweet music to my ears. I looked around at the sad, frightened, innocent faces of the other children on the plane and realized what a toll the war had taken on them. Most had no family left. How could they ever relax, smile, laugh, or have any fun again?

To coax some smiles from those kids on the otherwise dreary, noisy plane, I started to tell some Yiddish jokes and sing and play songs on my mandolin — mostly old familiar Yiddish and Hebrew songs, plus some Czech, Hungarian, and Russian tunes. Many of the kids joined me in singing; some continued crying for their lost loved ones and fear of not knowing what awaited them. Soon we were high up in the air, smiling through our tears as we left behind our Czech Republic and any feeling of belonging to our country of birth.

Our flight became bumpy as we approached the British channel, and the fears we were all trying to quell tumbled around in our minds. We were about to enter a new country, with strange customs and a foreign language. We would have to rely on grown-ups whom we did not know. After all we had been through, we had no sense of security. Fear of the unknown, combined with the rough flight, made some kids sick to their stomachs.

As the turbulence increased, I suddenly became very aware of the loss of my beloved parents. It hit me that they were really, truly gone, and I began to miss them more than ever. I tried to console myself as I looked forward to my upcoming reunion with Rosalyn. I looked out the plane's small windows as it bounced over the rough clouds, and I continued to play my mandolin loudly and sing Yiddish songs to drown out my fears. I even tore some strings from playing so hard.

Everyone breathed a collective sigh of relief as we landed in Edinburgh, the capital of Scotland. We were met by some Scottish Jewish people who seemed very nice, then we boarded a bus for the orphanage and travelled through the beautiful, ancient city. Although we did not understand a word our hosts said and vice-versa, we quickly felt their warmth and eagerness to help us.

Our new home was a secluded but nostalgic place on a hilltop in Lasvaile, on the outskirts of Edinburgh. The view was breathtaking. We could see the ocean in the distance; we were surrounded by castles, centuries-old buildings, farms, and trees. The scene was made more beautiful because Rosalyn was part of the welcoming party. We hugged, kissed, and cried, happy beyond words to be together once again.

The hostel was very old, with beautiful, large trees. Its Scottish farm-like atmosphere was good for us, as we desperately needed the peace and quiet. Our living quarters were very nice and spacious, compared to our housing in Prague — and they were worlds away from life in the camps. The food we were served was a little strange to our palate at first — and it certainly was not my beloved Mother's sumptuous Yiddish home cooking — but it was nutritious and tasty.

The Scottish people — and specifically the Edinburgh Jewish people — were wonderful from the beginning. They understood that it was traumatic for us to start a new life in a strange environment, and they patiently helped us adjust to the Scottish way of life. Despite the frustrating language barrier, we wanted to show our love and build a good rapport with them. But we were so accustomed to lies and mistreatment, and we had not been permitted to talk to or associate with anyone for so long — many of us had trouble believing that these wonderful caretakers were for real.

Some of our caretakers were very special — they calmed us when we cried out in the middle of the night for our lost loved ones. They soothed our bad dreams as we relived the horrors we had endured. Even during the day, children who cried received loving reassurance.

Our guardians were never too busy to smile, give hugs, and reassure us that our ordeal was truly over. They tried to help us understand why God had allowed the fascist hate-mongers to murder our loved ones in the prime of their lives, just because they were born Jewish. It is a mystery for which no one had answers, but our Scottish caretakers helped us cope as best they could.

I decided that I could be of great help to those hurting, motherless children — as well as to myself — by assuming a positive, loving attitude, without hate or prejudice. I knew it would take time to turn our lives around, but I endeavored to nurture them along and make our little world better.

Aside from managing our fears, we had many other adjustments to make before we could begin feeling whole again. The Scottish people helped us relearn to stand properly, look up, and walk straight with pride. We played often outside in the fresh air, which was very healing.

The language issue was very complicated because we did not speak English at all, nor could the Scots speak any of the languages that we knew. Most orphans spoke Yiddish; some spoke Polish, Hungarian, Romanian, Czech, or other east European languages. In fact, sometimes we had difficulty communicating with each other even in Yiddish, because of the different dialects. So we used actions, signs, and body language. Some Scottish volunteers came to tutor us in English, which somehow did not penetrate my mind. But at least they helped me feel welcome.

Some of the kids from very religious backgrounds wanted to start prayer services, but most of us were not in a proper frame of mind to accept God so quickly as we had been taught in Hebrew school or by our parents. The Sabbath was most difficult because it rekindled fond memories of attending synagogue every Friday evening, Sabbath morning and Sabbath evening. We also missed our festive meals, socializing, and singing ritual songs. But it was hard to act religious when, for many of us, our hearts simply weren't in it.

By Scottish law we had to attend school, so they sent us to public schools nearby. Learning was no easy task: the Scottish teachers and students did not understand a word we said, no matter how hard we tried to express ourselves. And of course we did not understand their customs or language. But the Scottish children, especially the girls, tried to reach out to us through their actions and attitudes. We boys especially appreciated that — particularly because the Scottish girls were so pretty. Sometimes they would come up the hill to our hostel and sit on the stone wall, waiting for us to come out and flirt with them. We boys made an effort to oblige them. Even though we could not communicate verbally, we had no trouble flirting.

Besides being exposed to English and developing other academic pursuits, we were encouraged to participate in school sports — primarily because it would help restore our confidence and physical health. I became involved wholeheartedly in sports. I trained very hard to strengthen my legs, learned to run again, and improved my soccer skills. Besides learning ping pong and other sports, I earned a spot on the Lasvaile school running team. The soccer skills and strong legs I had developed as a young boy paid off (and had probably saved my life many times in the camps). For me it felt natural to get back on the soccer field. I practiced every free moment from early morning to late at night — especially when I could get someone to play with me.

That season our sports team participated in the annual Dolkieth National Scottish Youth games. We did very well, and I earned the coveted blue ribbon for participating in the most events and scoring the most points. I also won the 100-yard dash and the 500- and 1,000-meter runs. When the winners were presented with their ribbons, I felt like I had won the gold medal of the Olympics.

Our ribbons were awarded by a prominent Scottish businessman named Lebo, from Glasgow. Of course, he spoke only English (with a Scottish accent). The lady in charge of our hostel, who spoke both English and German, translated how proud Mr. Lebo was to present the blue ribbon to me. Mr. Lebo then invited me to his home for a day; I gladly accepted.

A few weeks later on a bright Sunday morning, Mr. Lebo picked Rosalyn and me up from the hostel and took us to his home, where we met his family. I was surprised and delighted to learn that his father spoke Yiddish, Hungarian, and Carpato Ruski. Amazingly, he was from our region of the Carpathian Mountains which, when he lived there, was part of the Austro-Hungary Empire (pre-World War I, before it became Czechoslovakia). As a young boy he had left home to find a better opportunity, probably in America. When a severe storm forced his small ship to stop in Scotland, he decided to stay.

Mr. Lebo's father explained that his name was originally Lebowitz, but he had shortened it to Lebo, which was easier for the Scottish people to pronounce. He had been a butcher back home, and his first job in Glasgow was in a meat-packing house. He eventually started his own meat-packing business, which grew to become one of the largest meat-packing companies in Great Britain.

I explained that Lebowitz was my Mother's maiden name, and of course it was also the name of my grandfather and my uncles on my Mother's side. Then it dawned on us — he was my Mother's first cousin! At first I cried, I was so excited and happy. I marvelled at the strange, small world we live in. What a joy to learn that yet another relative was alive! He and his wife were very cordial that day, and asked us to come back for another Sunday brunch soon. His children, however, acted somewhat distant to us. Looking back, I realize that maybe they felt threatened by me — perhaps they were afraid I would try to take advantage of their father's prosperity. But after our initial meeting, I never asked them for anything — nor was I ever offered anything from them. I would have been content to merely stay in touch with them, had they made any effort or indicated that they wanted to remain connected with me — one of the few relatives they had left on the continent.

I attempted to contact the Lebos in later years, but to no avail — I felt they did not want us in their family, so I eventually gave up. To this day I have no idea if any of them are still alive. I realize it was not only their loss, but mine also.

During our short stay in Scotland, Rosalyn and I continued trying to learn English and adapt to the Scottish ways. The act of studying was foreign to us — we had had hardly any schooling as kids, and we had missed so much of the basic life skills that many individuals take for granted. However, our lack of education and life skills were minor problems compared to our continuous struggle with the harrowing past and our inability to speak of it to the well-meaning Scottish Jews who inquired. I coped by convincing myself that it had happened in another world or to others, not to me. And I kept busy with dreams of finding a job, earning a living, reuniting with my brothers, and eventually joining my relatives in America.

As summer approached, we learned that our orphanage would be closed down soon for economic reasons. Some of the children whom I had befriended were to relocate to hostels in Glasgow. Rosalyn and I, along with a few others, were assigned to an orphanage in Nellson, northern England, near the city of Burnley, Lancashire.

The night before we were to leave, I tossed and turned. I was scared about where we would wind up and what we would have to face. It seemed we were just getting acclimated — now we were being uprooted once again. I did not want to leave the nice Scottish people or the beautiful countryside. But what choice did I have as an orphan?

The next day I gathered my little bundle of clothing. By then I had a decent pair of shoes, an extra pair of socks, an extra set of underwear, and a decent shirt, but still only one pair of pants and a jacket. Then Rosalyn and I boarded an old military trooper bus bound for yet another strange land. But at least it was in peace, with no screaming, cussing, or abuse. I was frightened but optimistic. As the bus sped toward our new destination, I tried to keep everyone's spirits up by playing my trusty mandolin, singing happy songs, and telling funny stories. I continued trying to convince my fellow orphans and myself that despite our past, the world was indeed a good place to live.

Chapter Fourteen

England

Our new hostel was a nice little farmhouse on the outskirts of Nelson, close to Burnley, Lancashire, It was a pleasant enough place, but I was restless and eager to begin living independently. I was most anxious not to be dependent on handouts for me or my sister. I wanted to find myself, become self-supportive, and make a better life for myself and Rosalyn. I immediately started looking for ways to make a living, and my efforts paid off — I was the first of our group to find a job. I felt very fortunate to obtain work as an electrician's apprentice in a large knitting mill owned by a former Jewish refugee from Germany who had escaped to England before the war.

The ride to and from work was very long. I had to leave each morning before daylight and walk a half-mile from the hostel just to take the first bus towards town; then I rode another bus to the factory, which was on the other side of Burnley. Yet despite the early hours and long distance, I felt lucky for the opportunity to learn a trade, attempt the English language, and associate with people who weren't afraid to smile or laugh.

During my employment I came to know many nice people. Even though we struggled to communicate, I enjoyed associating with them — especially the girls who worked there. I tried hard to be social, and I had no problem establishing a rapport with them because of my profound love for life and people. I sincerely appreciated every human being, particularly those who were kind.

Even as an orphan, I was obligated to attend public trade school one day per week in Burnley. I enjoyed school very much, even though I could not understand what most of the other students were saying about me or even to me. Some were obviously making fun of me — sometimes I understood them only by the way they giggled and stared at me.

In spite of the well-meaning teachers, my difficulty learning to understand or speak English continued. I had even more trouble writing it, and to this day

I still do not comprehend the spelling and composition. There are so many more ways for a person to express himself in English than Yiddish — probably ten different ways to communicate the same thing more effectively. I especially wrestled with the various dialogues, slang, and cuss words, so I often resorted to motions. For example, to tell a girl that I thought she was nice, I would motion with my hands and whistle, or playfully exclaim, "Ooh-la-la!"

At school I met a boy named Burt Potts. (I doubt if he remembers me, even though we became friendly almost at once.) He did not make fun of me like some of the other boys — he was very kind and understanding, regardless of the language barrier. Burt and I practiced soccer during break time and whenever we had a free minute. I realized he was an exceptional athlete, but I had no idea how good a soccer player he was until much later: Burt became the first amateur player to be selected by Great Britain to play International Soccer for England. When he offered to get me a job working for his father, who owned the Burnley professional soccer team, I was very appreciative. But I was content with my current job and hoped to emigrate to America soon, so I politely declined.

One Friday after work I learned that my brother, Sam, had been transported out of Czechoslovakia to London, under the same orphanage program that brought Rosalyn and me to England. I desperately longed to reunite with him, so Rosalyn and I asked permission to go to London as soon as possible. After much pleading, we were given the go-ahead.

Coincidentally, we learned that our hostel would be closed down soon, so Rosalyn and I got our bus tickets and left for London as lost souls, very scared. We had no idea where we would stay or how we would get money to sustain ourselves.

When we arrived in London, we met Sam and were put up in the local shelter, then we bunked at the Primrose Club, which was organized for us by the British Jewry. It was the forerunner of the 45 Aid Society, which is still in operation today. I made many friends there, with whom I still keep in touch to this day. One of my closest friends was Jerry Hornstein. Jerry had a job with the George Nissel Contact Lens Company, which designed and manufactured full scleral contact lenses — from molded glass — which covered the entire eye. Early in 1947 Jerry helped me obtain an apprentice job there.

At that time contact lenses were very new to the world market. Mr. Nissel, the principal owner, was a Hungarian Jew who fortunately went to London before the war and was able to remain there for the duration. His partner was a mechanical genius whose first name was also George. They were very kind to everyone who worked there. Mr. Nissel took a liking to Jerry and me — we could communicate easily with him in Hungarian. At the Nissel Company I learned how to make excellent-quality glass contact lenses. I was happy and proud to do a good job for George Nissel, even though the apprentice pay was very low then.

Back then the optical field was different from today. The contact lenses were of molded glass, and they covered not only the pupil, but the entire eye — hence the name "full scleral" lenses. The ophthalmologist had to take a mold of the patient's eyes before we could make the lenses. I was very excited to be in this new field — I felt that once I had mastered the trade, I could become self-sufficient and earn a decent living. I worked every day and evening when they would let me, and often on Saturday without overtime pay. (The union did not allow overtime because back then people were out of work.)

I felt very privileged to work for George Nissel and especially with Jerry, and to be able to experiment and work with famous eye doctors and ophthalmologists. Often I would be sent to Harley Street, where some of the best eye doctors and medical specialists in the world had their offices. Sometimes I would observe the patients — if the lens was putting too much pressure on the eyeball, I would take it back to the lab to grind, adjust, and polish it.

I remember once when a beautiful, tall princess from India was having problems with her contact lenses. We kept adjusting, remolding, and regrinding them until they had been ground so thin that they finally broke. She just could not tolerate any pressure on the scleral part of her eyeball. The doctor asked my boss and me what we thought; then he decided to experiment. He had heard of a Scottish eye specialist who had experimented with a lens that covered only the corneal portion of the eye, not the entire eye. He told us to remove the portion that went over the sclera. I went back to the shop and cut the scleral portion off both lenses, then beveled and polished the edges so that they would fit perfectly over the corneal portion of the eyes. After a few adjustments it worked — the princess was able to wear the corneal lenses comfortably and see perfectly. She was so grateful; she was the happiest person I had ever seen with those contact lenses, so we were happy too.

As a result, our company pioneered the corneal contact lens manufacturing business in England, then overseas, and most eye doctors thereafter learned to fit only the small corneal contact lenses. Jerry and I established ourselves as the specialized corneal contact lens grinders for our company. The Nissel Company eventually became one of the world's largest manufacturers of corneal contact lenses. It also began manufacturing machinery to make the lenses and selling the machinery to companies around the world.

Sam also got a job soon after his arrival in England, so he and I were working evenings and weekends, scrounging and saving every penny to rent a room big enough for Rosalyn and us to share. Even if it wasn't in a good area, it would be cheap and we could finally live together.

The cheapest room we could find was in a boarding house in the worst area of town, just around the corner from the Maida Vale subway station. First, Sam and I shared one room with Rosalyn, then she shared a room with a very nice orphan girl named Mala. When we first moved in I could not figure out why so many women were standing around on the street corners every night and the weekends; much later I realized these women practiced the oldest profession in the world. However, this area was close to our work, we could not afford anything better, and we did not want to stay in the hostels or orphanages anymore. When Mala moved out, Rosalyn moved in with us. We hung a sheet to separate Rosalyn's small bed from ours. Sam and I had narrow bunk beds, but we felt very proud of them. It was so wonderful for the three of us to be together again, living independently. Now we could support Rosalyn while she got an education.

The British Jewish welfare agency most generously established the Primrose Club for child survivors of the Holocaust (and other English teens who cared to come); some of the orphaned boys bunked upstairs. It was a pleasant place where we could meet and socialize with Jews and other British people, get involved in sports, and learn all kinds of games — all free of charge. Jerry, Sam, Rosalyn, and I went to the club whenever possible.

I especially liked to dance, and to my delight the club provided free dance lessons. Many of my friends decided to take lessons so that they could go out dancing with us — that was our only source of entertainment in those days. We also took photography classes there, and the club formed soccer teams, so I started playing soccer again. We played in a London youth league, with challenge games from other cities. We had a fairly good team, and you had to be quite good to get on and stay on it — there were several hundred boys vying for spots on our team.

The best part of the club was the strong bond among the boys, especially those who played soccer and other sports. Jerry, a few others, and I were nearly inseparable — we went everywhere together. We reminisce about that time whenever we get together for our reunions in England, Israel, or the States, and we try to see each other whenever we can, even fifty-five years later.

I was also introduced to boxing at the Primrose Club, which quickly became my second love. In addition to training hard for soccer two nights a week and on weekends, I trained under Jack Delaney, the former British Empire and European heavyweight boxing champion who fought Joe Louis and another world-renown featherweight (Jewish) boxer. All training people volunteered their time free.

Jack made me run five miles each session to keep in shape. I became fairly good at boxing, and tried out for the equivalent of the Golden Gloves in the 114 lb. weight division (which coincidentally was to be held exactly two years to the day after my liberation from Buchenwald). Jack insisted that I train at least two evenings every week and on weekends for upcoming fights. Since I had no money for transportation, I either walked, ran, or rode the same broken-down bike which I took to work. Despite that several-mile commute, Jack still made me run five more miles each training time. As a result I began to hate running, and still do today. He also made me spar with heavyweight boxers to prepare me to take punches. I fought several good fights and won some.

By that time I had begun understanding English better. We often had guest days in the Primrose Club where Jewish Londoners came to meet and get to know us. They brought cookies and refreshments and encouraged us to socialize. We met a lot of very nice people this way, particularly a wonderful family by the name of Ralph. Sam met the Ralphs first in the hostel where he used to stay; then they met Rosalyn and took a real liking to her.

The Ralphs lived in a town called Croydon, just outside London. They invited us to visit for a weekend, and we spent many wonderful weekends with them afterwards. I fell in love with this kind, loving family — they were the most considerate people I had encountered in England.

Love radiated especially from Mrs. Ralph. Rosalyn, Sam, and I immediately felt at home with them. They had two sons about my age — Gerald and Derek — and one daughter, Maureen, who were as kind to us as their parents. At the Ralph's request we started calling them mom and dad, which was not difficult because we loved them (and longed for a real family tie). Mom Ralph never treated the three of us any differently than her own flesh-and-blood children.

The Ralphs were generous with us to a fault. Soon they asked us to move into their home, and we happily agreed. Their children never showed any jealousy or seemed to object to our being taken into their home. We became one big, happy family, sharing with and caring for each other. However, Sam, Rosalyn and I knew our place and did not take undue advantage of their generosity. At first we kept our room at the boarding house, in case things did not work out. I wanted a life of my own, and the boarding house was closer to work and the Primrose Club.

Mom Ralph insisted that we join them Friday evenings for Sabbath prayer and on holidays at the synagogue. At first I did not desire to go after all I had been through. I was not sure about the existence of the Almighty or the power of prayers, or whom to pray to or why. However, after attending Synagogue with them a few times, I started to enjoy the prayers and met many nice people

— such as the fine rabbi, and Dr. Fry, a friend of the Ralphs. But I had difficulty relating to an Almighty who had allowed so much suffering and such unholy, devilish things to happen to us. I thought that the Almighty might have turned into Satan — how else could He permit so many innocent people, especially children and elderly, to be tortured and murdered? Still, as I went to synagogue more often, I began to accept that it was the people who committed those heinous crimes, not God. I also started remembering the teachings of our parents. Ever since I was young I had gone to Synagogue every day, especially on the Sabbath and holidays. Back then it was as natural to me as breathing. Soon that practice took hold of me again, and eventually I willingly went Friday evenings and some Saturday mornings with the Ralphs. I became eager to get closer to God and other people, and not to dwell on the bad things of which humans are capable.

Our quality of life slowly continued to improve, thanks to the Ralphs' loving care and our Primrose Club activities. My biggest boxing fight for the equivalent of the Golden Glove semi-finals was also my last fight. I had the fight almost won and became over-confident, thinking I could knock my opponent out whenever I wanted to. I felt I could play with him a little and he would surrender; if not, I could knock him out with one last punch.

I let my guard down because he was bleeding and badly cut. Somehow he managed one good uppercut, which caught me by surprise and flipped me over. I came down head-first on the canvas and suffered a bad cut over my eye. Dazed and bleeding, I was counted out by the referee.

I stayed in my room every evening that week and did not go to Croydon to see the Ralphs. Some of the boys with whom I played soccer came to see me, but I was despondent.

When I came home to the Ralphs the following weekend, Mom noticed a patch over my eye and asked me what had happened. I fibbed that I bumped my head on some equipment at work and got cut over my eye. Of course, she did not buy it — she took me immediately to Dr. Fry, who declared that I had suffered a bad concussion. Mom was very upset with me and insisted that I tell her everything right there and then. I admitted to Mom Ralph that my injury was from a knock-out in a boxing match. This upset her very much, and she immediately made me promise that I would never box or put on boxing gloves again. As a result, I have never done either since — I would never break my promise to her.

Now that the war had been over for some time, Holocaust survivors everywhere were becoming increasingly aware that to avoid another Holocaust we would have to establish our own Jewish state. Jews in Palestine and many other countries were struggling to reestablish the State of Israel for the massive number of Jews still homeless and considered undesirable refugees in many lands, including Europe. Sam and I felt strongly that the rebirth of a Jewish state would help other destitute Jews like us who could not return to their former homes and needed a safe haven. We wanted to help our people reclaim their rightful place in the family of nations, and we felt it was very important to follow our convictions — although at that time it was very dangerous to try and enter what was then Palestine under British mandate. The British, and especially the Arabs, were arresting and killing Jews who tried to enter Israel and attacking those who were already there.

We had learned of an underground movement to smuggle Jews in to Israel, and I told one of the organizers that I would like to volunteer to go and fight for this most righteous cause. I signed up and was told to prepare to leave soon.

A few days later, Sam told the Ralphs and me that he had volunteered to join the Hagganah, a semi-military Jewish force in Palestine. While we both wanted desperately to go, one of us had to stay with Rosalyn. So we tossed a coin, and Sam won the right to leave for Palestine.

Sam himself had to furnish all equipment for his mandatory military training, including boots, clothing, and even a blanket. We had to buy these items in England with the little money we were able to scrounge up and ration coupons, as all clothing in England was rationed at that time. Soon Sam left for military training in France with our blessing It was a sad day for me but I was happy for Sam, even though I was afraid his ship would be impounded by the British and he would end up in a Cyprus prison.

After a tearful goodbye, Sam boarded a not-so-safe ship, hoping it would last long enough to reach Israel's shores. Unfortunately, we learned later that the British Patrol had seized his ship three miles from shore and forbade the boys to enter Palestine. Sam and some of the other boys jumped overboard, swam several miles to shore, and were able to join the Jewish Defense Forces. This movement was instrumental in reclaiming the soil of Israel, given by the Almighty to our forefathers, Abraham, Jacob, and Moses, many thousands of years ago.

As part of the fighting forces for independence, Sam unfortunately suffered severe injuries to his face, head, and ear from grenade attacks by the Arabs. He quickly recovered but was scarred forever, and he chose to remain in Israel awhile. He missed us and we missed him. We wanted badly to be reunited in America with him, but he ended up staying in Israel for several more years.

Shortly thereafter, Ben, Bill, and Bernie — along with Bernie's wife, Ruth, and their infant son, Eddie — got their visas, and our uncles in Ellwood City, Pennsylvania, sent them tickets to immigrate to America from communist-dominated Czechoslovakia. Meanwhile, our American relatives (especially

Aunt Rose, Uncles Gene, Adolph, and Ben and their families) were trying to obtain visas for Rosalyn and me. We prayed each day for the arrangements to be finalized so that we could all meet in America. We felt certain that our parents up in heaven were urging us all to be reunited in America. It had been so long since we had seen each other.

Finally, in December 1948 Rosalyn and I got our precious, long-awaited visas, allowing us to immigrate to the United States. Rosalyn left immediately; however, I stayed behind. Mom Ralph had become very ill with a brain tumor, and Dr. Fry felt she would not go for the operation if I left. He and the rabbi asked if I would postpone my immigration and stay with her until the operation was over and she regained enough strength to get on with her life. I was somewhat reluctant — I had dreamed of living free in America with my family for so long — but I was glad to oblige because Mom Ralph was so special and had been so very good to us.

Mom Ralph's operation fortunately proved successful. After several months, when she had gained her strength back and we felt she was out of imminent danger, I asked her if it would be O.K. for me to leave. She readily agreed that I should go, and she urged me to save money to pay for my trip and some decent clothes.

I happily proceeded with finalizing the arrangements to leave for America, consumed with thoughts of rejoining my family and finally meeting my only surviving uncles, aunts, and cousins. I gave up renting my Maida Vale room in London. Thanks to the Ralphs' generosity, I did not have to pay for rent or food, so I was able to save a good portion of my earnings for my passage. The Ralphs kindly matched my savings, which gave me enough money to travel fourth-class on the elegant Queen Mary.

I was very proud that my uncles did not have to pay my fare. They had already helped the rest of my family with transportation costs and setting up a home for them, which I am sure drained them financially. It felt gratifying to pay my own way; I was sure they would appreciate it.

By the time I was ready to depart for America, Rosalyn was married and Ben had found a job as a kosher butcher in Pittsburgh, Pennsylvania, close to my relatives in Ellwood City. Ben had also met Sylvia, the love of his life, and decided to marry her, but they had held off the wedding date until they were sure I would get there on time to be Ben's best man. After all my transportation arrangements were finalized, the wedding was set for December 20, 1949.

As the day approached for me to leave for Liverpool to board the Queen Mary; mixed emotions gripped my heart. I was very excited to finally sail for the land I had dreamed about and be reunited with my family. I was also sad to leave Mom and Dad Ralph, and Gerald, Maureen, and Derek. I hated parting with my many wonderful friends, fellow orphans in the Primrose Club and the 45 Aid Society, with whom I still keep in touch and feel a brotherly bond. I would also miss my fellow employees at the George Nissel Contact Lens Company — I was afraid I would never see or hear from any of them again.

Life and business in Great Britain were very rough after World War II, so the Ralphs decided to emigrate to South Africa with their two sons as soon as possible after I left. One son married a child survivor who was a friend of ours, and their daughter, who was a Zionist, emigrated to Israel. I have visited her family, as well as Gerald's son, in Israel several times. The Ralphs came to visit me, Sam, and Rosalyn in America, and we have been to visit them in South Africa. Both Mr. and Mrs. Ralph unfortunately have since passed away, God rest their souls. But their children are alive and well, and we try to keep in touch.

Because of the Ralphs, I entered the United States with self-confidence. The love that they gave so generously reestablished my faith in humanity and reminded me how important it is to truly love others. The Ralphs, England, and its people will always remain dear to my heart and precious in my memory; I will forever appreciate their healing kindness, understanding, and help.

IMAGES

BEFORE THE WAR

THE GROSS FAMILY

FILIP, MOTHER, BERNIE, BEN, BILL, FATHER, SAM,
ROSALYN, ALEX

FIVE MEN FROM THE OLD COUNTRY
UNCLE YOSEF LEBOVITZ, FATHER, THE WAGON DRIVER
THE RITUAL SLAUGHTERER, GRANDFATHER

THE MEN ON THE HOMESTEAD
BILL, A WORKER, BERNIE, A WORKER, SAM, FATHER
ALEX

AT HOME

OUR HOUSE AND THE BASTION BEHIND IT ON THE HILL
MOTHER, ROSALYN, FATHER

THE WEISS FAMILY

———

MOTHER'S SISTER, HUSBAND, AND CHILDREN
ALL KILLED IN AUSCHWITZ

AUSCHWITZ, 2001
THE BARRACKS IN WHICH ALEX STAYED

AUSCHWITZ, 2001
THE CREMATORIA

AFTER THE WAR

REFUGEES IN PRAGUE, 1946

ARRIVAL IN ENGLAND, 1946

CHILD, ALEX, AND TRANSPORT AIRPLANE

UNCLE EUGENE, AUNT ROSE, UNCLE BEN, UNCLE ADOLPH

ALEX'S SPONSORS

MOM AND DAD RALPH

MY ADOPTED PARENTS, ENGLAND (1967)

AMERICA

ALEX AS SOLDIER IN THE KOREAN WAR

ALEX AND LINDA GROSS

NEWLY WEDS, 1960

ALEX AND BENJI

———————

LIKE FATHER, LIKE SON

THE ALEX GROSS FAMILY

PROUD AND HAPPY, LATE1960S

BENJI AND ALAN GROSS
COUSINS AND BEST FRIENDS

BNAI MITZVAH, NOVEMBER 24, 1973

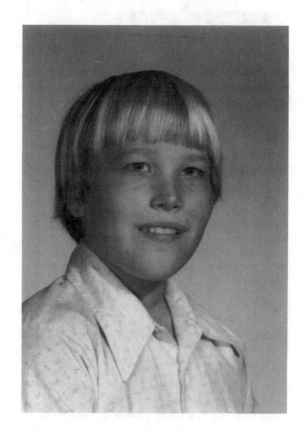

BENJI

JANUARY 28, 1961 - JUNE 18, 1975

ALEX AND LINDA GROSS
AUGUST 1983

LINDA, MAY 1, 1939 - NOVEMBER 11, 1983

THE HONORARY DEGREE

CHAIR OF THE BOARD OF TRUSTEES, PRESIDENT OF THE UNIVERSITY, ALEX, A DEAN
JUNE 1995

THE HONORARY DEGREE

DAVID BLUMENTHAL, ALEX, URSULA AND BENJAMIN BLUMENTHAL
JUNE 1995

FAMILY 2001

THE SIBLINGS, 1998

BILL, BERNIE, SAM, ROSALYN, FILIP, BEN & ALEX

ALEX AND DAISY

MARRIED AUGUST 18, 1996

ETTA AND LEYA

ROBIN AND BENJI

STEPHANIE WITH ELIANA AND HANNAH

ALEX AND THE GRANDCHILDREN

BENJI AND LEYA
HANNAH AND ELIANA

PALANOK 1967
OUR HOME

ALEX AND LEYA, PALANOK 2001
OUR LOT

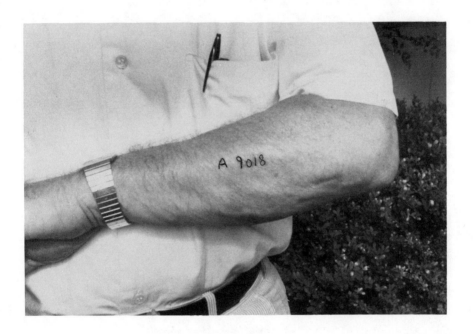

MEMORY

————

ALEX'S TATOO

LIFE IN THE THE NEW WORLD

CHAPTER FIFTEEN

THE "GOLDENE MEDINA"

I barely noticed the chill in the air that momentous December morning in 1949 as I approached the embarkation docks in Liverpool. The majestic Queen Mary beckoned me, and its breathtaking magnificence filled me with awe. Even though I was leaving the Ralph family behind, this trip was the fulfillment of a lifelong dream. I had never felt happier — after years of waiting and hoping, I was really and truly on my way to the "Goldene Medina": the Golden Land of America. The game of hide and seek with myself was over.

The ship's loud whistle sounded and soon we started moving. What a miracle! I felt my life begin anew as the beautiful ship passed through the slips and out into the rainy, rough Atlantic Ocean.

Sumptuous meals were served in the ship's huge, luxurious dining room. At first I was too excited — and intimidated — to eat. I felt that the beautiful dining room was intended for royalty and wealthy people, not young paupers like me. But I soon adjusted to my surroundings and began eating up a storm. I was ready to be treated like a normal person and quickly came to appreciate the ship's stately beauty.

As a fourth-class passenger, I was put in a very small four-person room on the lowest deck, with double bunks above and beside me. This portion of the ship had not been remodelled since being used to transport troops during World War I, but I felt as if I was traveling to heaven in first class. My roommates and I sang happy songs in crazy combinations of Yiddish-Polish-Czech-Hungarian — we were giddy with anticipation but I expected nothing from anybody except the opportunity to work and be with my family.

Every evening after dinner I went dancing, which I enjoyed very much. I even entered the dance contests, which combined all classes of travelers, and I won one of the final ballroom dance contests. After that I was asked often to dance by several good dancers, including many lovely American girls. (Some were probably married; most were obviously well-to-do.) We flirted playfully with each other, and they let down their hair to entice the men to dance with them. Of course, having never been exposed to such luxury and graciousness, I took the bait. Dancing with them all night was great fun — I have fond memories of it to this day.

On board the ship I befriended some very nice people from all over America who tried to stay in touch with me afterwards. But I had no money even to return the long-distance phone calls, and I did not know how to write well enough in English — or what to write about. I suppose I could eventually tell them I got a job in a knitting mill in Ellwood City, Pennsylvania, earning a measly $18 a week — a lot to me, but probably peanuts to them. Or I could write about how tough it was to get started in a new country without money, among strangers with weird customs and a new language. Or we could discuss the difficulty of trying to get a job in my trained profession. Somehow I didn't know if they would relate. I wanted to be part of the people of hope; no longer the target of hate. I wanted to flourish in this haven.

I constantly pondered my future as an American during that journey. I felt very upbeat about the American way of life and its opportunities — I had confidence in myself and my American family, and above all, I had faith in the American system and its people. After all, millions of poor, uneducated people came here from all parts of the world, where they had struggled to succeed but could not. In America, most people who were smart and worked hard succeeded — some beyond their wildest dreams. From the time I was a child, my parents and grandparents had taught me that honest, hard work brought its rewards. I was looking forward to working and living in a democratic society, practicing my religion (or what I could remember of it), becoming the best person that I could be, and trying to help others whenever possible. I felt my chances for succeeding were just as good as anyone else's.

As the mighty vessel navigated the often stormy sea, I was lucky not to become seasick. My expectations of soon touching American soil, seeing my siblings, and meeting my American relatives was exceedingly overwhelming. As if that weren't enough to anticipate, I would be serving as best man in Ben and Sylvia's wedding the day after my arrival. So much to think about and look forward to — I felt immune to seasickness (and any other type of illness, as well).

Our arrival in the New York harbor was magical, a fantasy come true. Not so long ago I was in dire pain, on the brink of death, clinging to the faintest hope of survival. I could hardly believe then that this journey would indeed happen. As we excitedly prepared for disembarkation, I felt like an infant being reborn.

It was still dark, but the Statue of Liberty radiated in all her glory. She was a pinnacle of splendor. In the background, the New York lights sparkled like precious gems. I could hardly wait for daylight so that I could get off the ship to kiss the land of America — "the beautiful bastion of freedom and land of opportunity" — especially for me and my family. At that moment I fully realized and appreciated the fact that America was indeed a haven for everyone, regardless of race, religion, or nationality — including this once condemned Jewish boy.

My happiness was marred only by thoughts of my wonderful parents and the millions of others who had been inhumanely tortured and murdered in Auschwitz and other killing centers. I wondered what my arrival in America would have meant to them. I knew they would have been overjoyed to realize that Lady Liberty was to be the new guardian of their beloved children. Never would they have suspected that all their children would survive the Holocaust and eventually call this new land their home. I was delighted not just for us, but for our future generations. I wished only that my parents could enjoy this experience with me.

As I walked down the plank and my feet touched earth, I immediately went down on my hands and knees. I cried, prayed, and kissed the American soil.

Soon thereafter I thought I heard a porter paging me — or at least it sounded like my name. He called for a Mr. Goos, which I guessed was New York Yankee slang for Gross. When I asked if he meant Gross, he ignored me.

Then others came to look for me, again mispronouncing my name. Apparently, Aunt Rose Meyerson had sent someone to look for me, but they were having difficulty finding me because they were looking for a young man at least 5 feet, 10 inches tall, of normal weight, with thick blond hair and a mustache. I spoke to several porters before convincing one that I might be who they were looking for. I certainly did not fit Aunt Rose's description. Even though I had gained back most of the weight and some of the height I had lost while in the camps, I now weighed only around 110 pounds and I no longer had a mustache. After finally convincing one of the porters that I was who they sought, I was led to the gate where I met my wonderful Aunt Rose for the first time, along with Uncle Aaron Gross, my Father's brother, who had brought her to pick me up.

I was overcome with tears of happiness, and they also started crying. Aunt Rose exclaimed, *"Oy-vey,* I thought you were much taller!" I was stunned by her immediate warmth, her smile, and her uncanny resemblance to my beloved Mother. I was touched that both Aunt Rose and Uncle Aaron had come to the docks to meet me.

As I waited to be cleared through immigration, I felt immense pride and happiness. I bid farewell to the new friends I'd made, as well shipmates from the orphanage and the Primrose Club. Then I gathered my one-and-only suitcase and left arm-in-arm with my newfound family. I always thought of my Mother, her smiles and loving personality. She was present in my heart and mind as though a screen was in front of my eyes. I tried to keep her radiant smile on my own face.

As Uncle Aaron drove us away from the busy harbor, I was amazed at the hundreds of automobiles, buses, taxis, trucks, and vans buzzing around. The streets of New York were jammed with people and vehicles of every description. What an exciting, bustling city! It seemed New Yorkers had very little patience — everyone was in such a great hurry to get to where they were going, blowing horns, screaming, and cutting in front of each other. Yet I felt none of the hate and divisiveness that I had been exposed to most of my short life. I felt as if I could see the opportunities awaiting me more clearly than ever. Finally I would truly be rid of the hatred and persecution that had once ruled my every waking moment. Here I would be surrounded by hope, love and freedom. I would never again go hungry or be a burden to anyone.

There was so much traffic, I could hardly believe my eyes — I never imagined there were so many vehicles in the entire world, let alone in one city. In the backward area where I came from, most of the residents walked everywhere; a few had a horse or cattle to pull their wagons. The most fortunate rode bicycles. The vast majority of automobiles in our area were military vehicles. We didn't even have paved streets! Clearly, New York was worlds away from the Carpathia, Russia area.

We sped toward Aunt Rose's house in Brooklyn, and I gawked in awe at New York's many tall buildings. They loomed even taller than the highest mountains near my village. The sights were overwhelming.

Along the way my Uncle Aaron pointed to various buildings, saying each one was "his." At first I thought he was indicating that he owned them, but I soon learned that he merely owned a contracting business that cleaned windows and offices in those buildings — including some of the tallest skyscrapers in New York. I was very proud of him, just as proud as if he actually owned those buildings. I listened with great interest as he confidently recounted his achievements. He kept saying, "Just look at what you can accomplish in America when you put your mind to it." That was music to my ears.

After an overnight stay with Aunt Rose, we left very early the next morning for Pittsburgh, Pennsylvania, where Ben and Bill lived. Bernie, his wife Ruth, and their son, Eddy — our first nephew — lived close by in Ellwood City. Rosalyn and her husband lived in Erie, about 100 miles from Pittsburgh. I could hardly wait to see all my disjointed family and finally meet the rest of my American relatives — it had been several years since I had seen or talked to my brothers. I was also proud and excited to be the best man in Ben and Sylvia's upcoming wedding.

Time passed very fast on that trip. I spent the entire eight-hour ride probing Aunt Rose and Uncle Aaron with all kinds of questions about life in the United States in my limited English or in Yiddish. They forthrightly told me about the good and bad things that were happening on this side of the Atlantic, but they emphasized the positive — especially the prospects of getting a job and making a good living in a safe, equal opportunity environment. As the miles sped by, my hope increased as I thought of the good times ahead: being with family, especially for the holidays, sharing their joys, and being there for them in times of need.

As we approached Pittsburgh, my happy mood suddenly turned to panic as I noticed the tall smokestacks of the steel mills belching out dark soot. My mind immediately flashed back to Auschwitz — that unforgettably putrid scent of burning flesh, and the ever present black smoke. Before I lost all control, I reminded myself that I was not back in the camps but safe in America with my family, and that the smoke was from coal for making steel, not from the burning bodies of innocent Jews. I forced myself to concentrate on the rolling landscape with nice trees and homes, the pleasure of meeting the rest of my beloved relatives, being reunited with Ben and meeting Sylvia's family at the wedding.

Our first stop in metropolitan Pittsburgh was Homestead, the site of Sylvia's synagogue. It was very traditional — small, old, and beautiful, and the Smooke family had attended it for many years. Sylvia and Ben were a lovely bride and groom. Sylvia was a wonderful addition to our family — she immediately became one of us, and we felt instant acceptance by her and her family.

The ceremony was truly moving, and a perfect occasion for me to meet and get to know my new American family — including my Aunts Hilda and Helen and my uncles Eugene and Adolph. My only regret was that our murdered parents and relatives could not experience the wonderful joyous music, sing Yiddish songs, and dance the Horah along with us. That memorable event was the start of many long, satisfying relationships with my American family that would remain so for generations to come. I felt truly blessed to be related to those wonderful people.

Soon after the wedding we left for Ellwood City to see the rest of my aunts, uncles and cousins, plus Bernie and Ruthie and their three-year-old son, Eddy. Each made me feel welcome in their homes. They gave me the guidance from their heart that I needed and they encouraged me to be a good Jew, a good human, and a loyal American. Because of this I felt that I could never disappoint them or myself — succeeding was my only option.

Getting to know my wonderful family gave me strength to handle anything that life had to offer in this new land. I know that my beloved parents were looking down on me from heaven that day. And they loved and appreciated their American brothers and sister even more for embracing us in America. With the Almighty's help and the fortitude of familial love, I was ready and willing to begin my new American life through honest hard work, positive attitude, and determination. The future beckoned me, and I couldn't wait to get started.

CHAPTER SIXTEEN

THE AMERICAN WAY

Adapting to the American lifestyle was a challenge, to say the least. I was a typical refugee, full of hope and energy, eager to work hard, and learn the ways of Americans. I was in awe of the luxurious lifestyles and opportunities that were available in America.

My generous aunts and uncles graciously assumed the role of surrogate parents, which made for a smooth initiation. Yet despite their staunch support and unconditional love, my new life was so different from the way I was brought up, in a backward area of the old country. Language and communication problems evoked my most profound frustrations. I had learned very little English in Britain because I was mostly around fellow orphans, refugees like myself. Here I struggled mightily to grasp, for example, the various meanings for a single English word. A few years before I had been comfortable speaking many dialects — Schwabish-German, Czech, Polish, Rusky, Hungarian, and most of all, Yiddish. But mastering English was vexing. Having no alternative, trial-and-error was my most successful method.

In America, when I thought I had said one thing in English, I was told I had said something quite different — sometimes the opposite of what I was trying to convey. For example, the English word "pots" means a man's vitals in Yiddish. That mix-up caused plenty of confusion and embarrassment, for sure.

It must have been amusing back then to hear me talk with my broken accent and limited understanding. Your imagination works in strange ways when you are not sure what a person asked you and whether or not you answered properly. I remember one such incident with Uncle Gene that occurred just a few days after I arrived in the States. Uncle Gene, who always dressed immaculately, took me for a ride to the nearby town of Koppel — a deserted town which he and his business partner had purchased after selling their insurance business. Most of Koppel was very run-down, and the factory that had supported the town had gone bankrupt during the depression. The previous owners of the factory had at one time owned most of the homes and the land in and around Koppel in the late 30s and early 40s. The plant had been the town's sole source of livelihood, but after the war it closed down. Most residents had been drafted, began working for the military, or moved to wherever they could find employment.

As we left Ellwood City and rode along a narrow twisting road, I began to notice signs that read "curves" and "danger," I knew that "c" was sometimes pronounced "k," and "kurves" meant "prostitutes" in Yiddish. The more "curves" signs I saw, the more I became convinced that Uncle Gene was taking me to a house of ill repute. I protested to him in Yiddish, "I do not want it and I do not need it! Please don't worry about those things for me, I am quite capable of taking care of myself." He looked at me, confused — he had no idea what I was referring to. We continued in silence on our journey.

Although my parents had taught us to love and respect our family members, I began thinking that Uncle Gene was overly concerned regarding my needs in this delicate matter. When he handed me a $20 bill, I was convinced more than ever about his intentions. Refusing to take money for that purpose, I politely shoved it back to him, again protesting that I did not want it.

Soon we stopped at an old hotel which I thought looked like a European brothel. Uncle Gene parked his car in front, got out, and began walking towards the entrance. I refused to go with him. Again he held out the $20 bill to me. Mortified, I refused once more. As he stepped onto the front porch, he was greeted by a lady whom I thought was the madam — just like in the old country, when the Hungarian military took us Jewish youth to Munkach to clean the houses of ill repute as part of the anti-Jewish edicts.

He introduced the woman to me, and she seemed very nice. As they chatted, I realized that this was not a brothel but a run-of-the-mill boarding house, owned by Uncle Gene and his partner, and that she actually managed the place. What a relief to discover that he had only come to collect the rent!

Many years later we would have a good laugh over the incident, but it sure wasn't funny at the time. More importantly, it proved to me how naive I was and that I ought to learn to communicate better in English — fast.

The more I got to know Uncle Gene, I realized just how smart, resourceful, and ahead of his time he really was. For instance, he was instrumental in helping to complete the Pennsylvania Turnpike — the forerunner of major American thoroughfares. He did this through a land swap of some property he had owned, which enabled construction of the Turnpike all the way to the Ohio border. I believe this was accomplished through "land for discounted turnpike" bonds. The privately-run Turnpike Authority was short of funds to complete the thruway that went from New York through New Jersey on through Pennsylvania. Now the turnpike goes through Ohio and Indiana all the way to Chicago.

I take considerable pride in the fact that my uncle played a big role in pioneering this effort and contributing to the orderly growth of America's economy. Also because of his business acumen, the economy of Koppel was eventually rejuvenated and it ultimately became a vibrant community.

Thanks to a friend of my uncle's, it wasn't long before I was employed. My very first job in America involved many hats: I worked as an electrical and plumbing apprentice/maintenance man/assistant to the main cutter in the Campus knitting mills in Ellwood City for $18 a week. The pay was low, even for those days. Still, I felt very fortunate to get the job — especially considering my weak language skills. Ellwood City was a small town with no opportunities in the contact lens field for which I had been trained.

I felt like a millionaire when I got my first paycheck. After Social Security and taxes were deducted, I netted about $14. When I showed my precious paycheck to Uncles Gene and Adolph, they introduced me to the American-Jewish charitable way. They felt that 10 to 20 percent of one's earnings should be given to charity, if possible. My mother and her father, my wonderful Zeidie (grandfather) Moishe Aharon, felt the same way. They told us, "When you give to those less fortunate than yourself, it always comes back to you many fold." So I kept $10 to live on and immediately joined the B'nai B'rith organization with my first $2 allotted to charity. (I am still a member today.) I even managed to save $2 for a rainy day. With my next paycheck I planned to use the allotted $2 to join the synagogue or contribute to another charity.

I worked long hours in the knitting mill, seven days a week when I was permitted by the union. I learned not to spend money on food, clothing, dating, or anything else that I could do without. Of course, I never went hungry — there was always good food at our uncles', and Bernie and Ruth were always generous with their open house and wonderful home-cooked meals. I developed a close relationship with my first nephew, their young son Eddie, while enjoying many delicious dinners there. And Aunts Hilda and Helen always had extra food ready, just in case one of us stopped by with a good appetite. Their kids, my cousins, were also exceptionally good to us, for which I remain most grateful. They never treated us like refugees — we were always part of their family.

My precious Aunt Hilda (may she rest in peace) filled part of the gap left by my dearly departed Mother. She advised me on how to dress and got rid of most of my clothes — suits that I had thought were the finest available, at least in England. Aunt Hilda also taught me to be punctual. One time I arrived at her home for dinner about ten minutes late, so she made me sit and wait for my food. It was a lesson that served me well my whole life.

Good jobs were so hard to get and keep at that time, so Uncles Eugene and Adolph often tried to guide me and help me understand the way business worked in America. They helped me comprehend many things, like American likes and dislikes and the peculiarities of the culture. They gave of themselves very generously, and I accepted their guidance in the spirit with which it was given. This gave me the determination to work harder so that I could someday show them my appreciation through my accomplishments. I wanted to be successful not only for myself, but, hopefully, for my very own future family, if I was to be fortunate enough to have one.

As I worked to carve a place for myself in America, my other transplanted siblings struggled to do the same. When Ben, Bill, Bernie, and his family had arrived in America almost a year before me, Ben worked first as a butcher in a grocery store in Ellwood City, then in a kosher butcher shop in Pittsburgh (where he met Sylvia). Later Ben and Sylvia opened up their own kosher meat market in Pittsburgh, where they built a reputation for offering good kosher salami, bologna, corned beef, and other meat products. Then they began making their own kosher sausage and salami, which soon became known as the best in the area. But in those days there was little profit in being a butcher, especially when starting out with very little, mostly borrowed money. They could not afford any help — they worked long hours and made their own deliveries at day's end, often carrying their children with them to save money and spend time with them.

Meanwhile, Bernie and Ruthie were establishing their own tailor shop in Ellwood City. They were working very hard to earn a living, despite their inability to speak English or understand American ways of doing business. Bill had found work in the tailor shop of a large Pittsburgh department store. Rosalyn was married by the time I arrived in America, and soon had a child. She lived in Erie, Pennsylvania. Sam was still in Israel, recuperating from injuries received while fighting there. Unfortunately, Philip and his family were still trapped in Communist Russia.

It was initially very difficult to become accepted by the general American public. Some people responded to us as if we were aliens, because of our accents and foreign behavior. However, soon we were on our way to becoming productive members of American society.

Uncles Adolph and Ben owned thriving Army-Navy stores in Ellwood City and nearby Beaver Falls. Uncle Eugene had spent many successful years in the business world. Besides acquiring Koppel as a partner, he remained very active in other real estate ventures. Time after time he told me how much the United

States needed savvy, hardworking entrepreneurs, and he implored my brothers and me never to be complacent, never give up trying. My uncles were all living proof of the successful American dream, and I constantly contemplated ways to follow in their footsteps.

There were very few new homes built during World War II because there were no able-bodied men left stateside to build or buy them. Also, the men and women who stayed stateside during the War had suffered cramped, substandard housing just to be near their jobs. Now that peace was restored and the GIs were returning home, many were marrying the girlfriends they had left behind, and the "baby boom" was just beginning. The need for decent, affordable housing was greater than ever.

Bill and I decided that America definitely needed "starter" housing, as well as upgraded housing. Although we had no money to get started in the housing business, we had desire, nerve, and all the good business advice we could handle from our uncles. I listened to Uncle Eugene carefully and retained what he told me. From Uncle Adolph I learned about retail sales. Uncle Bernard, also in the Army-Navy surplus clothing business, was another great source of support. A bachelor who loved children (especially his nieces and nephews), he wanted to help since he knew we had no parents to guide us. The love and encouragement of these great men planted the seeds of confidence that Bill and I sorely needed to get started.

We also realized that we needed to be able to read and understand English well to succeed in the building business. I wanted to communicate properly with suppliers and prospective purchasers, and understand all the legal documents. Bill and I also wanted to help our customers obtain financing and understand the associated paperwork.

Bill and I had no money to invest, no financial background or collateral, and we were unable to borrow funds. But thanks to Uncle Eugene's guidance and connections, in 1950 we started a business as dealers in a line of pre-cut packaged garages and utility buildings. We began with small structures, expecting to expand as we gained experience and capital. Our goal was to eventually sell pre-cut packaged houses to handyman do-it-yourselfers who wanted to own a home but had limited funds. We approached our prospects with enthusiasm, encouraging them to purchase our low-budget homes and do most — if not all — the erection work themselves. The customer first had to purchase a lot for his particular house, then he had to finish the basement or foundation himself before we shipped his pre-cut, bundled, and numbered material to the homesite. We delivered the material directly onto the foundation, so that it could easily be erected (with the help of friends and relatives). The buyer had to do almost everything, but if he needed help of any kind we were always available (with our broken English and limited but growing knowledge) to guide them in building and finishing their home.

We worked long, hard hours. We had a mighty financial struggle, even though we bought our materials directly from a manufacturer whose plant was located just outside Pittsburgh. But our excitement was genuine. Bill even began talking of eventually expanding into other areas, so we were constantly on the lookout for opportunities outside Ellwood City.

Of course, shortage of cash, language struggles, lack of education, and other problems arose, and we tried to address each situation as it occurred. We made very little profit at first, but we persevered. Bill and I were very proud of ourselves. Uncle Gene was proud of us too, and praised us whenever we made a sale. At that time I was still working in the knitting mill eight hours a day, five days a week, and Bill continued to work as a tailor in Pittsburgh. We worked evenings and weekends for the business, and it took every cent we could muster just to keep it going. Each month seemed harder than the previous one. We had no money of our own and no automobile to visit prospective customers. (For that matter, we still did not know how to drive in America — in England people drove on the opposite side of the road.)

Although we continued to work 18 to 20 hours a day, seven days a week, we were not able to make ends meet. We realized that we desperately needed some capital if we were to make progress.

We also realized that both of us could not be supported from this business. Then Bill lost his tailoring job. We struggled to keep the business going for a while, but my job at the knitting mill did not pay enough to keep both of us in food and shelter. We had no assets or inheritance to fall back on. Something had to be done and quickly or our business would fail.

Around that time, the Korean War had broken out. I immediately applied to be drafted, but I was turned down because I had been in America only a few months. I also had flat feet and other minor health problems, so I was assigned a high draft number. But I remained hopeful that I might still get drafted if the war escalated.

Then I received a call from Jerry Hornstein, who had been with me in the English orphanage and with whom I worked in the contact lens field in England. Jerry was setting up a contact lens manufacturing division for the Ritholtz Company, a large Chicago optical firm operating at that time under the name of King Optical Company. The owner was looking for people with experience to help manufacture and market contact lenses first in Chicago, then eventually nationwide. Jerry had immediately thought of me.

The job paid $50 a week to start, which at that time was very good pay. They would even pay my fare to Chicago. The offer sounded too good to be true. I discussed it with my brothers — especially Bill — who advised me to take the job. Uncle Eugene agreed: he said good jobs like that were hard to find, particularly for immigrants with limited language skills. What's more, I would be building on my experience.

When Jerry called back, I accepted the job and left immediately by overnight train for Chicago.

Upon arrival I met the owners of the company — including Ben Ritholtz, the president, who was very nice, and his brothers, who were a little "kooky" and not very friendly at first. I explained to them that while I was happy to work for their company (and especially with Jerry) and would continue for as long as possible, if the war should get out of hand in Korea I would like to be drafted into the U.S. Army. I felt very strongly about this, and they agreed to it.

I began work the next day. At $50 a week I felt sure that I could send Bill some money to help keep our business going — that was all that mattered to me. I wanted to depend on no one but myself and make my uncles proud.

My new job was rewarding. I truly enjoyed working with people from many different ethnic backgrounds, including some of the most beautiful, sweet African-American girls I had ever seen. As time passed, King Optical became a large success across the U.S. I felt a small part of that success and yearned for the same for Bill and myself someday.

Perhaps more than anything, I gained valuable business experience. I realized that Bill and I lacked more than just a command of the English language — we lacked a solid understanding of the American financial system. But the biggest lesson I learned came from witnessing the Ritholtz Brothers' constant nagging and quarreling with each other. I saw firsthand how this upset the employees (myself included) and caused costly mistakes. I vowed that Bill and I would never reach that pain. After all the suffering we had gone through, we certainly didn't need the heartache of bickering between ourselves.

Meanwhile, the Korean War was escalating sooner than expected, and the United States was suffering many casualties. As a loyal American, I wanted so badly to repay this great country for liberating me and my brothers from Buchenwald, and allowing me to immigrate here. My dream was to serve in the Army, then re-enter the housing business so that I could help other Americans fulfill their dreams of home ownership.

In Chicago, Jerry and I enjoyed many exciting adventures. We went out dancing (on a very tight budget) every Friday and Saturday evening at the Aragon and Trianon ballrooms. We did not drink, but because of my dancing ability I attracted many girls. Usually they came in pairs, which always worked out well for Jerry and me — especially if they could give us a ride home. Often my dance partners asked me to stay for a meal, and I never turned them down.

I was living on a very strict budget, so I welcomed any chance for free food. (I was renting a very small bedroom in a boarding house at the time, with no refrigerator or cooking facilities.)

On Sunday afternoons Jerry and I sometimes went to watch soccer games. One Sunday Jerry was disgusted with the soccer players' bad plays and mistakes, and he let them know it. Then he started screaming at me to get down on the field and show them how to play. The next thing I knew, one of the coaches came over and asked me to come the following Tuesday evening for practice.

Two days later Jerry and I did just that, and I really enjoyed practicing with the team. Afterwards we even got a free meal. That night I signed on as an amateur to play for the very popular Hansa semi-pro soccer team. Despite my sore muscles, the following Sunday I played in the starting lineup as a left winger for my new team. We played well and won the game. I was asked to return to practice every Tuesday and Thursday and to start for the team each Sunday, and I enthusiastically agreed. I looked forward to the workout, the games, and especially the good food. Soon after that I was selected to play in the All-Stars against a touring Dutch team.

As busy as I was in Chicago (and as much as I loved Jerry's company) I still missed my family back in Pennsylvania very much. My cousin, Sonny Lebowitz (Uncle Adolph's son) was attending school in Chicago, studying optometry. Whenever his family came to town they would include me in their dinner plans. They liked to eat at a restaurant called The Stockyard, where the specialty was world-famous steak, juicy and thick. Also, Moty Schwartz, a former neighbor from my village in Europe, would invite me to his home sometimes for dinner. His friendship meant very much to me — it was a link to my long-gone roots. Without their occasional visits, my life would have seemed empty.

My knowlege of Jewish religion left much to be desired. Holidays meant little to me. My first Passover Seder in our uncle's homes in America had most of the reading in English. I didn't know much English and hardly remembered how to read Hebrew or any of the religious practices I had been taught. I thought, the religion of my parents, grandparents, brothers, sister, and myself was the same one for which we were condemned to death.

That Midwestern winter was very harsh. Late one afternoon I was walking home from work along the lake (I did not have money for the bus). Suddenly a terrible chill went through me. My body had not yet fully recovered from the camps — the dampness and wind from Lake Michigan intensified the cold and aggravated my arthritis and frostbite. I realized that I had not felt that cold since the winter months when I was incarcerated. I then started remembering the horrendous, painful cold in the open coal cars that had transported us from Gleiwitz to Buchenwald. I could actually feel the freezing torture of the death march from Buna to Gleiwitz. As I forged on, I recalled my beloved family, lost in the Holocaust. I started feeling lonely and my will became frighteningly weak. The thought of my American family so far away — in Pennsylvania, Israel, and communist Russia — made me feel even worse.

As I dragged on, I felt as though I might freeze to death. The howling wind, the blizzarding snow, and the sub-zero chill pierced right through me. I walked faster and faster, hitting and rubbing my frozen body with my hands, trying to get back to my tiny room to find a little warmth for myself. But it seemed I could not run fast enough.

I told myself that I did not survive the hell at Hitler's fascist's hand to freeze to death now or be separated again from my family — even if most of them were only a few states away. I continued plodding through the blizzard along Lake Michigan, all the way to my room at 6700 North Hermitage. As the wind and snow smarted my face, I made a decision about my future right then and there. I would immediately do everything possible to be drafted into the Army and serve America. Then I would return to Pennsylvania. Somehow Bill and I would make our business succeed, just by being there for each other and working as hard as we could. I knew that we would not only make a living, we would someday be successful. But I also knew that I must first go back to the draft board and ask to be drafted.

Unfortunately, the Chicago Draft Board could not help me, so I turned to Aunt Hilda, whose relative was a Supreme Court judge in Pennsylvania. He made the necessary political connections, and a week later she called, telling me to come back as soon as possible.

I gave my notice of resignation to Mr. Ritholtz, who assured me that anytime I wanted to return to Chicago, a job would be waiting for me. I said goodbye to Jerry Hornstein, my soccer team, and dancing partners with mixed feelings. Then I returned to Pennsylvania.

Back in Ellwood City, I resumed my work with Bill while waiting to learn of my fate with the Army. I called the draft board and was instructed to go to New Castle, Pennsylvania, where my application was being processed. There the recruiting officer said that my application was being approved in Washington. I went home and waited. When the wonderful letter came announcing my acceptance, I felt so proud! It seemed that my life was heading in a positive direction, and the future held only brighter things for me.

CHAPTER SEVENTEEN

THE U.S. ARMY

Before I went into the Army, I remembered my first Passover Seder in America in my uncle's home. As we recited the Haggadah, I was very uneasy because my Mother, my uncle's sister, was not there with us. The Haggadah teaches us about the four sons and their attitude toward the question of why we recite the four questions and keep Passover. The first one knows the question and assumes responsibilty for it. The second knows the question and rejects it. The third endures the question with indifference. And the fourth does not even know the question. I was not sure which one I was.

Most people did not want to be drafted to serve in the Korean war. To avoid the draft, many went to college and then came up with all kinds of ailments, but I hid mine. I wanted badly to serve the country which had offered me a safe haven and I was assured that, after I finished my military duty, I would be eligible for the GI Bill of Rights which would support me while I attended school.

On February 29, 1951, I bid my family in Pennsylvania good-bye and left by train for Ft. Mead, Maryland, for induction and basic training. I was honored to do my share for my beloved adopted country — I was willing to die for it. I wanted only to go and fight the facists, communists, and other extremists who were harshly ruling and murdering people. I was very proud when I was ordered to report for induction and sent to Ft. Mead, MD.

Upon arrival there, I was pleased to learn that my fellow inductees included Holocaust survivors who had been in the orphanages in England with me. I heard that testing for the Army Intelligence Units would be given soon, so I decided to go for it. When the scores were announced, my name was near the top of those who had passed. This was truly a great achievement for me — I would be a proud member of the prestigious U.S. Army Intelligence.

As the doctor gave me my physical, I could tell by his accent that he was a Czech. We began conversing in our native language and became fast friends.

Afterwards he asked me to help him in the medical section so that we could continue our talk. As the recruits arrived in bunches for their check-ups, we chatted while I took blood samples.

Later that morning, the new recruits were sent to my post for "short arm" (genital) inspection. The group included an entire college football and basketball team. Apparently, those athletes had been suspended from school for cheating on tests, so they were all inducted in the Army at the same time. As they stood in line watching the blood being drawn, one by one they started passing out. It was quite funny to watch all those big, tough, muscular guys faint, falling like dominos. I can't help but grin when I remember it.

Before basic training, I had to pass many tests, physical and for aptitude. As I spoke seven languages, I was given a hint that I would be assigned to military intelligence. This was very exciting for me but I knew I must stay cool. I was assured that they were waiting for approval of my transfer.

Meanwhile, the first six weeks of basic training were very challenging, both physically and mentally. At first, I couldn't do one push up or chin up but, with practice, I learned to be as good as the others. There were so many things to learn, but the most important was discipline — especially how to carry out orders properly and promptly. Besides learning to march, salute, and handle discipline, we practiced how to shoot and care for all kinds of weapons, including machine guns, rifles, pistols and heavy weapons. Training also involved getting physically in shape, how to survive long marches in all kinds of weather, and how to read compasses to navigate through an obstacle course. Of course, none of those things was as important as carrying out orders carefully and quickly, particularly in the intelligence units — we especially could not afford mistakes.

Some of the guys in basic training came from the hills of Kentucky and had never seen a Jew before and, unfortunately, they had been taught some horrible things about Jews. Certainly they knew nothing about the Holocaust. This was very disconcerting. The words of my Mother reassured me, "Tomorrow will be better, Yankele."

The drill instructors were charged with getting us young recruits into shape and making us into good soldiers. I had heard of the terrible drill instructors, but I must say that our instructors seemed like angels compared to the monstrous German officers, kapos, *blockaeltesters,* and guards in the concentration camps. Most young draftees came into the military straight from their parents' homes — no doubt many had lived sheltered lives. Whenever fellow recruits put the drill instructors down, called them abusive, or questioned their orders, I tried to explain to them that there was no room for question or error in a soldier's life during war, and our drill instructors were simply trying to get us ready for military service.

Our sergeant's name was Royster and he was rumored to be "tough as nails." Some thought him mean but I saw him as a tough but fair man. At times he smiled at us and responded gently, making you feel he listened and cared. I got along just fine with him because I was totally on the ball. He picked me to be his personal jeep driver, even though I had never passed a driver's test and had no license. I enjoyed the extra duty for many reasons. I often drove him into Baltimore for an evening of pleasure. Once when we were in a Baltimore strip club, I noticed that one of the dancers kept blinking and rubbing her eyes — she seemed to be having trouble with her contact lenses. (Very few people knew how to properly fit contact lenses in those days.) Sergeant Royster also noticed the dancer, but for other reasons — she was very good-looking with a very sexy body. I called her over, introduced myself, and told her that I had been a contact lens specialist in England and I would be honored if she would allow me to adjust her lenses. (Most of all, I wanted my sergeant to spend some time with her.) She agreed, and we all got along fine. As a result, we made several more trips into Baltimore, ostensibly to adjust her lenses — but mostly for the sergeant's relaxation. I even finagled a part-time job adjusting contact lenses for the doctor who had fitted hers.

I was fortunate to meet up with several more survivors who had lived in the orphanages with me. We enjoyed reminiscing about the Primrose Club days. We often wondered about the fate of our buddies whom we had not seen since we left England.

Even though I enjoyed basic training, at times I suffered from the recall of Nazi abuse — especially when an extremely loud command was made. I shivered as the painful memories came to life in my mind. I tried to push them far back into my consciousness so that I wouldn't have to deal with them. I wanted to be like the other American soldiers, with a clear mind and body, so that I could protect my country and comrades to the best of my ability.

I befriended most of the men and women I served with (as well as the civilians around our bases). Our unit consisted of boys from every part of America. Some had never been outside their home town; some had never seen the ocean and others had never seen the prairie states. It was amazing — and often humorous — to experience firsthand the differences between them. I enjoyed discovering how many things we had in common, despite our differences. It was gratifying to know that in America, rich people, poor people, and those of different color and religion could bond together and live peacefully under one roof. This made me feel less of an outsider, as my English was still not very good — although by now I was beginning to understand more than I could speak. We often laughed at each other when I misunderstood.

After basic training, I was initially assigned to be shipped to Europe, which upset me greatly. I could not yet face stepping on bloodied Eastern European soil, especially Germany — the loss of my beloved parents and the horrors of my past were still too fresh in my mind. I could close my eyes and hear the hateful screaming of the SS, and my nostrils would fill with the acrid smell of rotting bodies as if it were still happening. I knew it would be many, many years before I could think of returning to Eastern Europe. And I did not know what to expect when I did return. What if I ran into a former SS officer or guard? Could I contain myself, or would I lose my cool and do something impulsive?

I was very happy to leave the training at Fort Mead and enter my new occupation as a U. S. soldier. But, when I lay down at night, I found myself exhausted thinking of my childhood as a young boy in our village in Czecho-slovakia, then Hungary, and seeing those goose-stepping Hungarian gendarmes and German SS.

I spoke to my superiors and fortunately, my request was granted and I was reassigned to Ft. Bragg, North Carolina, where I worked in the M.I.S. 210 Censorship section of the Intelligence. They would utilize my ability to communicate in six languages and my knowledge of Eastern Europe. I felt very privileged for this assignment, and I hoped that maybe eventually there would be an opportunity for me to work in the optical field for the Medical Corp.

Just at that time, Ben and Sylvia were blessed with their first child — a girl. So I pulled some strings to get a weekend pass and arranged a ride with a fellow GI to see them. I was in seventh heaven when I got there — I loved holding and kissing my precious new niece, Cindy, and being with the family. I also enjoyed a few scrumptious home-cooked meals — so much tastier than basic training food. Unfortunately, my visit was short-lived — the day after returning to Ft. Mead I was headed for Ft. Bragg.

That trip was the beginning of my love affair with the South — particularly the weather, the Southern hospitality, and the beautiful countryside.

As I began to settle in at Ft. Bragg that spring of 1951, the Korean War was at its height. Training was intensified. Besides all kinds of intelligence and the required military methods, we were taught parachuting — this involved being taken up a very tall tower and ordered to glide down, which was supposed to simulate a parachute fall. I did not like it, but I had no choice.

Our section was also required to partake in "Maneuvers Southern Pine" — the biggest military maneuvers to date — to prepare for a massive offensive airborne drop in Korea. Our chief duties were to review the intelligence, censorship, and interrogation procedures necessary for our mission. Our headquarters was a big tent we had pitched in the forest. We had laid out our individual sleeping tents, some in wetlands, some on the mushy forest ground. One day we were deeply engrossed in work when suddenly one of our men came rushing into the tent, petrified. He pointed outside and rambled hysterically. I asked him to slow down and tell me what was wrong. He pointed to where his tent was pitched. One end of the tent, which lay on the earth, was moving. We yanked the tent with a bayonet and out came a huge rattlesnake, its head in the air, hissing and spraying venom everywhere. It must have been 12 feet long — most people were scared to go near it.

I immediately began looking for a loaded gun. (As part of the Intelligence Group, all we had was a handgun with no bullets.) I ran over to the Military Police to borrow a rifle with dum-dum bullets. One of the MPs came with us — a good ol' boy from Kentucky. He started pumping bullets into the snake's head, but even after several rounds, the tail was still moving. Of course, this greatly concerned us — we were sleeping in tents in this forest with nothing but a blanket under our bodies. Because snakes only attack when disturbed, we became very careful about our comings and goings. Needless to say, we did not get much sleep that night, or the rest of our nights in the woods. The snake incident made us extra cautious about everything we saw in the forest.

We had heard from the non-coms that had recently returned from Korea that unfortunately a bunch of improperly trained soldiers had been killed. As a result, they were committed to giving us very rigorous training in order to save our lives. Several times we were told we were bound for Korea. Most of us were scared but I kept calm and tried to relieve the other soldiers' worries.

In preparation for Maneuvers Southern Pine, our duties included monitoring wind and weather conditions. The morning of the big "enemy drop," a strong wind was predicted. We were concerned that this wind could push the "enemy paratroopers" — in reality, our own men — away from the clear landing zone into a wooded, snake-infested, swampy area. After all, these were U.S. Airborne boys — we did not want them to be hurt. We immediately brought it to the attention of the superior officers from both "sides." We pleaded with them to either postpone the drop or move it over a few hundred feet, but we were ignored.

When the designated time arrived, heavy winds pushed the paratroopers into the dangerous area, as we had predicted. It was not a pretty sight to see our boys stuck in the tall pine trees, some badly injured, their parachutes caught in the branches — or lying in the swamps with poisonous snakes all around. Unfortunately, by the time they were rescued there were quite a few casualties which could have been avoided if the opposing commanding officers had listened to us and verified our information.

I was heartbroken to see so many young men unnecessarily injured. We helped get them out of the trees and the swamp as best we could, but for some it was too late — we were not able to move around the swamp very fast, and we were scared because they were badly injured. It was an event that I will always regret.

Unfortunately, the U.S. Army had a small share of hate mongers, Ku Klux Klansmen, fascists and anti-Semites. But in my two years as a soldier, I experienced just two anti-Semitic confrontations.

One of the corporals in my new outfit was Italian American. His parents were Nazi sympathizers before the war. He and his father were fascist; he also claimed to be anti-communist and openly did not like Jews. He baited me every chance he could, always threatening to "finish the job that Hitler and Mussolini had started."

One day after lunch, I was standing in line at the canteen truck to buy Cokes and candy, right behind this corporal. He was bragging about being a proud member of the fascist Youth Group during the war. He made all kinds of anti-Jewish remarks — he even exclaimed how happy he was that they had tortured Jews from his area and deported them to the German concentration camps. He added that he hoped the Jews of America would soon see the same fate.

I first asked him nicely to stop the anti-Semitic remarks and threats. Then I warned him to stop harassing and baiting me. No one in line told him to stop or tried to defend me — perhaps they were afraid of him.

Clearly he was looking for a fight. He stepped on my foot and bumped into me on purpose a few times. I continued to politely tell him to leave me alone. Of course, this was to no avail — he was an anti-Semitic corporal and I was a Jewish private.

Suddenly he dropped some of his change in the sand. I "accidentally" stepped on his hand, and the hot summer sand burned it. Screaming, he began to kick and punch me, cursing me and calling me a bloody S.O.B. Jew. He said loudly that he would finish what Hitler had failed to do. To make sure others would hear, I warned him in a loud, clear voice that I was a trained boxer, but he continued to scream, punch and kick me. I went into a boxing pose and with a couple of left defensive jabs and a right hook, I knocked him down. He got up and attacked me again. I hit him with a solid right on his chin (which hurt my wrist), then I utilized my soccer skills and kicked him hard a few times, especially in the groin. I managed to punch him a few more times before knocking him out cold.

I helped carry him to the medic tent. Besides a sore jaw and a few other sore spots, he was okay. I believed he finally learned his lesson that day not to harass me or any other Jew ever again. Afterwards, word spread quickly not to mess with Alex — the Jew boy is tough.

The other confrontation involved a big, strong master sergeant who looked and acted like an SS man. An Arab from Palestine, he fiercely hated Jews — especially me, because he knew that my brother had fought for Jewish statehood and was living in Palestine.

This hateful sergeant tried hard to make my life difficult. He assigned me extra evening work details and extra duty almost every weekend — especially Saturday afternoons — and I tried to put up with it, hoping he would change. If not, then I would request a transfer. I was sure he did not have the backing of the U.S. government or military officers; I tried to stay away from him whenever possible.

One weekend I had plans to go into Durham, North Carolina, with some other GIs. It was always fun to get away with a group of soldiers from our base. One GI would rent a cheap hotel room in town, and several of us would stay in it and share the expenses. None of us had much money — we only received $84 a month as privates. But I looked forward to those weekends and anticipated the fun of dancing with the beautiful city girls (who really appreciated soldiers).

When this sergeant found out I was leaving Saturday after roll call, he was furious. He tried to stop me by giving me extra work duty, hauling lockers up some stairs after inspection that afternoon. Luckily I found another soldier to fill in for me, and I agreed to teach him dancing and introduce him to some girls in return.

I got dressed in my clean, tailor-fitted "Ike" uniform and proceeded to the bus stop with my friends. I wanted to leave town before he realized I was gone. Just before the bus arrived he found me and immediately tried to stop me from going.

He began physically and verbally harassing me, which attracted the attention of some paratroopers from the 82nd Airborne, as well as guys from my outfit who were also waiting for the bus. They encouraged me to fight back, saying that the sergeant was out of line. The sergeant grabbed me by the middle and pulled my chest hair out as he lifted my 130-pound frame into the air. He continued to shake and curse me. Finally, after warning him to leave me alone, I utilized my boxing and soccer skills, kicking him hard between the legs. While he was bent over in pain, I used my best moves to finish the job he had started. Laughter and applause came from the bystanders. When the bus arrived, I rushed onto it, happy to see the door close behind me before he recovered.

Seeing all the commotion, the bus driver hurriedly left the base and sped towards Durham. When we arrived at the hotel, I called my former commander from Ft. Mead, Major Stern, who was had moved to Ft. Bragg. I explained what had happened and the events leading up to it. I pleaded that he speak to my present major, the commanding officers of the base, and the intelligence unit on my behalf, as I had never been in trouble before. He assured me that he would — in fact, he was going to talk to the commanding officer, the colonel of the entire intelligence unit, that day. He set up a hearing as soon as I got back.

The following Monday morning Major Stern had a military guard escort me to the hearing, where I was given an opportunity to explain what had happened. Witness after witness came forth on my behalf and corroborated how the sergeant had picked on me, the discriminating, Jew-hating remarks he had made, and the extra duty he had repeatedly given me. They told how he had baited and physically abused me at the bus stop. As a result, the sergeant was stripped of his rank and transferred out.

Soon thereafter I requested transfer to the optical unit of the Medical Corps in St. Louis, Missouri, and my request was approved.

It was gratifying for me to utilize the optical knowledge I had acquired in England and Chicago. Contact lenses were still a new concept, and I felt my experience would be a significant contribution. Working in the medical unit in St. Louis, I made eyeglasses for several prominent dignitaries. I am almost positive my group made glasses for General Eisenhower, President Truman, and General MacArthur, but since this was classified information, I can't be sure. I felt my work was a way of thanking them for liberating me from the Nazis.

Soon I was promoted to corporal, and I wore my uniform with bursting pride. Since corporal pay was still very low, I had to cut corners on my expenses. I wore my uniform most of the time because it saved me money on civilian clothes (and also because of the looks I received from the girls — especially on the dance floor). I was still trying to send money home to Bill for our business; I also wanted to save for a car after active duty.

In St. Louis I spent my precious free time at the USO Club or the YWHA (Young Women's Hebrew Association), where there was always good food and cute girls. I went to the dances free because I taught dancing two evenings a week I spent many joyful hours on the dance floor, teaching ballroom and Latin dances. I even entered some competitions and gave exhibitions on boat tours along the Missouri River. I had fun, made some extra money, and got free food — it was heavenly.

One day, a friend told me about an optical company that might be looking for part-time help. At first, I thought that I would never have time for a job in the private sector because I was busy making glasses for the military forty hours a week. But I became intrigued with the idea of making some real money, so I began working part-time helping eye doctors fit contact lenses.

At the same time I began studying for my high school equivalency diploma. After passing, I eagerly enrolled in a logic course at Washington University in St. Louis. With my job fitting contact lenses and teaching dancing, I had only Saturday night for dating, dancing and relaxation — consequently, I dated very little during that time. But in spite of my busy schedule, I befriended a lovely Irish girl who helped me with my studies. She and her grandmother were great cooks, so many nights when I worked or studied late, I stayed with her, then she dropped me off to work the next day. We became the best of friends, but love was the last thing on my mind — and I informed her so on several occasions.

I thoroughly enjoyed my logic classes — they would eventually help me understand the tough business world and family entanglements I experienced later in life. I also saved most of the money I earned for a car, which would also be handy in the business. It felt great to put money away for a rainy day.

My two years of active service were nearing the end; I was happy for that and grateful to have served my country. Now I faced only the five years of reserve duty. I was offered a big promotion to officer's rank if I signed up for five more years' active duty, but I declined. I was anxious to return to Pennsylvania and rejoin Bill and our business.

Shortly before I was released to civilian life, I received a letter from Mr. Ritholtz, President of Ritholtz Optical and Contact Lens Company. He wanted to fly me to Chicago to discuss coming back to work for his company. I was intrigued and eager to talk with him. The day after my discharge I said goodbye to my friends and coworkers and made the trip to Chicago. There Mr. Ritholtz offered me an immediate incentive to manage his new Pittsburgh office. This would be perfect — it was close to Bill's and my business, and because my income would be based on commission, I felt it was a chance to earn some decent money. However, I explained to Mr. Ritholtz that I would work for him only a short time — as soon as I trained his people and got the business going, I would return to my housing business.

As soon as I returned to Ellwood City, I bought a new stripped-down 1953 two-door Chevrolet for $1,720 cash from my military savings. I could not have been happier. When I slid behind the wheel I felt like a king. To me it was a Rolls Royce, even though it had no heater, radio, or any of the "luxury" things that are standard in cars today. It was reliable transportation with four wheels, which was all that mattered. More importantly, it was a symbol of my financial independence and a fresh start on the road to my American dream.

CHAPTER EIGHTEEN

GROWING ALBEE HOMES
ONE NAIL AT A TIME

The first year of rejoining Bill and growing our company — which we named Albee Homes Co. for *A*lex and *B*ill) was the most frustrating and disappointing of my early career. Despite long hours and aggressive efforts, we were not able to sell enough homes to keep us going financially — and when we did make sales, we often had difficulty getting loans to finance them for the do-it-yourselfers. Nor could we make enough money to draw a salary, let alone build a sales office and model homes to lure additional business.

I worked for Mr. Ritholz in Pittsburgh as promised, helping establish the new office there. After a month or so, I pulled out (per our agreement) to devote my all to Albee Homes, but many times I was tempted to call him and ask for my old job back. I was even thinking that maybe Jerry Hornstein and I should start our own contact lens manufacturing company. Whenever I mentioned these feelings to Uncle Gene, he would say, "Give it time. Rome was not built in one day." He constantly reminded Bill and me that working smarter and harder is the only way to success. He felt that as brothers we were obligated to be loyal to each other and give it our all. I took Uncle Gene's fatherly advice and pushed even myself harder, trying to think smarter, working as much as 20 hours a day, 7 days a week.

Uncle Gene also pointed out that I should use my brain for thinking and my personality for selling. So every time I approached a potential customer, I did just that — and I slowly learned to improve my sales and communication skills. I told myself that my business problems could not compare to the inhumanity and suffering I had endured only a few years before. Most of all, I wanted to help people help themselves — this goal kept me going, even when I was ready to give up.

The long hours, hard work, guts, and genuine effort slowly started to pay off with time. It gradually became easier for me to communicate in English, which made selling easier as well. I found that I was able to motivate more and more prospects. I felt fortunate to show them how home ownership did not have to be a luxury for the rich — it was a necessity that everyone in America could afford. I explained how owning a home was more than just a roof over your head — it also provided a tax shelter, a place to build roots, a feeling of pride from not renting, and a source of equity over the years.

I also reminded prospects that with equity they could build a financial safety net for their children, and perhaps provide for their education. To me, my work was about so much more than selling homes — it was a way to show others that all of us have the ability to succeed if we only use our time, energies, and heads, with a little help from family or friends.

My enthusiasm knew no bounds. I wanted to sell homes to all my prospects. I had set goals for myself each hour, each day, each week, each month. Sometimes I cried myself to sleep from exhaustion and disappointment because I was not meeting those goals. Nevertheless, if I was unable to meet them one day, I resolved to start over again the next.

In those days we sold a complete packaged home with the electrical wiring, light fixtures, furnace, plumbing materials, drywall, paint, and all, for a mere $4,500 to $5,500. By today's standards that's very reasonable, but after the war, most of our customers had very little money to pay down. I worked constantly to find innovative ways to help customers finance their dream — I was always ready to do whatever it took.

Often, the only way our customers could get financing was by personal guarantees, as well as Albee Homes guaranteeing their loan for up to five years, until they finished building and could afford to refinance and get a permanent loan of their own. As a guarantor, I had to make sure all the loans were current, plus Albee Homes had to set up cash reserves with each bank loan as security, in case purchasers did not pay the mortgage on time — in that case we had to make it good. The banks would not release us from the guarantee until the homes were finished and our customers could get a permanent loan from a local bank or savings and loan. We built up sufficient funds in reserve at the banks, but it was putting a hold on our profit and cramping our cash flow.

Often we encouraged buyers to entice family, church members, fellow workers, or friends to help with the construction, after the loan was approved. This built a lasting bond among those who helped build each others' homes. It was amazing to see how many people were willing to gather their tools, roll up their sleeves, and get started. Friends helping friends, neighbors helping

building homes, but he gave that up and opened up a tailor shop in Atlanta. Each of us now had 25 percent ownership which was what I had intended when we originally set up our Atlanta operation.

By the time the Atlanta venture was solidly underway, I had been commuting to Conyers for about a year without a salary, spending my own money to travel frequently back and forth. I sorely missed my family — every time I left home, it became harder to be away. While I did not want to uproot them from family, friends, and our beautiful Youngstown home, I wanted us to live together. Etta, Benji, Stephanie and Robin were young; I felt they need the presence of both Linda and me, perhaps now more than ever. I was a family man, and I wanted to live like one. Although I spent a little time in Ben's and Bernie's homes, especially during the Sabbath, my wife and children were my life — I wanted and needed to be with them after a long day at work and to celebrate each Sabbath.

After cautiously approaching the subject of moving to my wife, Linda reluctantly agreed to come with me to Atlanta to seriously consider the area as a possible future home. Although she hated the idea of leaving Youngstown, she admitted that she missed me when I was gone and would probably like the Atlanta climate.

Linda visited several Atlanta schools and talked to many people about life in the South. She realized how much she had missed Ben and Sylvia and Ruthie and Bernie. She was, for the most part, pleased with her findings. When she said yes, I was elated! I could hardly wait to be with my precious wife and children on a daily basis. But we decided to hold off until after Benji's Bar Mitzvah, which would be celebrated that fall in Youngstown, the same time as his cousin, Alan's (Bill's son).

As planned, Linda and the kids came down to Atlanta after Benji's and Alan's Bar Mitzvah and the tragic passing of Bill's wife — our beloved Aunt Estelle, and we began to search for a new home — near Ben and Bernie. Ruthie and Bernie had joined an orthodox synagogue, but strict orthodoxy was not for us — Linda and I planned to join a conservative synagogue. But we decided that the synagogue decision could come later, after we found the right home and school to suit us.

I deeply loved all my children equally, but Benji and I were extra close. Our kids used to come with us to the Albee factory office and model homes. Benji was a very hard worker. He was always anxious to use the farm and construction equipment to help out, and he especially loved beautifying the land. In Ohio, he, Alan, and some of the others would come with me on weekends, operating the trucks, straddle carriers, and other machinery. His ambition was to work in the building and development business someday, hopefully with his cousins. He worked the land with Robert, our loyal and trusted employee who oversaw the maintenance of our land. He often talked of his desire to provide people with a nice place to live and play. Benji loved nature — especially the many fish in our lakes. He loved to watch them swim, and how they jumped up to bite the bread he threw them. Benji also adored his Uncle Ben — he would listen intently as Ben told him of the plans for our property. Benji was very smart, and he retained almost everything he heard. He was concerned about the best way to utilize the land without hurting its natural beauty. Benji was truly a unique child — and fast becoming a man.

Just before Father's Day 1975, we were finishing a new office building on our Conyers property. I had purchased and shipped a travel trailer from one of our Ohio companies and placed it on the beach at Gross Lake. Benji, Ben, and I decided to camp overnight in the trailer, while Linda stayed in a nearby motel with Stephanie and Robin. (Etta was away, working as a counselor at a summer camp then.)

We joyfully celebrated Father's Day together that Sunday; I felt so happy to have most of my family with me. It was a glorious day. The kids enjoyed playing at the motel pool, and we spent most of the day at Gross Lake.

The next day, Monday morning, started in the usual manner. The sun shone brightly — it looked like a wonderful day was in store. Little did I realize that that day would be beyond a doubt, the most painful, tragic day I had ever endured as an adult.

I had a busy day planned, beginning with an early morning meeting in Atlanta. I left Benji and Ben sleeping in the trailer at Gross Lake, and headed for my meeting.

When I returned to Conyers it was almost noon. I was talking with some people in my office who had stopped to see me on business when Benji came by to remind me to take him shopping at lunch time for some new jeans. He was going through a growth spell — at almost six feet tall, it seemed everything he wore was suddenly too small for him. I told him I would be ready to leave soon and that he should stay a few minutes and wait for me to finish.

Just then, Benji heard from the front office that a group of elderly Atlantans were coming to Gross Lake for a picnic that afternoon. He was anxious to make the area look beautiful for them, so he decided to cut the grass around the lake with the bush hog.

I was just about ready to go fifteen or twenty minutes later when Robert and our foreman, Mr. Capps, came running into the office looking for my brother, Ben. They called him outside and told him something in hushed tones. I could tell by their expressions that something bad had happened — when they kept looking in my direction I realized it concerned me. Immediately I thought of Benji. I asked where he was but got no answer; when I did not see him, I panicked.

I ran out of the office towards my car, but Ben overtook me and got behind the wheel. He drove directly to Gross Lake. He said that Benji had been in an accident. His pained expression told me it was bad. As we rode, I shivered and my mind raced a thousand miles a minute. I wondered if, God forbid, Benji had fallen and broken his arm or leg, or if he had been bitten by a snake.

The accident sight was only a few minutes away, but to me it seemed like an eternity before we reached Benji on the left side of the lake. Never in a million years would I be prepared for what I saw. My son was lying on the ground, his handsome, young body bloodied and lifeless.

In the few minutes since he had left me to cut the grass, the leg of his jeans had gotten caught in the blade of the bush hog while he was mowing, pulling him down underneath and into the bush hog's razor-sharp rotating blades. His insides were literally torn out. By the time our workers had reached him it was too late — his blood was spurting everywhere and he was lifeless.

I could hardly believe the nightmare my sore eyes were forced to witness. There was my handsome, precious Benji, lying dead on the ground, his beautiful face covered in blood, his light-blond, slightly bloodied hair moving gently in the wind.

I felt as though my mind and heart had left my body. I could hear myself scream, *"Nein, Nein! Gottenyu Ech, beit Dich! Nein!"* ("Dear God, I beg you, please no!") I looked up to the sky for an angel from the Almighty, crying, "Please let this be just a nightmare! Please tell me it is not true! It could not have happened to my one and only son. Why couldn't it be me?" But my voice seemed very small and far away, unheard by the Messiah.

I screamed, "Benji, Benji, my dear, sweet, precious son, don't leave me." I pleaded again with the Almighty, "Dear God, this tragedy could not and should not happen to me and our family, and not to my only son. After all the suffering, torture, and tragedy I have endured in my young life, please do not do this to me and my family." I even looked up to heaven for help from my beloved parents who had been murdered in Auschwitz — I was certain they could hear me. But my pleas for mercy were in vain. No one came down to save him. I could not put life back into that gorgeous boy, that dear one and only son of mine. I would gladly have given up all my money and material possessions just to have Benji alive and well.

Sinking to my knees, I gathered his torn, lifeless body in my arms and placed my head on his head — or what was left of it. Unfortunately, there was no life left in what just minutes ago had been a vibrant, smiling, handsome young man, who was always on the go. My precious, good son was dead.

Completely numb, I sat on the ground holding, hugging, and kissing his still-warm body as I watched his blood slowly soak into the red Georgia clay. I remember thinking that it was just like the summer rain. I wished it was mine and not Benji's; I wished I could transfer my life into his body and bring him back alive.

I was mad at the land development business, the world, and especially the bush hog that had robbed me of him. My mind raced. I had immediate flashbacks of the concentration camps — I saw my dead and dying comrades all around me — I relived the pain and torture, and I mourned anew the millions who were exterminated. My heart bled as I held Benji, thinking over and over again of those terrible days when I was about his age. I asked myself, "Why could my precious Benji not hold onto his life for us, as I was somehow able to do?" The pain I felt — and still feel — for the loss of my son is beyond words.

Strangely, I remembered the Seder prayers we recite on Passover to honor our forefathers' release from years of Egyptian bondage. They came across dry bones in the desert, and the Almighty restored those bones with new skin. Why couldn't the Almighty restore my son's life?

As I sat there dazed, holding Benji, I felt sorry for every father who might lose or has lost a child. This seemed the end of my life. I remembered the many joyous trips Benji and I had made here, stopping by the surplus bakery store or the bread plant beforehand to buy bags of stale bread to feed the ducks and fish as we strolled around our lakes, talking of everything and nothing. All my children enjoyed the lakes, but Benji seemed to enjoy them most. How ironic that he should lose his short life so painfully in the place that he loved so much. He was the same age as I was when the Holocaust engulfed me.

I flashed back to the many adventures he shared with his sisters and cousins, and all the places we visited as a family. There was no doubt that Benji was the apple of our eye. Everyone who met him loved him; he brought constant love and pleasure into our hears. I had put so much hope in his future — I had only begun to prepare him for the time when, if something happened to me, he would be the caretaker of the family. There was still so much to teach him and share with him! Now I was robbed of those priceless pleasures forever.

Oh, how I wished it had been me instead of my son, who was so young and good. Over and over I asked myself as I held him, why had he been taken from me. He had so much to live for. I wept uncontrollably for Benji and the life he could have had. He had not even reached the prime of his youth. I cried for myself and what I would miss by never again having my only son with me, may God rest his soul. I prayed that God would unite him in heaven with his dear

Aunt Estelle, my beloved parents, and the rest of our family lost in the Holocaust.

I cried for my dear Linda — who, like me, would forever mourn her handsome, adored son. I cried for our daughters, who would never again have the pleasure of their tall, caring brother showing them off and protecting them.

It seemed that time stood still as I held my Benji. I don't know how long I sat there. I thought and prayed again and again that it was just a bad dream, like the nightmares I had in Auschwitz. I survived that hell of hells — surely my son could also survive anything and everything! Once again I begged God for Benji's life. Hadn't God tested and punished me enough?

I tried to face reality. He was dead. How could I ever say good-bye to him? There was no way I could ever say good-bye to my Benji. How could I go on without him? I just could not give up my one and only son.

The wailing of the ambulance siren brought me back to physical reality. It reached us in minutes, followed by a doctor friend who practiced nearby. Of course, there was nothing to be done. As soon as they arrived, they pulled me away and placed Benji's partially stiffened body on a stretcher, then lifted him into the ambulance. I tried to reach for him; I could not give him up. I wanted to hold him forever — I did not want them to take him away from me. I did not want to remain with anyone — not even my brother and friends — while Benji was taken to the hospital. The doctor and Ben held me back as the ambulance left, its sirens crying out noisily as it carried my Benji — and my shattered heart — away.

Moments later, Abe arrived. We cried together for the unspeakable loss. Ben confessed that it was like losing one of his own sons. Benji had been Ben's sidekick — not only did he have Ben's name, he shared some of his looks and mannerisms. (Actually, he resembled Ben even more than he did me.) I knew how much Ben hurt as we hugged each other and cried that sunny day in the field overlooking Gross lake.

Suddenly, reality started to take hold of me. I had to face many terrible tasks ahead. What I feared most was telling Linda and my girls. How I hated and feared what would come. How could I tell his mother, the person I loved so much, that her one and only son — her future, her universe, was no longer alive? How could I tell the girls?

As I was led to the car, my body shook with pain. I was enveloped by the memory of the many young men dying all around me as I relived yet again my teenage years under the Nazis. The pain tortured me afresh as we drove towards the motel — I felt as helpless as when the SS guards had forced us to watch them repeatedly torture fellow inmates. I thought I had gotten past those horrible memories — but I had only hidden them. Now they overcame me as if they had happened yesterday.

I steeled my mind to purge those ungodly memories. I had enough to deal with. I kept telling myself that this could not be happening to me. How could it? Only a short time ago I was with my son in the office and he was fine — smiling, safe, and healthy.

I realized how much I longed for guidance and comfort — even at age 46 — from my parents. I prayed desperately for them and the Almighty to help me through this horrible crisis.

I tried to think about how I would tell Linda. Where and how would I get the strength? I knew for sure it would shatter her heart forever. Never again would she be able to kiss or hold him, take him shopping, show him off, or guide him in the nurturing way that every good, caring mother does innately. How on earth could I tell her that she would never see his face or hear his laughter again? I wanted the ride to the motel to take a long time, maybe forever, so that I would not have to face her. I knew that once I told her, it would all become real — it would no longer be a product of my imagination, and I could no longer hope he would come back.

But the ride was over in only a few minutes. When we arrived at the motel, I went directly to our room. Linda, Stephanie, and Robin were not there; Ben went to the pool to look for them. I could see them as I walked in what seemed like slow motion towards our room. Suddenly I was aware of how very much Robin resembled Benji. She was also tall and had Benji's blond hair and blue eyes. And her expressions and mannerisms were very much like his.

As Ben neared Linda, she looked startled — her mother's instinct told her that something was wrong. She was probably asking herself why Ben had come to the motel in the middle of the day. She started looking for her son — she knew that he would (or should) be with us. When she didn't see him, she asked Ben where he was. Ben told her to bring the girls and come to the motel room with him.

When they opened the door, I tried with every ounce of my life to act as strong and composed as I possibly could for their sake. I told them that I needed to tell them something important, and that they should sit down. My mouth felt mushy and full of cotton, yet it was heavy as steel. My lips wouldn't move. Never, even in the camps, had I prayed so hard or was I so weak to act. I felt so desolate, and the pain in my heart was overwhelming. My stomach was in knots, it hurt so badly.

When at last the strained words came tumbling out of my mouth, Linda and the girls were speechless. I had to continue convincing them that it had really happened. They began to shriek and cry in disbelief. I answered their questions with what little poise and strength I had in me, but I lost my composure almost immediately. We embraced, shaking and crying very hard and loud for what seemed forever. We were utterly devastated and physically ill.

Linda and the girls screamed over and over that it could not possibly be so — they had seen him just awhile ago. In hysterics, Linda cried out to me that she wanted to die — that she could not possibly live. "How could this happen to us, especially to a good person like you? What more punishment can the Almighty force upon you? How can you still believe in God after all the horrors you have endured? Have you not been punished enough," she asked. Her questions — like mine — fell on empty ears. We did not know why; we did not even know if the Almighty knew (or cared) about our tragedy. I pleaded with her that she had to live for my sake and the sake of our children.

We also had no idea where the ambulance had taken Benji's body. We assumed that he had been taken to the hospital to see if by some slim chance his life could be restored. But — God forbid — if not, we hoped that they would take him to a funeral home. After all, there was no Jewish synagogue, and certainly no Jewish funeral home, in Conyers, Georgia.

We were literally lost souls, so new to the Atlanta/Conyers area; we didn't know what to do, where to go, whom to call. We only knew that now Benji was with the Almighty, his wonderful Aunt Estelle, my beloved parents, and the rest of our deceased relatives. Hopefully he would not know of worries, grief, or pain anymore.

We faced more pain and heartache as we bore the bad tidings to the rest of our family. We sent someone to get Etta from her camp counseling job. By the time she got to the motel, she was a basket case. Then we notified Linda's sister and mother in Florida; they left immediately for Atlanta to be with us.

We stayed that night at Bernie and Ruthie's house. Ben, Sylvia, Bernie, and Ruth were kind enough to contact the rest of the family for us and make most of the funeral arrangements. I don't know how we could have made it without them.

Ben and Bernie belonged to Beth Jacob, an orthodox synagogue in Atlanta. Their assistant rabbi, Herbert Cohen, offered guidance and prayers. (The head rabbi and renown scholar, Emmanuel Feldman, was on sabbatical leave in Israel.) Rabbi Cohen and Fred Glussman, the Executive Director, came to see us immediately. Those wonderful, compassionate people were so helpful — they walked us through all the final arrangements. We then bought plots for Benji, Linda, and me in Atlanta's Greenwood Beth Jacob cemetery.

Our extended family members arrived the next day for the funeral and to share our grief by sitting Shiva — the traditional Jewish seven-day mourning period. I don't know what we would have done without the love and support of our wonderful family. In fact, Gene Halpert (a survivor and long time family friend and employee) relocated to Atlanta and remained with the family business until his untimely death a number of years ago.

The service was very dignified according to Orthodox tradition, but it was sheer torture. It seemed to last forever, and at the same time we did not want it to end because that meant leaving our Benji. We cried as we said Kaddish — the prayer honoring the dead. His casket was lowered into the ground, then we each put two shovels of soil over the casket to cover Benji's body as his soul was returned to the Almighty, dust to dust. The graveside services were over, but our lifelong grieving had only just begun. A huge piece of my heart and life was buried with him.

We spent the entire Shiva in Bernie and Ruthie's home. Many people came for the morning and evening minyan prayer services held there. A minyan requires at least ten males to be present — although we knew almost no one in Atlanta, we had three to five times that many each morning and evening. Many people brought and served us food; some stayed late to console us or just keep us company. Knowing that we were grieving and totally shattered, many kind strangers generously gave of their time and love. The wonderful rabbis constantly reminded us that only time would help heal our wounds, but it seemed nothing would ever help alleviate our pain.

Out of every tragedy, good things come. During that horrible time, the care shown to us by the people of Beth Jacob would be our motivation for joining that synagogue, even though at first we were a little uncomfortable with the strict orthodox rituals. But we forged many wonderful relationships as a result of Benji's death — strong, time-tested friendships that we might not otherwise have made. One was Dr. Ephraim Frankel, the director of the Hebrew Academy in Atlanta. He would arranged for Stephanie and Robin to join the Hebrew day school, even though they had not attended such a school before. The Sunday Hebrew classes they had attended in Youngstown weren't sufficient preparation — they had to learn the new language, take more intensive studies, and work much harder than before, but it was good for them. We were so grateful for his kindness. And thanks to our friend, Mr. Robert Maran, who at one point was president of the synagogue, Linda and I would become involved in many charities and committees. Eventually I even served on Beth Jacob's board of directors for several years.

Our association with Beth Jacob was a blessing in every sense — without it we never could have pulled through Benji's death or built a new life in Atlanta. That association would continue to sustain and enrich us as the years passed — through good times and bad.

CHAPTER TWENTY-FOUR

PULLING TOGETHER

How do you go on with life after losing a child? Linda's perpetually cheerful face suddenly started to show wear and tear; her smile was not as bright — or as frequent. The burden she suffered was palpable. I was wracked with grief, anger, guilt, fear — you name it. And the girls were beside themselves, as well. It was a terrible time for all of us.

Our beautiful Youngstown home, full of happy memories, was up for sale, but Linda wanted to go back just to be in Benji's room. I was afraid that doing so would be devastating for her. She and the girls were so fragile; I felt it would only hurt her more to be surrounded by the artifacts of Benji's former life.

I had to do something quickly. I invented reasons for an immediate business trip to Pittsburgh. When I got there, I rented a car and drove directly to Youngstown to meet with the realtor. I told her to sell our home right away at any reasonable price. When a doctor made a ridiculously low offer of less than half the listed price, I told her to either find another buyer immediately or accept that offer — as pitifully low as it was — so that I could honestly tell Linda and the girls that our home was sold. I simply could not take the chance that Linda would go back to that house and prolong her heartbreak.

The next day, the realtor claimed that she could not get in touch with the doctor who had made the offer, so I signed the contract. The financial loss was tremendous, but it was only money — my surviving family's well-being was more important to me than anything else in the world.

My dream of relocating to Atlanta was severely soured, but now that our Benji was buried there, I had even more reason for moving. At least I could be close to his body in Atlanta.

We did the best we could, hanging on to whatever thread of strength we could muster. We took one day at a time, constantly trying to console each other. We had joined Beth Jacob — that was a start. For the first year after Benji's death, I attended synagogue to say Kaddish seven days a week, every morning and night, which was a great comfort. Linda talked of finishing her art studies. We tried to find meaning in life wherever we could.

The economy around that time was down in Ohio as well as in Georgia. Properties weren't selling, which heightened my humongous loss on our Youngstown house and hurt me in the stock market. I had no choice but to sell stocks and securities at a big loss. After that I had very little left — the Atlanta and Ohio entities constantly needed an infusion of funds so that they would not be foreclosed on by the banks or other creditors. I even started to sell my children's stocks and borrow money on their insurance policies. So I was very glad when Linda told me that she would like to go to work selling real estate, besides continuing her art studies in the evenings. I felt she was making great strides in self-help. Even though neither of us would ever stop grieving about our son's death, we both needed to stay strong for our girls. It was a great relief to know that she was looking for ways to keep her mind occupied and feel productive.

So Linda went to real estate school, passed the test with flying colors, and got her license. We were very proud of her, and she seemed to have found renewed hope in her life. She chose to work for a small, reputable company — a husband-and-wife team who ran a small but well-established real estate firm. They appreciated Linda's congenial attitude to customers and her natural sales savvy. She wanted to be the best in her field, which helped her make sales immediately — but more importantly, she made many good friends with her clients. I was glad she had found her niche.

Staying so busy helped her handle Benji's death somewhat, but we all struggled constantly to cope — some days were terribly dark; others we managed to slog through. It was more difficult than I can ever describe. We continued to make friends and find solace through Beth Jacob; we also joined the Atlanta Jewish Federation and a number of other charitable and civic organizations. I became very involved in the Rockdale County Youth and Adult Soccer Association, as well. These activities helped keep our minds occupied; helping others — especially young and elderly people — felt very healing.

As a student at the Hebrew Academy, Stephanie was now around more religious kids. Consequently she had begun practicing all the strict Orthodox Sabbath observances. She would not get into an automobile, use electricity, carry anything or perform any kind of work on the Sabbath, according to Orthodox law. She stayed weekends at Bernie and Ruthie's — because they were very Orthodox. Their home was around the corner from the synagogue, and they walked to and from synagogue for services each Friday evening and Saturday morning and evening. While Stephanie influenced us to become a bit more observant in our already kosher home, our home was too far to walk to the synagogue — so I drove there each Sabbath and holiday that first year to say Kaddish for Benji, even though a father is supposed to say Kaddish for a departed son for only the first month. In over 25 years I have rarely missed honoring him at a Sabbath morning or holiday service since.

Linda had quietly and anonymously become much more involved with helping the less fortunate. Sometimes she drove visually impaired people to the grocery store, or she took sick people who had no transportation to the doctor. She bought clothes for orphans and helped the unemployed find jobs. She was always busy helping those who needed it; especially those whom she found out about from the Beth Jacob congregation. In many ways her generosity mirrored those of my wonderful Mother — just like in my home in the old country, no one was a stranger to her or unwelcome in our home in Atlanta.

By 1975, our Atlanta property was thriving. People were drawn to the natural beauty of our developments, especially the lakes and recreation areas. We provided not only free regulation soccer fields, but also free fields for other activities, such as softball, baseball, jogging, and touch football. Our property — especially Gross Lake — was utilized seven days a week for recreation. Ben was becoming known as the father and chief organizer of soccer in Rockdale County and Atlanta — this was several years before it became popular in the U.S. He provided instructions, equipment, and uniforms — particularly for children whose parents could not afford them. But his biggest challenge was exposing soccer to the many people who had never heard of it. Most Americans knew only baseball, basketball, or football; he worked hard to educate the parents first so that they would let their children play. He continued to coach and referee for many years.

I, too, enjoyed coaching soccer. Anything I could help others do — especially young boys — was a joy. I helped coach the Rockdale Soccer Classic young boys, plus I coached an adult ladies soccer team in a community league. Eventually I became vice president of the Rockdale Youth Soccer Association, which was very rewarding. During my tenure as V.P. the program grew from 138 boys to over 300. We also started our own adult men's soccer league, and later that year, a ladies' team — both of which are still active to this day. Largely as a result of Ben's and my interest and involvement, our area became the soccer capital of the South.

Linda and I continued to immerse ourselves in work, our girls, and the community. We felt as if we were slowly but surely becoming whole again. But no matter how busy we stayed, we missed Benji terribly — nothing or no one could ever take his place. Every time I saw a young boy with blonde hair like his, I had to quell the urge to run up to him and hug and kiss him. I still feel that urge today. Even though we constantly grieved for our Benji, we worked hard to be a happy family. We were grateful to the Almighty that he had given us each other, and the strength to go on each day with our lives.

It seemed that almost overnight, our daughters were maturing and beginning to date. The girls had a multitude of friends — our home became a second home for other boys and girls because they felt welcome there (and, of course, Linda was a sensational cook). It was an exciting but worrisome time for all of us, with choosing and preparing for colleges, new boyfriends, break-ups, engagements, and broken engagements.

As my daughters grew into lovely women and independent adults, Linda and I tried hard to respect their decisions — even if we did not always agree with them. Despite the immeasurable emotional setback of their brother's passing, Etta, Stephanie, and Robin seemed to gradually pull together and carry on with their lives fairly well. Linda related and interacted beautifully with all our children, as well as with her nieces and nephews.

After much consideration, Etta picked the University of Miami, located in Miami, Florida, which pleased us because Linda's mother, whom we affection-ately called "Mamma," lived near the school. Etta enjoyed Miami and the many wonderful friends she made there; we enjoyed going there to see her, her grandmother, and our other extended family members. Our Etta was a good student and a wonderful daughter, so full of joy. She had a prosperous career in commercial real estate. In 1988 she blessed our family with my first grandchild, Leya Edelstein. She is happily married to Raymond Zimmerman.

Stephanie was a good student and chose to skip eleventh grade, graduating a year early. She initially attended the University of Georgia and, after Linda died, she completed her studies at Mercer University in Atlanta. Following college, she went into advertising and later became an early childhood educator. Stephanie is lovingly married to Avi Weiss. Avi's mother, who is still alive, and his now deceased father were survivors of the Holocaust. In 1999, Avi and Stephanie blessed our family with precious twin girls, Hannah and Eliana.

Robin chose the University of Florida. She was an honor student. Because of her love of politics, she selected George Washington Law School in Washington, D.C. After graduation, she decided to stay and practice law in Washington, D.C., working in various political and government positions. She is also happily married to another attorney, Anthony Lehv. In 2000, they blessed our family with my first grandson, Benjamin, named in memory of Robin's beloved brother, Benji.

I was, and continue to be, so proud of my girls and their accomplishments. They have weathered emotional storms that would have paralyzed many young people. I would like to think that our personal family losses have somehow strengthened them. In turn, their strength has given the rest of our family strength that has enabled us to live for tomorrow. My own faith has been enhanced by these challenges.

CHAPTER TWENTY-FIVE

YET ANOTHER TRAGEDY

During the Arab oil crises of the late '70s and early '80s, interest rates had soared to an all-time high. Consequently there was a real estate market crunch and the we found ourselves in financial trouble once again. Interest grew to 18 and 20 percent just when we had started borrowing considerable money to further develop our properties in Conyers and some other land we had acquired in the city of Atlanta. Because of escalating oil prices and long lines at the gas pumps, commuting was becoming less popular — as a result, homes closer to downtown were being renovated, and new homes were being built to accommodate people who wanted to live in the city and save on the high price of gasoline.

Prior to the oil crisis, our properties in Rockdale had appreciated considerably — but now nothing was selling on the outskirts of town. So we thought we should tap the inner-city housing market. We went deeper in debt and bought several properties close to and in the city — some with partners, others by ourselves. We also started building fee-simple homes and duplexes in the west end of downtown with other partners.

We developed an exclusive midtown all-brick fee-simple town home project called Ansley-Monroe Villas, just before interest rates really started to climb. Pre-sales were good, but by the time we finished building, it was difficult or impossible to qualify for a loan — interest rates had jumped from 8 percent to 18 percent or more very quickly. So we purchased a forward commitment from a local lending institution to assure financing at a fair interest rate for our buyers from the same lender that had provided the acquisition and development loan for the project. We paid plenty for the commitment, which helped that bank go public and boosted the value of their stock.

Unfortunately, that bank did not honor their commitment to give our purchasers the financing at the agreed interest rate. For us to avoid filing

Chapter 11 or a lawsuit against the bank — or them going after us (which could have been very harmful to all involved) — we agreed to turn the project over to one of their chosen builders. We took a very large financial loss — all the cash, time, energy, and equity we had invested in the project added up to around a million dollars. It was a very painful lesson, but it would not be the biggest loss in that deal when all was said and done.

Part of the land purchased from the original owner of the Ansley-Monroe Villas included a few lots across the street, where we built some single-family homes. We listed some of those homes with Linda's real estate company, and she brought many prospects there. She worked hard to show those properties, despite the exorbitant interest rates.

With the girls out on their own, Linda and I were putting almost all our time and effort into work, trying to recoup our financial losses. To celebrate our 25th anniversary meaningfully, our children gave us a party and we took a much-needed holiday and went back to Grossingers in the Catskill Mountains, where we had spent our honeymoon so long ago. There we relaxed, reminisced, and talked of enjoying at least another 25 blissful years together with our children — and hopefully, many grandchildren. After a well-deserved rest, we returned to Atlanta and settled back into our work.

One night shortly thereafter, I came home early expecting to have dinner with Linda. When I entered our home, she was not there. Thinking that perhaps she had a late appointment with some customers — which was not unusual — I sat down to watch television and dozed off. When I woke up, I realized that she still wasn't home because she hadn't called me to bed. It was late, and I became worried because she had not called. After a little while and I still had not heard from her; I really became concerned. It was not like her to not call — if she was going to stay out that late she would definitely have let me know where she was and when she would be back. So I called her office to see if anyone there had heard from her, but I was told only that she had had a late appointment.

After waiting impatiently, I started calling some friends and family members, but they had not heard from her. Trying not to panic, I showered and lay down, but I was troubled and could not sleep. Finally, at about 4 a.m., I started calling everyone I knew to see if they had heard from her. No one had. I then called Ruthie's nephew, Marty, who had bought one of the Ansley-Monroe homes from us. I explained that I had not heard from Linda and asked if he had seen or heard from her. He said he saw her car parked across the street when he had come home late that evening from work.

I asked him to go and see if her car was still there — he came back to the phone and said it was. Scared and heartsick, I began to panic and shake. I feared the worst, even though I tried to be calm and hope for the best. I prayed that by some miracle her car would not start and she had fallen asleep in it while waiting for the prospect. Marty then went outside to look in her car; but she was not in it. I told him to call an ambulance and the police, just in case we needed them, and that I would be there in 15 minutes.

I drove the 10 miles to Ansley-Monroe like a maniac, faster than I had ever driven before, but it seemed to take forever. By the time I arrived, the police had cordoned off the house. They would not allow me to enter the house. To my horror, they told me that they had found Linda dead.

I couldn't believe my ears. All kinds of crazy thoughts went through my head. I thought that perhaps she had suffered a heart attack, God forbid, and that she would surely recover completely when they got her to the hospital. Or maybe, I thought, it was someone else they had found, not her. I hoped and prayed that the police were wrong, and that she would be alright.

I wanted so very badly to go and see my precious loving wife, the one and only Linda. I wanted to hug and kiss her, and make her well if she was sick, but I was frustrated that the police would not let me near her. I wanted to give her my life — or whatever it would take — to have her back and well. I reminded myself of the Hebrew prayer, *Dayenu*, which means "enough." Had I and my family not suffered enough? The Almighty brought us out of Egypt, He performed miracles, He rescued me from certain death in Nazi Germany — couldn't He please manage another miracle and give my Linda's life back? Somehow God was ignoring my pleas again — just as with Benji.

"My dear Mama," I prayed, "please help me. My heart and soul gaze at you and seek you. Your eyes make mine sparkle; your eyes glow in mine. Please try to bring back my Linda." I remembered a song of Shabbat that I had been taught as a kid, and it lifted my up a little. My heart was pounding in my chest. All I could do was to remember the song.

After only 15 or 20 minutes, the ambulance left with Linda. I wanted so much to go with it and be with her.

They did not tell me what happened at first; I found out later that Linda had been raped and murdered in that house. I was completely numb. I felt that my very life depended on being with her again, to tell her over and over how much I loved and needed her, but I couldn't even see her one last time.

I was gently but firmly led away by a policeman and Marty. Just as I had had the horrible misfortune to hold our precious son's dead body ten years earlier, I wished it was me instead of him when they took his body away. Now again I wished it was my body, not Linda's, being taken away in that ambulance. It is a feeling no one should ever have to experience — ever.

Marty tried to comfort me, but he too was in shock. He had found her, and would later express to others that he could not get the horrifying vision of what he had seen out of his mind.

I began to panic. I realized that not only had I lost my precious wife of over 25 years — just as I had lost my son ten years before — but again I faced the task of telling our precious daughters that they had lost their mother. I had to be the bearer of unimaginably, grim, painful news. Twice in one lifetime! How could this be? I hoped my daughters would not fall apart, but what else could I expect?

I tried desperately to collect myself. I took some long, deep breaths and repeated to myself, "I have got to be strong." I somehow managed to pick up the phone and dial their numbers, shaking and crying as I gave them the news. As I expected, they became hysterical, crying and screaming and challenging the Almighty, asking me to tell them that it wasn't true.

I will never forget how painful it was to hear their cries to the Almighty, and their pleas that it could not possibly be true, it could not happen to their wonderful mother, just as it had happened to their baby brother ten years earlier. They wailed on about the grandparents they'd never met who were murdered in the Holocaust. I wondered angrily, why should my children be punished — had they too not suffered enough? How much more could the Almighty punish us before we lost all faith in God and humanity? How much more could we possibly endure before dying of broken hearts?

CHAPTER TWENTY-SIX

FAREWELL, LINDA

Under Jewish law a deceased person must be buried as soon after death as possible. I was inconsolable; the funeral was torturous. My daughters and I clung to each other, with my sister and brothers nearby for physical and moral support. Linda's mother, sister, and family were lost too, as the casket with that precious body was lowered next to Benji. Again, it felt like my body was also being lowered into the ground. My heart and my spirit went with her. Now I had lost not only my beloved son, Benji, but also my beloved wife, Linda.

I have no idea how I got through those days after Linda's death. At first I went to the Atlanta homicide division, meeting with detectives every day, hoping to come up with some clues as to the killer (or killers). But the Atlanta police were totally inept. After becoming disgusted with their lack of progress — and being overcome by the pain it caused me — I then went every second day, then weekly. The police were utterly incompetent and leaderless. They never found one clue, let alone the murderer (or murderers). The real estate office could not be of help, either — they only knew that Linda had had an appointment to show one of the homes across from Ansley-Monroe Villas. I was bereft with heartache and frustration.

The last time I looked upon Linda's beautiful face was the morning before her death, as I was getting ready for work. I tried to feel grateful for the short time that she honored the world — and me — with her presence. But I could not bear the thought of going on without my Linda. Surely I never would have survived without my support system — once again, my family, friends, and the Beth Jacob Synagogue congregation rallied around us — but it would never fill the void she left. If Benji's death broke our hearts, Linda's broke my soul, my very being. It changed my life forever.

We sat Shiva, huddling together with the rest of our family. We stumbled through the ritual of morning and evening prayer services, hollowly reciting Kaddish. I wanted very much to forestall my daughters' pain so that they could at least try to get on with their lives. But I couldn't fix it for them — there was no way I could bring her back.

People came out of the woodwork, it seemed, to pay their respects. While we sat Shiva, the entire Rockdale Youth Soccer Classic Team showed up with their parents after winning their championship playoff game. They told me they had won it for us. Many people whom I never knew also visited us that week, including two women — a mother and daughter. These ladies were not Jewish, but they told us how much they had depended on Linda for transportation to and from the doctor's and the grocery store. They were basically blind — they could not see to drive and had no car. The women cried for her, and worried about finding another person who would give so generously of their time to them now that Linda was gone. I knew Linda was the epitome of loving and giving, and that she cared deeply for others — during Shiva I realized that Linda had touched more lives than we had all ever imagined. I felt somewhat strengthened.

In honor of Linda's involvement in quietly helping the needy, a group of women at Beth Jacob eventually set up a charity organization called the Chesed Society. (*Chesed* is Hebrew for doing good for others.) Those ladies could not have paid her a more fitting tribute. The Chesed Society evolved into a strong organization throughout the community as a result of its good work, and to this day it is used as a model in other American cities.

In her short life, Linda managed to accomplish enough for many lifetimes, and I shall always be grateful to the Almighty for lending her to me even if it was only for such a short time. I know — and my children know — that she lives on in her good deeds and loving ways. We know that she is in Heaven with the Almighty, and she's in good company with our beloved Benji, our dear Estelle, and my precious parents, grandparents, aunts, uncles, and cousins who perished in the Holocaust. May Linda's soul be bound up in eternal joy. We shall always love her and miss her.

EPILOGUE

For 20 years after liberation from the extermination camps I could not talk about my experience to anyone. I held it inside me until a dear friend, a Catholic priest who later became a Cardinal, convinced me that talking about it would benefit society far more than my silence. Speaking of it the first time made me sick for months. It is still very painful to recall that dark realm of brutality, trauma, and degradation. To this day I can close my eyes and still feel the pain and smell the horrible odors of burning human flesh. The horrific sights, sounds, and smells are forever embedded in my memory. They continue to haunt me and return to my mind, like ageless ghosts come to remind the living of a bygone existence. Sleeplessness, too, has stayed with me.

Very few people today know of the Carpathian Mountain region — the area I came from — or my village of Palanok, or the nearby city of Munkach, now called Mukachevo. Before the fascists took over, sixty percent of the people in that area were pious orthodox Jews. Today there are no Jewish people left in our village, and barely any in Munkach — only a few elderly. In many other places, too, the fascists succeeded in destroying the entire Jewish people and culture because the Nazis craved murdering us, pilfering, robbing, burning, and confiscating our homes, and raping our people. We Americans like to think that we were victorious in the war against Hitler and his fascism, but to the relatives and friends of the six million who were slaughtered in the Nazi killing centers, there were no victors. Generations were wiped out.

Memories, like dreams, come back to me. Family roots and Jewish values that were locked inside for over fifty years remind me that we were whipped by Nazi volunteers and stoned by peasants, especially on our way from Auschwitz III to Gleiwitz. Sometimes, much of this is like an unreal nightmare.

Understandably, I still struggle emotionally with many issues from my past. I will never understand why no one — not even the leaders of the United States, Great Britain, France, or initially Russia — cared enough to stop Hitler and fascism when they had the chance. They stood by apathetically and watched. All the borders were closed to the Jewish people. There was no opportunity to escape or emigrate to another country that Germany did not control. Even the millennium-old option of conversion to another religion was denied to us Jews in Nazi-occupied Europe. Freedom was certainly not an option. There is evidence that the leaders of America and Great Britain knew and that major newspapers and radios worldwide reported our starvation, sufferings, and killings, but apparently the news fell on deaf ears. Apathy and prejudice in the majority prevailed.[27] Why was there no escape? Why did no one stop this extermination?

For the American soldiers and other allied liberators, the days immediately following liberation of the camps were probably among the finest hours of their Army lives — and, no doubt, the saddest and most painful. In most cases, they stumbled, in complete surprise, upon the extermination camps without previous knowledge of the horrors they would find. There was no official or military policy on how to go about liberating a death camp or treating the survivors. The Allies were caught completely unprepared. Yet the courageous men I encountered when Buchenwald was liberated acted with kindness and generosity according to their innermost sense of humanity and strength. They represented the finest American commitment to democracy and decency, displaying a true sense of justice, compassion, and caring. The American people should be very proud of their soldiers' humane acts. That humanity is why America reigns as the world leader, as the longstanding haven for the oppressed, and as the land of opportunity.

Fortunately, we are now learning of many heroic acts that occurred, such as the Auschwitz revolt, where my uncle was involved in blowing up the crematoriums, and the Warsaw Ghetto uprising. Even without weapons, that uprising lasted longer than the battle for Poland with all its military weapons and thousands of fighters. Many of my fellow prisoners chose to die with pride, to fight the enemy even with bare hands and no ammunition, rather than continue to suffer or exist as slaves. For others, the instinct to survive sustained them until freedom. Their courage is another reason why so many Jews and Gentiles live freely today.

Since my liberation from Buchenwald over 55 years ago, my mind and heart have been haunted constantly by the legacy of the suffering that my fellow inmates and I endured. Even today this legacy challenges me to live with the knowledge of how inhumane humans can become. I can only hope and pray that my daily efforts to inform others through lecturing and writing will help us all become better humans and avoid another Holocaust.

Yonchi, who used to be my best friend and then became a Hitler youth, screamed at me, "Dirty Jew, we will kill you. You Jews are worse than snakes. We have to kill you. Long live our leader, Hitler! *Heil Hitler!*" This left lasting scars, especially when I remember eating and playing with him. I was very young when my trust, faith, and friendship suffered these shocks. My naive, young mind and spirit were not prepared for so much abuse and suffering. And, when those demons of memory creep back into my mind, they help me remember how imperative it is to share with others the horrors I experienced, to pass that dark part of history on to future generations, because those who forget are doomed to repeat history.

Who but the eye witnesses and victims can give an accurate account of what happened when Hitler and his Nazi cohorts ruled almost all of Europe, when our whole world turned to grief, vulnerability, and desolation? Atrocities like these must never be permitted to happen anywhere. Future generations must learn to live together in harmony and respect each other. They must not judge by skin color, sex, religion, ethnicity or race. Each of us has a great responsibility, a heritage that has been handed down from our forefathers. Our freedom is our most precious birthright, and we must never take it for granted. There is nothing more important I can do than make sure other people will never be subjected to — or permit — such inhumane acts. Of those who survived the Holocaust, only one percent are alive and able to tell the story. So I am making sure our story is told.

Every single person must be aware of the German industrial giants who benefited from our suffering, such as the I. G. Farben Industries, Kaiser Steel, Mercedes Benz, BMW, and Krupp steel company, to name a few. These firms enriched themselves through the use of incarcerated Jews, gypsies, gays, and other concentration camp inmates for slave labor. They continue to benefit from our enslavement and suffering to this day.[28]

Another sobering fact: The right-wing Nazi executioners did not come from a strange planet or an uncultured other universe. They came from the most civilized and advanced countries in the world. The Weimar Republic, where Buchenwald was located (where I was liberated), was once the center of German culture. Famous personalities such as Goethe, Schiller, Liszt, Herder, and many others made their homes in that area. There are museums dedicated to them today. We have to ask ourselves, "What does it mean to be civilized?" Is it a dream we thought we had achieved before World War II but forgot to pursue? Many times I wonder where education, humanity, and civilization went wrong. I don't have the answers. I'm not sure anyone does. All I can do is share my story, first hand — from one who has survived the worst tortures, nightmares, humiliation, pain, and failing spirit — as fully as I can.

I recognize, too that, although I live peacefully, the same frightening hatred, racism, and mass murder exist in today's world in Bosnia, Yugoslavia, Africa, Asia, the Middle East, and other areas. It is very sobering to realize that such extreme hate and anger still exist. It is all the more reason why I am compelled to tell my story. I tell it to fight hate, ignorance, and apathy because, on many occasions, episodes surface in my memory of the Nazi beastiality.

The message that bursts from my heart is that we cannot ever be apathetic to injustices anywhere. Even if they don't directly affect or concern us, we must act courageously to stop them. It is our duty as human beings.

We must all be vigilant. Whenever prejudice or hate raises its ugly head, we must all confront it immediately, with every ounce of our energy. If we choose to ignore it or look the other way, we are guilty of an indefensible atrocity.

My religious teachers taught that there are no accidents in history. People make things happen, and everything that happens has a meaning or purpose. Life can be beautiful and meaningful if we see each other in a respectful light. No matter if your skin is red, yellow, black, or white; regardless of your religion, sex, or ethnic background. A Jew cannot be a Jew without God; nor can any religion exist without God. Whether you believe in God or not, respect for fellow humans is respect for yourself. It is not optional

Developing an understanding of the Holocaust is the key to a safer, saner world — whether you are religious or not. To preserve our freedom and survive as humans we must learn from our past. If we fail to learn from our mistakes, who will be the Jews of the next Holocaust? Which dictatorial government will use its power to destroy an entire people? Many times people ask, "Could it ever happen again? Could it happen here?" The answer is: "Yes, certainly and unequivocally. It can happen again, and it could happen here — if we are apathetic to others' sufferings and permit evil to succeed."

It could happen at any time. If not now, then in our children's or grandchildren's lifetime. No society is immune to widespread hate. If future generations have no one to teach them these horrors, there will be a dangerous void in their understanding. All of us must study the past to learn from the errors of our ancestors. We must continue to honor those who cannot speak for themselves.

In the years since Linda's death, I have been privileged to remarry to a wonderful woman and to see my family grow. My wife, Daisy, and her family have been a great comfort to me. My daughter, Etta, together with her husband Raymond and my granddaughter Leya, have made me very happy and have continued the tradition of caring for others. My daughter, Stephanie, together with her husband Avi and her twin daughters Eliana and Hannah, have warmed my heart over and over again. And my daughter, Robin, together with her husband Anthony and her son Benji, named after my own son, have given me great joy. My brothers and I have sold most of the business and I am now retired and living in Florida, though I travel a great deal to be with my family. My health is fairly good, despite the toll Auschwitz and the other camps took on my body and my spirit. For the most part, I am in better shape than many people my age, especially those who survived the Holocaust, though I have to work hard, watch my diet carefully, and exercise to keep my spirit and myself in good mental and physical condition. Thank God, I also live freely in a civilized democratic country.

In 1995, I returned to the concentration camps and our home town with my brother, Bill, his two daughters Erica and Shelly, and two of my daughters Stephanie and Robin. I returned again in the winter of 2001 with my wife Daisy, my daughter Etta, and my oldest grandchild Leya. Each time profound and painful memories returned and my questions remained unanswered.

I also have good friends all over the world. There are so many that I could not possibly acknowledge them all or tell what they have meant to me. However I must take a moment to express my love for the Blumenthals. They have been very close to me, particularly Benjamin who has been a second Benji to me. I also want to say thank you to all those who have helped to bring this book to the light of day, especially David Blumenthal, and to express my gratitude to Emory University for all it has done for me and for the survivors.

Finally, we are the only family to have had all six brothers and one sister survive and we are all still alive.

With all this, I feel that my life has been blessed — in spite of the Holocaust and other traumatic experiences, especially the deaths of my one and only, precious, fourteen and one-half year old son, Benji, and my beloved wife and great mother of twenty-five years, Linda, who was a victim of rape-murder, may God bless their souls.

Because of the blessing I have received, I have always tried to help those less fortunate or in need. I try to practice good personal and professional ethics, putting others first, and most of all, treating everyone with compassion. In a nutshell, I try to treat others the way I would like to be treated, and I feel it has paid off in many ways.

In re-reading this book and in thinking back over the experiences I have had, several final thoughts stick in my mind which I would like to share with the reader.

To survive was daring. To do it with honor and dignity was nothing short of a miracle. At times, I am angry with myself that I could not help someone who needed me because I was so weak.

My hatred and fear of the Nazi killers grew. Even in death, they will not let go of me. I am desperate as I go between triumph and defeat. I felt they pushed me toward oblivion and certainly toward madness. Such is my life as I try to be a survivor.

We hoped that, after the punishment we received, surely redemption would come. We prayed for the Messiah to save us, but we felt that the Messiah may well come too late, when there would be no one left to save. Nonetheless, I shall wait, as I have been waiting, for a long time — because I have no choice — just as our people have waited for centuries. I have waited and hoped to find my Father and Mother, and I want desperately to meet my other lost relatives soon.

From time to time, I stop and pick up a book on the Holocaust and leaf through it. I put it down. I open it. A shiver runs through me. At times the pages are blank and confusing.

Losing my one and only son in an accident and then losing my beloved wife after twenty-five years of marriage led me to become much more committed to bearing witness and to embracing my religion.

Dream — that is what I must do. To dream is to invite a future and to deny death.

CONCLUDING INTERVIEW
WITH ALEX GROSS

November 1999
David R. Blumenthal

Ed. note: This interview lasted about 90 minutes and ranged over many subjects: writing, memory, pain, health, helping others, the second generation, various audiences, Jewishness, and Alex's personal life. I thought to edit the interview by topic, but that proved impossible because, like all conversation, the topics were interwoven. Instead, I have chosen simply to eliminate phrases that were repetitive, to make minimal corrections in grammar, syntax and continuity for the sake of the written format, and to let Alex's voice speak for him. Alex, too, has edited the manuscript to remove certain personal, family remarks. The original tape and transcription are available upon request.

DB: Tell me, Alex, what led you to decide to write this book after having spoken in so many places? After all, we have a videotape of you and we have transcripts of the tape.

AG: I have been urged by many teachers and by organizations at which I have spoken. I finally got to the point that I am not getting any younger so I decided that I had better write down the horrific events that I don't get a chance to speak about. So I proceeded to write and somehow things started to come more and more to my mind. I wrote of a lot of things that were on my mind, but I could not talk about. I have finally completed it, I have edited it a few times, cut it, and re-did it. Most of all, I have some wonderful friends that are helping me to finish it.

DB: Were there things that you remembered in the writing that you just hadn't spoken about at all before?

AG: There were a lot of things, especially the real painful events which at first I did not write about but, after I wrote it, I took them out again because I realized that people could not believe that this actually happened to me. So I did remove a lot of those horror things that are so difficult to believe, specifically some of the bad things in my village, some of my experiences upon my arrival in Auschwitz and the camps, and then, of course, the death march, and the final trip to, and time spent in, Buchenwald where we were mostly dead. Those horrible occurrences just have had to be set aside in the back part of your mind because I don't think you could live with something so horrific in your memory.

DB: Did you have nightmares while you were writing this?

AG: Well, you could call it nightmares or whatever you want to call it, I suppose. I have a difficult time sleeping anyway but I have been getting less and less sleep since I got involved in this. If I get three to four hours of sleep, I am very happy, very satisfied because a lot of these things come up. For instance, I'm bringing back my memory of some of the boys that I was in camp with and the suffering and death that happened to them. I even went back especially to Auschwitz to bring back and remind me what had really happened. I couldn't believe that it was true, and lo and behold I looked over to where we arrived on the cattle cars and remembered what the poor children went through being separated from their mothers and fathers, their brothers. I remember seeing my Father being led straight forward — they said to take a bath. I realized many years later when I was there with my daughters that it was the gas chambers that they had taken him to. And he was still a young man, in very good shape. He was not even fifty years old. He was a tall and strong man. He was considered too old for Auschwitz. Those people who were not yet eighteen or over thirty on the day you arrived were just taken to the gas chambers.

DB: I've been moved by what you have already written and I've heard you talk about it any number of times, and yet you say that there is much more that would be even more difficult to talk or write about. You even say now that you did write about these things in the book and then consciously took them out. What was there about those experiences that you took out, as opposed to the horror that you have already talked about?

AG: Number one, you don't want to remind yourself of the horrific suffering because it seems so unbelievable. I can't see how, if I can't believe that I survived the horror, anybody that might read the book could ever believe that this actually happened. Also, can anyone believe how vicious a fellow human could become? And remember that these people were perfectly normal human beings. Still, once they were there and they had joined the nazi[29] movement, they were just unbelievably vicious.

DB: Was there a moment or set of experiences in the debarkation, in the ghetto, or in the camps which is most difficult for you to remember?

AG: There were a lot of them. For instance, when we were rounded up to be marched into the ghetto which was nothing but a brick factory, suddenly we were surrounded by electrified fences and watch towers. We had no shelter whatsoever. It was the last day of Passover and it was still very cold in our area and we had to sleep outside. Even though we were quite used to cold weather, we at least always had a roof over our head and this time there was no roof. Finally they let us sleep in the ovens where they baked the bricks, but it was full of black soot. We were crammed in there with several other families. There was no room to lie down to sleep; we had to stand up. We were miserable and, of course, it was still impossible at that time to believe what was happening to us. As another example, they forced us to throw these very rough industrial bricks and we had to catch them with our bare hands. After a few minutes we didn't have any skin on our hands, but God forbid if you dropped a brick, they were there to beat the hell out of you. You didn't want your mother or father to see you being beaten up; so you had to be very strong and pretend that it wasn't hurting you. How can you pretend when the pain is there?

DB: I think we are moving too quickly. There are two types of pain you mention: one is the physical pain and physical discomfort of catching the bricks and of being cold, and later of constant hunger and then searing thirst — all this is physical pain. But there is definitely a psychological pain that I'm hearing — of not wanting to be embarrassed in front of your family and friends, of having to stand and watch others being tortured, of not being able to help, and the powerlessness of all this.

AG: Well, I was very fortunate, at least compared to others, to have been raised to age eleven or twelve years by very loving and caring family. My grandfather, may he rest in peace, always had an open heart. My Mother, may she rest in peace, always had an open heart and an open home. We had more strangers and poor people pass through our home. We were very caring. And suddenly not to be able to do anything when your fellow humans are being tortured and beaten was very difficult to take. I was still a very young boy, and it was very, very difficult for me to take. I wanted to go up and tear that SS man apart but there were other SS men or guards if you stepped out of line who would beat the hell out of you; so you couldn't do anything about it. That was very, very painful for me — not to be able to help my fellow human beings.

DB: Is it silly for me to ask if it was more painful not to be able to help or more painful just to have the physical stress and strain and hurt?

AG: I would say it was more painful not to be able to do anything about it. There is no doubt about that. As far as physical pain is concerned, I had plenty of that too. One didn't help the other. On the contrary, it just made it so much worse because, let's face it, I had — I had a difficult time with my bleeding hands to be able to catch those bricks and throw them on to the next person and not be able to drop them and the pain was there. I think it was probably even more painful to see my Mother having to see her children exposed to such cruelty. Father had to work too so he didn't see so much of it except what he was involved in directly. But sometimes Mother was just standing out there, maybe forty, fifty, or a hundred feet away, just watching her children being tortured and abused. It was a very, very painful and difficult for me to see the agony in her face.

DB: It is interesting that the survivors we talk to mention all the things that you have mentioned so far. First, that you take the story that you have and then narratize it; that is, you get it down to get to a story that you can tell which will not be too upsetting to you or to your listeners. Second, that every once in awhile, memories come back which are so painful that you either can't say them or aren't sure that you yourself really believe what happened. And third, that there is something we can call *the moral pain* — of not being able to help, or of knowing that your father was watching you while you were being beaten or, if you were a child, of seeing your father beaten — and that this *moral pain* was a piercing and terrible kind of pain, in addition to all the physical pain.

AG: Even more so because you couldn't do anything about it. Many, many times I wanted to jump out of line and go and attack one of those guards, but I had seen what happened if anybody did that — they were beaten or shot. And I did not want my Mother and Father to see me being shot because they suffered enough and I did not want to add to their pain; otherwise I probably would have done something.

DB: I know you have told your story hundreds maybe thousands of times, and in different setting — in settings with children and in settings with adults and even on Army bases. How has this been received in these different settings?

AG: Well, for the most part, unbelievably well. I just couldn't believe that they received it as well as they did, even though I have been to some schools, for instance one school in Cobb County where I was called in by the ADL [Anti-Defamation League] and, when I got through talking to the whole filled auditorium, some students came over to me crying because they were afraid to ask me any questions. I wanted to know why and they told me that, behind one of them, there were KKK boys, and in another area of the auditorium, there were skinheads. It just so happened that the principal at the school overheard this and immediately came down and apologized to me and said that he would take care of it. I don't know whether you remember it but it was publicized — this was some fifteen odd, maybe twenty, years ago — that these kids got expelled from school. Later I went back to that school and the receptionist told me it was different now.

DB: Do kids ask different kinds of questions than adults do?

AG: Yes and no. Some kids come up with some tremendous questions, many very good questions, some very well thought out. Some questions in some schools are not well thought out, and well phrased. But I find it depends on the school. If it is a good school with good teachers, you get fantastic questions. And, if it is an ordinary school, I still get some good questions, some are extremely good. But you also can't help but detect that they have experienced some anti-semitism, some hateful comments, or have been brought up in a broken home and that there is a lot of pain and hatred in their homes too. You can detect that immediately in the students and you try to give them an answer that they can understand, so that they are able to hear the answers to their questions and feel comfortable with them. In other words, I don't insult them or take away anything from their parents even though their parents might be hateful people or whatever the case might be. I try to make them feel good and make sure that they continue on the road to becoming good Americans and good human beings.

DB: And, adults — questions from adults?

AG: It all depends, again. When I spoke to the trauma specialists of America, I had totally different questions that had to do with mental things more than anything else; which is fine. Some of these questions were very, very good questions and I think they are important. But, if you go to speak to a Chamber of Commerce or to a real estate group or whatever, you are going to find different types of questions. It also depends on what area it might be. Obviously, if it is in a backwoods rural area, you get one type of question and, if it is in the city, you get a different type of question.

DB: What constitutes a good question in your mind?

AG: Most questions are very good as far as I am concerned; all questions are very good; though some of them are not well thought out. More important, some of them are not compassionate. For instance, some people don't feel that Hitler was a bad guy, or that communism was necessarily bad, or that any dictator is necessarily bad. And, you have got to make them realize that we are human beings and that we should be caring for each other, and not just be selfish and want to accomplish our goals whether they are right or wrong.

DB: I gather, Alex, that there have been tensions between you and your brothers over the years. Still, you have always tried to keep the family together. Was this part of the command that came from your parents to stick together?

AG: Yes, but it goes deeper than that. Remember that Bill, Sam, and I were liberated together in Buchenwald. When we found each other, we were more dead than alive. Bill was strong enough to get us some food and he gave me the first bread that I saw. To me, he was like an angel at that time.

DB: It means really that the bond between you — having survived and found each other in Buchenwald — was deeper than any possible family conflict could be.

AG: Well I don't look at it as conflict. Yes, it cost me a lot of money. For instance, I sold a lot of the properties in Ohio for maybe twenty cents on the dollar; still, I am happy as a lark. Because my brothers didn't want to sell properties there, as well as in Atlanta, we got into deep financial trouble which gave me a heart attack. As a result, we were forced to sell very cheap to get rid of the debt, and it was very low, like twenty or twenty-five cents on the dollar, and I am very happy about that. To me, it was the best thing we could have ever done, and the best thing we have done, in a long time. I was reaching sixty-eight and the heart attack was a warning to get out of debt and not have any more of these types of strains and aggravations. I have more than sufficient to

live on, and I can spend the time and energy to do good with my time and my money. I have hopes that I will be able to stay alive and in good health to be with my wife, children, grandchildren, and friends.

DB: The heart attack that you had — when was that?

AG: It was about four years ago.

DB: Did lying there in that hospital bed bring back memories or associations of the camps?

AG: Well, at first I couldn't believe that it was a heart attack.

DB: I know, you believe you are indestructible.

AG: Yes, the hospitalization brought back not just memories. Some of the pain that I experienced from the angio-plasty and the fact that I wasn't able to go and meet some of the appointments that I had set up at some schools was very difficult for me. Thank God, I made a good recovery and was able to go on with my life without the stress of that tremendous debt of over fourteen million dollars. Now that we are out of debt, I am able to now take more time for myself and my family.

DB: But while you were there in that hospital bed — you were obviously close to death or they wouldn't have operated on you — did that bring back memories of having been close to death in the camps?

AG: You can't help feeling that way every time you are in pain and, now especially, because I take Coumadin I get injured very easily — the slightest bump and I show terrible marks. Yes, it brought back a lot of horrible memories of suffering, but you are prepared a little more for it now and, in my effort to write my life story, I think I have prepared myself a little bit better to handle some of these stressful, traumatic things that I see my friends going through. Anytime I see someone suffering I want to help but I am able to handle it better now.

DB: It must be difficult with Fishi being as sick as he is and Ben having had a stroke.

AG: Well, my oldest brother has had his lung removed because of cancer — he is, thank God, all right — and Ben has had several strokes and has been paralyzed for a long time. In fact, he has Abe driving him around, back and forth to the office and properties. Our brother, Bernie, has a pacemaker. The next brother, Bill, has had open heart surgery — he had lung problems after we were liberated — and they found that he has cancer of the pancreas, which very few people survive. Then there is my brother, Sam, who has Parkinson's disease. Then there is me, and I just have to stay strong. Then my sister has problems too. But we are the only family that had six brothers and one sister survive the holocaust and are still alive, thank God.

DB: How old is the oldest of you?

AG: The oldest one is, I believe, eighty-one or eighty-two. I just turned seventy-one. I am the youngest of the six boys. Our sister is the youngest and I am two and one-half years younger than Sam, and Sam is two and one-half years younger than Bill, and Bill is one and one-half years younger than Bernie.

DB: What is interesting is that we know that survivors, when they get into hospitals, really have a hard time because, all of a sudden, they are back in the same helpless state in which they are in pain and people are doing things to them and all of the instruments surround you. This is pretty terrifying for ordinary people too, and normally this is a very difficult time for survivors. I remember going in and telling your nurse that you are a survivor and that she should put that on your chart, and I think she did.

AG: It is understandable why we are so scared because anybody who went to the so-called hospital in the camps was usually sent to the gas chambers. Very, very few people ever survived there and a lot of these so-called hospitals were used for experimental stations, especially in Auschwitz. Whether they experimented on the breasts, or cut fingers off, or whatever the case may be, they used you strictly for medical "experiments," and it is scary even now. Even when I drive past a hospital, it brings back horrific memories.

DB: They also say that survivors approach death differently. Somewhere between seventy and ninety that thought occurs to everybody, but that must also be a pretty scary experience. Having fought and survived for so long, you kind of believe that the laws of nature don't apply to you and confronting death must be a very frightening experience.

AG: Yes, you used the right word that "the laws of nature mostly don't apply to us" because we have survived so many horrors and so many difficult times that you say to yourself, "Well, if I survived the horrific traumas that I did, I am sure I can survive this, or at least I'll try," and sometimes we don't make it.

DB: One of the things that makes you and your pain — both moral and physical pain — easier is the ability to help other people. That is one of the things that comes through in the book more so than in the talks that I have heard you give — your ability and willingness to go out and help the folks that you were with and talk them out of suicide, to talk them into going on and holding on to life a little longer.

AG: Well, of course, lately a lot of these thoughts have been popping back into my mind and one of them which has been coming back again and again was when they brought in a transport of well-established German Jews and French Jews, and this French guy didn't even know he was Jewish. He denied being Jewish. He was put in the same bunk with me and I had a terribly difficult time talking him out of committing suicide. He wanted to take his life — he wanted to hang himself — or do all kinds of things. But somehow we managed to talk him out of it, unfortunately he didn't last too long because he was used to a life of luxury even under the nazis. Unfortunately, this type of Jew didn't last too long.

DB: One of the things that Terrence des Pres talked about in his book, *The Survivor,* is that apparently it was the custom that some of the inmates gave gifts one to another. You could make something that you could give to somebody else. You could share something with another human being. Do you remember anything like that?

AG: Well, yes, for instance there was a boy I saw who had his tongue hanging out from hunger and I had learned real quickly that you should not eat your bread right away — I was already in the camp for two weeks so I broke off a piece of my bread and put it inside his mouth, which, of course, tasted better than any candy he ever had. He wanted another piece, and I said, "Just wait a little bit. First digest this" — because the stomach couldn't take it. Then, after awhile I gave him another little piece of bread and, suddenly, he was crying. Of course, I didn't have much. I had to save it because we never knew whether we were going to get some food the next day or not. So, he somehow made it, and when he got his bread the next day, I told him, "Don't eat all of it. Just break off a little piece. Put it in your mouth, and let it dissolve slowly." Of course, most of the bread there was made of sawdust, and it was very dangerous to swallow it anyway. Somehow he was able to survive. Of course, I lost him after a while because they kept on separating us.

DB: Do you remember anybody making little boxes or making little things and giving them to somebody — just for gifts, as des Pres talks about it?

AG: Not in our camp. We didn't have boxes. We didn't have gifts. We didn't have any of those things. In Buchenwald there were some people who did that because there were different sections in Buchenwald. There was a prisoner of war section; they had a children's and political prisoners' section; and there was also a section where they kept people to show foreign diplomats or other people who were brought into the camp to show off and say, "Look how we take care of our prisoners." But, not in Auschwitz I, II, or III. Now, maybe Auschwitz II, because that is where they brought the people in, but I only stayed there a day or two. I was shipped to Auschwitz I, the killing center and, from there, to Auschwitz III which was Buna where I worked many, many long hours every day.

DB; Did you ever meet anybody who had been on one of the Hungarian transports that went to Switzerland in exchange, the Brandt program; that is, met people that had been saved, Hungarian Jews that didn't go to the camps? or Hungarian Jews who managed to remain in Hungary?

AG: Yes, I met them after liberation. As a matter of fact, we had some of these boys in England in the orphanage. We had been to the refugee center in Prague and I got to know some of them there. And I have met some since that time, at the different gatherings that we have had since. But really we didn't have any in Auschwitz III.

DB: Did you know Elie Wiesel in the camp? You seem to have followed the same trajectory that he did.

AG: I think I was brought to Auschwitz a few days before him. We were in the same camp. Certainly he was in Buna (Auschwitz III) and he was on the same transport to Buchenwald, where he unfortunately, lost his father. As a matter of fact, he was liberated in the childrens' section of Buchenwald. I was not in the childrens' section, but my brother, Sam, was, and I used to go there, especially right before liberation after we found each other. Of course, we were so weak and didn't look anything like we look now. When I saw Elie the first time in America, of course, I didn't recognize him, but after talking a while we recognized each other. Unfortunately, we had both gone through the same hell.

DB: How far was his village from the one that you were raised in?

AG: In today's distance it was a matter of only about an hour by car. But of course in the old days, we didn't have cars or paved streets or any of that sort of stuff. I would say it would have taken maybe a day and a half to get there by horse and buggy.

DB: When did you start telling the story and why?

AG: I became very good friends with a Catholic priest, an Irishman. We used to have lunch with a union leader who later on became a congressman and a Russian Orthodox priest in the Youngstown (Ohio) area. Every so often when we met for lunch, he used to ask me, and he kept after me, that I should come to the school to talk to his students. Of course, I ignored him and said that there was no way — I told him not to even think about it. He kept on bringing up the subject and one day I came back to the office and Father Malone was sitting there. I said, "Father, what are you doing here?" And he said, "I came to get you to come with me." I said, "No way, I have appointments lined up." He asked my secretary Miss Wolosyn if I had any appointments and she said, "No, Father, you made me cancel all of them." And that was the first time I went to any school. Of course, when my kids found out that I went to a Catholic school, they asked why would I go to that school and not to theirs. But, for a whole month, I couldn't look into a mirror, I was shaking all over. My world was totally devastated because it brought back a lot of memories that I had totally hidden and just didn't want in my mind. The students brought them out somehow. They asked me questions that were very very painful — about the hunger and the abuse, about my friends in my village, about how they suddenly changed from being best friends to being haters because they became part of the Hitler youth.

DB: So you began to talk about it in Youngstown?

AG: Yes, and when I came to Atlanta, I started to get involved in charity work, and before I knew it, ADL asked me to go to one of the schools — they found out about my talking. Betty Cantor just insisted that I go to this school and that school, and the next thing I knew, she would have had me booked twenty-four hours a day. But I had to limit it to two or three schools a week because of my business and charity work. I found that, when I got through speaking, some of the questions that were asked made me shake.

DB: What kinds of questions made you shake?

AG: "What happened to this SS officer?" "What happened in this camp?" "What happened to this and this boy who bunked with you, or this guy that was next to you?" For instance, somebody asked me about bathrooms: "Did we have toilets over there?" Yes, we had toilets there but they were not the toilets that we know of. They were rough stone with holes in them, and a whole bunch of us had to line up and jump on it and very little came out. We didn't get too much water and certainly didn't get much food, and many times it was so cold that our bodies froze to the toilet and some of your skin came off when you stood up. Those were the kinds of torturous things that were very difficult to describe, as well as the things that were constantly going on in the Auschwitz camps that were really unbelievable. I know it is difficult to believe — even in your case. You are a very learned man, you have studied it, and met many survivors; yet it is difficult for you to comprehend.

DB: Well, as you know, my exposure to Jack Boozer came to me around 1980 when I got here. He said that we needed to teach a course on the holocaust. I am second generation American. I was born in '38 in Texas and my father was in the Army. The closest I got to the war was at an Army base on Staten Island, NY. My grandparents were already in this country and my parents were born here, so I am not a survivor in any sense of the word. So, when Jack said we needed to teach a course on the holocaust I said, "No way; there was no way I would touch that." It was he who twisted my arm. What made me change my mind was that we brought Simon Wiesenthal here, and Simon Wiesenthal came out on the stage to talk, with these two big gorillas from the Georgia Bureau of Investigation around him, and began his speech by saying, "Everybody thinks I am the Jewish James Bond. But let me tell you that I am just an old Jewish lawyer with a heart condition." Then he talked about the need to do justice, and after that, I decided I would teach the course.

AG: It was before '80 because I got to know you just when we had this conference with Judge Cohen, Dr. Fred Crawford, and Bill Scott.

DB: Did you ever run across liberators in your audience, and how did they react?

AG: They cry. As a matter of fact, one of the guys who was a liberator is on the Georgia State Holocaust Commission. I have spoken to liberators, as well as to some doctors who were at a conference here. A few of the doctors came over, and they were liberators of the camp. Yes, I do run across some liberators. Most of them cannot speak about the horrors they witnessed. I was recently the main speaker for one of the veterans' groups that liberated the camps.

DB: When we began interviewing liberators, one of the things that we found out very quickly was that these guys had nobody to talk to. Jewish survivors at least could talk to other survivors, and they were within the Jewish community.

AG: Yes, but the Jewish survivors never talked about the holocaust to each other.

DB: Well, at least, they knew just by looking at each other. But a liberator might have come from nowhere in Georgia, and he went back to nowhere in Georgia, and he couldn't talk to his wife, and he couldn't talk to his pastor and, if there were other buddies, they might not be liberators. Do you think that films like *Schindler's List* or the big *Holocaust* television series really convey whatever you think needs to be conveyed?

AG: As you know, I was given the opportunity to critique the *Schindler's List* and, in the original film, they had a lot more; a lot of the very, very worst things; a lot of mean things, which they eliminated. So when it played the first time, I called them up and wanted to know why they had eliminated so many of the real horrors. Their answer was: "The public is not ready yet; people wouldn't believe it. We wanted to make it more calmed down, to eliminate some of the horror things so as not to make people sick."

DB: Were there what one might call "good" SS in the camps?

AG: If there were, we certainly never saw them. Not to us. If an SS man was mean in front of another SS man, we naturally expected that, and if he was not as mean when he was alone, to us he was an angel. We loved and respected him for it. But most of them were trying to outdo the other, and not just SS men. I am talking about the Ukrainians, the Hungarian fascists, the military, the Polish. They were no better and, in fact, they were often worse.

DB: There is a book written on that by a man named Katz, which I deal with in my book *The Banality of Good and Evil: Moral Lessons from the Shoah and*

Jewish Tradition. In his book, Katz calls this "a culture of cruelty" — that you scored points, that you got ahead in the nazi world and got good marks for inventing new ways of being cruel in that kind of environment. It is hard to believe that that existed, although subsequent studies have shown that this is true among torturers in general, and it is true among prison guards in general — unless there is really strong civil supervision in prisons.

AG: I think they should let us bring this out, some of the vicious, inhumane behavior. I had some things like that in this book, but I took them out. I thought it was unfortunate, yet I agreed with Schindler's producers who said that it was something that needed to be taken out. Still, he accomplished a lot with the film. At least people are accepting now that, yes, it did happen and those that don't believe it at least say it could happen.

DB: I saw *Schindler's List* in Germany, in Berlin. I was with a group of students. Do you remember Elke, the German theology student who studied here? She met me at a conference in Berlin. We had the evening off and they were going to show *Schindler's List* in English for the people attending the conference. But I said, "Why should we see it in English when we can see it in German?" So she and I got on a tram and went out somewhere in southwest Berlin and saw it. It was amazing. Everybody came in and sat, and at the end, there was total silence. You know, there are about fifteen minutes of credits and nobody moved, even when the lights came up. You could hear the people weeping as they were watching the film. You know, just hearing it and seeing it in that environment, with a group of people who were obviously sensitized to it and were ready to admit that it is part of German life today, was something. Still, I think that most Germans are not really ready for this.

AG: Remember, I introduced you one time to the German vice-consul here in Atlanta. He finally admitted to me that his father was a fascist, even though he turned against fascism later and that is how he got the promotion and posted abroad.

DB: Have you ever met with children of perpetrators?

AG: Oh, yes, although some of them denied it and only later finally admitted it. In fact there were two students from Germany in Carrollton, Georgia, who were adamant that NO, it couldn't happen; it is not true. I used to show films and, after awhile, they said, "Yes, my father admitted to me that he was involved but only because everybody did it."

DB: There has been a lot of study done on children — with the first, and now the second generation of perpetrators. And while a number of them, probably most, deny that it happened, or deny a family connection with it, they will eventually admit it. There are also a number who have acknowledged this and have really turned into themselves and worked very carefully and very hard on it. I know some of these people; we have gone to conferences together.

AG: Eventually they are going to have to admit it, for their own sake. And eventually some of these German companies — the big corporations, such as Mercedes, Krupp, and I.G. Farben — will have to admit to themselves that they exploited us and, yes, they were involved in these vicious things that happened to us.

DB: Are you going to apply for compensation if they admit their exploitation?

AG: Yes, I would rather give it to charity. I want it out of their hands because, look, I worked there as a slave laborer for over a year, and quite frankly, if you just take the interest on the money alone that they made on just my three brothers and me who were in Auschwitz, taking away the fact that they killed my Mother and Father, taking away the fact that a million other workers and I did the work for them — it comes out to a lot of money for these German companies. I don't expect anywhere near what I should get, but I would like to have them realize that they were wrong and that, maybe, some other people are not going to do that, that maybe others will realize that to use people as slave labor is criminally wrong and does not pay.

DB: I agree. I think it is a very important principle to establish in international justice, and I think that the kind of exploitation that existed in the camps was particularly cruel and particularly exploitative. There are other kinds of exploitative labor, and to set a warning for the world business community is a really good idea.

AG: Yes, and I think it has to be brought out to the world, whether it is right wing or left wing: If you are going to use or exploit people, if you are going to torture people, and are going to be mean to them, and rob them of whatever they have, you are going to have to pay for it.

DB: How do you think that your experience as a survivor has affected your children?

AG: No doubt it affected my children very, very much. I was aware of it and tried very hard to talk to them — not about my experience because I would never talk to them about it, it would be just too painful — but what to make out of themselves — that money isn't everything and success isn't everything; but that the greatest joy in life is to try to develop a good humble approach, a good way of working with people and helping people if you can, and helping yourself; and to know that you have to work to accomplish something, that nothing is accomplished without effort. I think my children basically have gotten a good part of that from me.

DB: Did you read a book called *Nightfather* which is the story of a child and her survivor father, or the *Maus* cartoon books, also the story of a survivor and his father? It seems that the effect on children — the second generation — has been really enormous.

AG: Most children of survivors have had tremendous difficulties in their lives because a lot of the survivors have had difficulty — I mean terrible difficulty. Some of us were fortunate enough to get away from that environment, to get into a new life, to be exposed to good people and a proper life, and have managed to overcome some of these so-called obstacles. But a great deal, a great part of the survivors' children do not come out too well.

DB: Would you say that one of your daughters is more affected than the others?

AG: Yes, I would say so. They are so much alike and yet they are so different. But most children are that way. I think I had more time with my oldest daughter and she was much more grown, so I was able to get across to her what I stand for, much more than to the others, before the tragic loss of my son and wife. I think she was able to handle it better, and get on with life a little bit more successfully. I know my middle daughter has had some big problems; she is fortunately coming through all right now and is blessed with twins. And my youngest daughter is bright but she still comes up sometimes with anger. She can't take the pain; she has a difficult time with bad things or tragic events.

DB: Most of the survivors married fellow survivors; that is just the general impression that I have had; yet you did not. What about your brothers?

AG: Well, two of my brothers did, but the rest of them did not. Number one, when we survived, nobody wanted to have anything to do with us. We were too weak, poor, and terribly sick. And when we went into the refugee centers and got together among ourselves, looking for a home, looking for some haven, most of the time people wanted nothing to do with us — we had no decent clothes, we looked terrible, and most of the people would have nothing to do with us — even some of our relatives. Some of them were not too good to us. Even those relatives that had gotten people out to this country, some of their children were objecting. They thought we might take something from them and they were not nice to us at all. So there has been a lot of resentment on that part. We were fortunate that our family — our uncles, aunts, and cousins in America — were so wonderful to us.

DB: When it comes to marriage, it seems to me that, as a survivor, the camp experience marked you as a person, and that it would be easier — or maybe not — just to be married to someone who had been through the same experience so that you didn't have to explain anything.

AG: Yes, but we wanted to get away from it. We wanted to be just like any other ordinary person. I didn't look for anyone. In fact, when we were in the orphanages, I got a job right away. I used to get up at 4:00 in the morning to hitchhike in order to get a job somewhere in Scotland. And, when they moved me to Burnley, I walked for miles to get a bus in order to go to work in a knitting mill. Then when I came to London, I had no money for street cars or anything like that, so I got up very early in order to go to work and learn the language and learn a trade.

DB: Certainly the girls used to pursue you, at least according to the book.

AG: I wanted to be just an ordinary guy, an ordinary Jew. And I wanted to be a good guy and give back for the kindness that I was shown by a lot of people. That yes, I can be a good man, and yes, I can give back some of it. I was very appreciative of how nice the people were to me. When I was in Youngstown, and especially when I moved to Atlanta, I met people that were simply angelic — they were wonderful.

DB: Still, did Linda not ask questions? Did she not....

AG: No, no. We had an understanding that I didn't want to talk about it. She was a young girl and all she knew was that I was a successful businessman, and yes that I was a survivor, but that didn't mean more to her than that I was a good person and that she wanted to be married to me.

DB: That's interesting, Ursula [my wife] had an aunt who was wonderful. She went through the camps and wound up at Bergen-Belsen at the end. She came out in the war and moved to Switzerland where she became a leading child psychoanalyst in Zurich, which was one of the great capitals of psychoanalysis. She went to her training analyst, where all psychoanalysts have to go for training, and said, "I will talk to you about anything, but I will not talk to you about the camps; take it or leave it." She too wanted to give back what she had. Tanta Rutchen worked primarily with abused children in Switzerland; the really tough cases were sent to her. She too just handled her being a survivor by saying, "I am not going to handle it" or "I am going to encapsulate it" — until somebody came along who would get it out of her and then she would talk about it. She talked about it to me.

AG: Well, my sister, Rosalyn, was liberated in Bergen-Belsen. She went through the Auschwitz camps. It is quite understandable. I can understand why Ursula's aunt said she didn't want to talk about it but I was no different, until Father Malone who later on became a Cardinal. He and I were very close and he got it out of me by forcing it out of me, and I could never say no to him. He was such a fine fine man, a fine human. Unfortunately, it was very difficult for me to understand how I could talk about it because I had it buried in the back of my mind for so long. I didn't want to believe that it had really happened to me because I had suddenly been exposed to decent people all the time. But, ever since the Hungarians had taken over our area — I was eleven years old — I was exposed to nothing but vicious, hateful people just because I was born a Jew. One time, I even asked my friend, Yonchi — my closest friend who became an SS Obersturmführer — and I said, "Yonchi, you and I were the closest friends. How can you after all these years of being my best friend — you even slept with me on the haystack — how come you suddenly hate me after you go to the Hitler youth meeting?" He said, "Oh, yes, but *du bist ein Jude* ("you are a Jew") and Hitler tells us in the movement that the Jews are our *Ungluck*, that the Jews are our misfortune." I had a very difficult time with that. And they attacked me coming back from *Cheder* (Jewish school), my brother and me. I was taught by my Father that when someone lifts up their hand to you, you lift up your legs and run like hell. And when you can't run, he taught us to make sure that person will never attack you again. Believe me, every time I had to fight back or throw a stone at one of these kids I was very much in pain, as though I was being hit, but I had no choice because it was the only way I was finally able to run away.

DB: I am sure you have been asked this question many hundreds of times and that is: Where do you think you got the strength from just to continue?

AG: Well, it came probably from the kind of background I was raised in. We had an angelic Mother who only saw good things in people, who always was very calm and giving. While we were in the ghetto, and even before the ghetto and especially on the train when they took us to Auschwitz, she kept on demanding from me, "Yankele, promise me that, no matter what, you will survive." I didn't know what she was talking about. I thought to myself what is she talking about? I am a young man, why shouldn't I want to survive? Why shouldn't I want to grow old in life? I think she just had a premonition that very few of us were going to be able to make it because she saw how mean these Hungarian and German soldiers and the general public especially the Ukrainians were.

DB: You think that it was really her command for you to survive that gave you strength?

AG: It was her pleading and the command from her and Father. But it was really a commitment on my part that I could never say no to her, that I committed myself that absolutely no matter what, "Mother, I am going to try." I kept that uppermost on my mind during the worst times that no matter what I would survive. I was too many times out of it and I thought, "Oh, wait. I committed myself. I can't give up."

DB: Viktor Frankel, who was also in the camp and was a psychoanalyst, says in his book *Man's Search for Meaning* that, insofar as your survival depended on you — and a large part of it didn't, it depended on fate — insofar as it depended on you, people who had some sense of loyalty, orientation, or purpose (as he calls it) were the people who managed to hold themselves together. For some of them, it was a word from parents or, for others, a commitment to God. For still other people, it was something else, as was his case. He made up his mind that he was going to write the book which he had brought with him to the camp and which they had taken away from him. For some people, it was revenge; for others it was other things. But there was always some moral commitment that made people survive.

AG: It had to be that because, quite frankly, in order to survive the hunger, the abuse, the pain, and the torture by fellow humans, it had to go way beyond just wanting to live. You had to have a commitment that goes very deep, and you were so determined no matter how much you suffered. You know we talked about the toilets as an example. Just to go and sit there. Just to sit down on the stone and concrete for a second. It was ice cold. And because your body was a little bit warm and it was so cold, you stuck to it. Many people's skin came off. You didn't have much blood to bleed but the pain was unbearable

DB: I truly want to ask this question too: How is it after all these experiences that you can still believe in the goodness of people?

AG: I was brought up that way. Mother was that way. Father was that way. My grandparents were that way. For the most part, my brothers and sisters feel the same way. And I was very fortunate that I met a lot of very good people in my life — good, caring people. There was a non-Jewish family that wanted to adopt me in Prague, Czechoslovakia, after the war and a family that wanted to adopt me in Budapest before when I ran away and, when I was taken to England after liberation, I had several families that wanted to adopt me.

DB: How did that erase what you had seen in the way of cruelty and inhumanity?

AG: It doesn't erase it. No, it doesn't erase it, but it proves that there are a lot of good people in this world. When the good people's actions are brought forward, it will overcome some of the bad people's deeds. It is only if you are under the fascism, communism, or a dictatorship that people have become conditioned to stop being humans. But for the most part, there are good people. I have met some unbelievably wonderful people and I've surrounded myself with a lot of wonderful people. I see that more than I see the hateful things which some not-so-nice people do.

DB: I'm sure this is a question you've been asked too: The price of being Jewish went up a great deal in our century; it skyrocketed out of the ordinary person's pocketbook, if you want to put it that way. I am sure you have met, as I have met, people who are Jewish who say, "After hearing about the holocaust, I would rather not be Jewish," and they either drifted off into nothing, with no identification, or some of them converted to Christianity or elsewhere. How is it that you have been able to keep faith with being Jewish in spite of the horrible price that you had to pay and that you know that others had to pay?

AG: Well, at the beginning after liberation I couldn't go inside a synagogue. I didn't believe there was a God. I thought God was Satan. But then I started noticing more of the decent people. Suddenly I started to realize how lucky I am. We have six brothers and one sister who survived whereas, in my family alone in Lavik, out of eleven children, only one survived. And out of eight other children in Lavik, only one survived. Another relative, our Mother's brother who had eight children, only two survived, and only one is still alive. Of my Mother's sister's family in Vari none of them survived — the parents and children were killed in Auschwitz. As a matter of fact, the Ackerman family, our neighbors, had eight or nine children and only two of them survived. I could go on and on. Very, very few of our family and friends survived, and yet in our family six brothers and one sister are alive.

DB: Why did not the survivors just stop being Jewish? I'm not talking about atheism; just stop being Jewish?

AG: When I was in London — a family (the Ralphs) wanted to adopt us and she insisted that I go to the synagogue with them and I absolutely didn't want to go. I found every excuse and finally on Friday night I told her that I didn't want to go to the synagogue, and she just made us go. So I went to please her because I couldn't say no to her.

Then I came to the United States and again I didn't want to go, but my uncle made us. He even made us join the synagogue, and still I kept away. Especially when I was in the Army during the Korean War, I had a couple of bad experiences. When I was stationed in St. Louis, they wouldn't let me in the synagogue on Yom Kippur and Rosh Hashana because I did not have a ticket. But once I started getting my life back together, started working in our own business, and making some money, there was no doubt about it that I wanted to become part of my religious community and its activities. So I joined a synagogue. And when I got married, of course, I started to keep a kosher home and have kept a kosher home since that time. I'm not glatt kosher necessarily, but I'm kosher at home. And I wanted to bring my children up Jewish and, thank God, I have succeeded in that.

I do not blame God for what happened to us because He didn't do the killing. He didn't do the torture. It was fellow humans that did it, and for me to blame God for something like that would be wrong. I feel very blessed, and no doubt very lucky, that I have become much closer to my religion and my people. I belong to a Lubavitcher shul (synagogue) in Miami that my stepson is president of and I enjoy it. I read the translation when I don't understand the prayers. I get a lot out of it. I think about how happy I feel that my Father, Mother, and grandparents would have wanted me to be this way, especially now that I am able to practice my religion. And I am happy that I wouldn't be a terrible disappointment to them. I feel very lucky that I was able to get involved in the charitable work — whether it is for the Jewish Federation, on the Board of ORT, or as Chairman for Israel Bonds, or with the orphanages — whatever it is, I feel very lucky that I am given the opportunity to give back a little of the blessings I was bestowed with.

DB: One could say in reading your book and following your life story that the most painful, or the second most painful, moment in your life, would be the loss of your son. It happened so suddenly and so tragically. How did you manage to survive that?

AG: Oh, well, David, to describe it is impossible. Your precious son that you have all your hopes, prayers and wishes on, the one you have built your whole life on, and suddenly in an accident with farm equipment, he is lifeless, his blood is soaking into the red clay. — There is no way to describe the pain it has caused me, and has been with me ever since. Every time I see a blond boy, especially somebody tall, a young boy his age, I am petrified — because that is the age I was when I was taken away to the extermination camps. There is just no way to describe it. Nor is there any way to describe losing my beloved wife, Linda, when she became a victim of a rape murderer. No one can ever replace her. Yet, I have been very fortunate and I am married to a wonderful woman. Daisy is an angel, very caring, and she knows my feelings — we have talked about it. Even now any time I go someplace I see something of Linda because she was a wonderful mother, a very caring and very involved woman. Nothing can ever replace either my wife or my son. I don't care. I love my grandchildren, I love my children, I love my friends' children, and as you know I love your son, Benji, as much as I loved my son, Benji. But that still can't replace him — not even your Benji can take his place, he will always be precious in my heart. You just don't replace anything like the wonderful son I lost, and you don't overcome that kind of tragedy easily. You can't ever overcome it. Yes, you can learn to accept the fact that it happened — I can't change it — I can't bring him back — and I can't bring my wife back....

DB: Is it silly of me to ask whether it is more difficult to overcome the loss of your son or the experience of the camp?

AG: They are totally different, horrific, experiences — totally different. You don't overcome either of them. You just have to be strong, learn to live with it, and go on with life. You cannot replace your son. You cannot take away the suffering that you endured in the camp or the meanness of fellow humans. That is probably even more difficult than the suffering itself — to remember how vicious, mean, and inhumane humans can become. It is very, very difficult and very painful to think about. How can I ever replace my son and Linda? Yes, when I had your Benji close by and living with me, he was like my son. It was great and I loved him, I still love him, and always will love him. And the fact that he is in New York now, I miss him terribly. But yet, at the same time, he has got to go on with his life. I feel the same with my children and grandchildren — I love them, I adore them — but they have to go on with their lives and you have to let them develop and lead their lives.

DB: It seems that you have done a great deal to put your life back together again after the camps, and you have done a great deal to put your life together again after the death of your son and after the death of Linda. Part of that, it seems to me, has been assuming a kind of mission, a kind of purpose, of getting out there and telling your story, of sharing the story of your life.

AG: Yes, I don't know whether I would call it a mission. I feel a responsibility, in spite of everything I might have accomplished with myself, which I never expected. I have lived a long life, much, much longer than I could have expected, in spite of my health problems, resulting from starvation, abuse, beatings, etc. that all of my brothers have had. But we are still around, still able to function and, yes, I feel a moral obligation, as well as a duty, to give back to this world, to make sure, at least try to make sure, that no viciousness and no meanness and no holocaust will ever occur again, whether in this country or anywhere else in the world — because we are all humans and we are very, very fallible. Some humans, at the drop of a hat, could become haters instead of being lovers and kind. So we have to work hard to make sure that not only this generation, but the future generation will not experience another hateful or tragic event or let a hateful person take over almost the whole world.

DB: I can't think of anything better to end on than that note.

AFTERWORD

It is inevitable. By now I should no longer be surprised at my reaction to his story or, for that matter, moved by it. After all, I have heard it for eight consecutive years and, for each of those eight consecutive years, it has been the same. Every year I am not only deeply moved, but I am also surprised by my reaction.

I have been teaching a course on the history of the Holocaust ever since I arrived at Emory University in 1993. I had taught the same course for many years prior to coming to here. From the very first time in 1977, I have devoted one class session to a talk by a survivor. In the early years I had to convince survivors to come. Most of them were not used to being asked to come and speak, particularly at a university. Many were not accustomed to telling their story to anyone but their family. If one survivor was truly reluctant to speak, I did not press the matter but tried to find another. I have been intent on doing this because I believe that the voice of the individual, the person who can speak in the first person singular, is a unique addition to any course, particularly a course on the Holocaust.

As a historian, I recognize that survivors often are not conversant with the historical detail or context of their experiences. Memories can fade over time. They can only describe one infinitesimally small piece of a vast and ugly mural. Therefore, we can not write definitive history based on the story of one or even a small handful of survivors. We need a convergence of evidence, of which survivor testimony can be a part, in order to understand the whole story. These shortcomings notwithstanding, survivors can personalize the story in a way that no document can. Moreover, we will not have such voices available for Holocaust courses for long. Most survivors are now in their seventies and eighties. It is not uncommon to hear survivors say, "First we used to meet at weddings and births. Now we meet a funerals." I have long been determined that, as long as it was possible to do so, the voice of the survivor be included in the curriculum of the courses I teach.

When I arrived at Emory my good friend and colleague, David Blumenthal, suggested I invite Alex Gross to my class. New in town and not knowing many people, I was glad for the recommendation and called Alex, who readily agreed. As he recounted his story of his boyhood in Hungary and his time in Auschwitz and other camps, I listened intently. His experience was not dramatically different from the stories I had heard from other Hungarian survivors. That, however, did not matter. It was his story. I immediately discerned from his manner of recounting the tale that he had told this story many times before. Nonetheless, I was touched by his straightforward and almost "naive" style of remembering it. He added no theological, philosophical, or psychological embellishments. He did not address the question, "Why?" It was just a simple — and quite terrifying — story. The fact that all his siblings survived and were reunited shortly after the war seemed to take a bit of the edge off the pain of the experience. At the least, he was not left completely alone as were so many other survivors.

Then Alex turned to his post war story. When he briefly mentioned his only son's death and his wife's rape and murder, I shuddered in pain. How could one man handle so much? Sitting in the front row of the large classroom, I did not want to turn around and see how the class was responding. My face was stained with tears and, for some irrational reason, I did not want the students to see that I was crying. Soon, however, as I heard sniffles coming from the rows behind me, I recognized that I was not the only one so affected. Though I was deeply moved by everything he told us, the most compelling moment was yet to come. Towards the end of the class session Alex looked at the over one hundred privileged students sitting in front of him at this highly competitive and respected institution of learning and said, "I consider myself blessed. I have a wonderful family and wonderful friends. I have been lucky enough in my business that I have the means to help others and to do some good in the world. I have beautiful daughters and beautiful grandchildren. God has given me all this and God has blessed me with good health. What more could a man ask for?" Looking intently at the students who, despite the fact that the class session was officially over, had, miraculously, not moved from their chairs, he said, "I have only one thing to ask of you. Appreciate what you have and work to do good for others. Thank you for listening."

Alex has continued to come to my classes and to tell his story. Every year when students turn in their class evaluations, many among them cite Alex's presentation as one of the significant moments of the semester. One of the consistent themes was the impact his story had on how they view their own lives: "Mr. Gross's speech will stay with me forever — and it is not solely because of the content — we have all heard survivor's tales; I have heard survivors speak before. The part that struck me the most was the fact that all this happened to this man and yet, he still was thankful for life. Mr. Gross could easily have been embittered by the world, by the lack of response of the Allies; however he has chosen to carry himself in a way that as a person I would like to live." "Alex Gross's outlook on life also allowed me to uncover a new perspective on my own life. After hearing about his hardships during and after the Holocaust, he still counted each day as a blessing." "As a major in anthropology and human biology, I am constantly studying human nature. Mr. Gross's story taught me so much about the strength of the human spirit. I've never known anyone who has seen and experienced so much hardship and is still able to have such a positive outlook."

After I heard Alex's presentation for the first time, when he finished and thanked the class for listening, I wanted to rise and say, "Alex, thank *you* for telling." I could not. The students' applause soon filled the awkward void. Now, with the publication of this memoir, those who have not had the opportunity to hear Alex tell his story can say, "Thank you for writing it down."

Deborah E. Lipstadt
Dorot Professor of Holocaust and
Modern Jewish Studies
Erev Pesach, 2001
Atlanta

NOTES

1. It is my custom, for ethical reasons, to use the word "shoah" and not "holocaust," and not to capitalize words such as "shoah," "holocaust," "nazi," "anti-semitism," etc. Alex prefers "Holocaust," and does capitalize; I have respected this in the main body of the text.

2. *Emory Studies in the Holocaust: An Interfaith Inquiry*, ed. S. Hanover and D. Blumenthal, vol. 2 (Atlanta: Emory University: 1988) pages 8-31. The tape is in the Emory University Library, Special Collections.

3. Most are still available from the Fred R. Crawford Witness to the Holocaust Project at Emory.

4. "Buchenwald: Liberator Meets Survivor," Fred R. Crawford Witness to the Holocaust Project (Atlanta, GA, Emory University: 1980).

5. On the banality of both good and evil, see D. Blumenthal, *The Banality of Good and Evil: Moral Lessons from the Shoah and Jewish Tradition* (Washington, DC, Georgetown University Press: 1999).

6. D. Blumenthal, *Facing the Abusing God: A Theology of Protest* (Louisville, KY, Westminster / John Knox: 1993).

7. Published first in *Emory Studies*, vol. 2, unnumbered pages at the beginning of the book.

8. Ed. note: Alex's name was "Yankele" (in Yiddish) or "Yaakov" (Jacob, in Hebrew). He was, however, the seventh boy in the family — Alex, five brothers, and a half brother — and he recalls that the custom was to honor families who had seven boys (the girls didn't count) with financial and other gifts. It was also the custom to give the seventh boy the name

"Alexander" which, for Alex, became his middle name. When he moved to England, he adopted "Alex" as his western name. According to Alex, "Alexander" was used so as to render homage to a famous Czech leader. I have not been able to trace this custom, "Alexander" being a Russian not a Czech name. One source tells me, however, that for a brief period after World War I, there was a "petit entente" between Czechoslovakia, Romania, and Yugoslavia. The king of Yugoslavia was named "Alexander."

9. Ed. note: Throughout this section, Alex, with the support of his siblings and friends, refers to Germans but he usually means the schwäbisch ethnic Germans of his village. There were very few actual Germans in Hungary at this time. Alex pronounces *schwah-bisch* and I have left that in the text, though the correct form is *schway-bisch* with an umlaut.

10. Ed. note: The local ethnic Germans who, after 1943, were recruited by the SS were taken to Germany for training and then posted all over Europe; they were not formed into local units. The round-up and then the deportation of the Jews which Alex describes was, thus, carried out by the Hungarian "gendarmerie," the Hungarian militia, which did not speak German. German forces formally took charge of the trains of deportees at the border of Slovakia. Nonetheless, Alex, here and in the next chapters, very clearly reports here having heard German as the language of command and, at points, maintains that SS troups were present. I do not know how to reconcile this contradictory evidence.

11. See above, note 10.

12. See above, note 10.

13. Ed. note: A *kapo* was a foreman or forewoman of a labor detachment or a prisoner in charge of a specific labor function, such as hard labor, supply, or record-keeping. The term is now often used generically for any prisoners in positions of power over other prisoners. As a matter of ethical judgement, the word is not capitalized. It is not in italics because it is common English usage in shoah related material.

14. Ed note: Alex cannot, of course, have known on arrival who the doctor was who conducted the selection. Dr. Mengele was the most famous of the infamous doctors who conducted these selections.

15. Ed note: A *blockaeltester* or "block elder" was a prisoner who had responsibility for prisoners sleeping in a barrack block. As a matter of ethics, the word is not capitalized though the original German is preserved because Alex remembers it that way.

16. Ed. note: There was no known formal incentive system for killing Jews despite rumors to that effect.

17. Ed. note: I.G. Farben's business at Auschwitz/Monowitz was the creation and production of synthetic rubber. Rubber is vital for any moving vehicle from jeeps to airplanes and also is necessary for parts for a variety of war machinery, including the machines to make war machinery. There were numerous plants established in the various subcamps of Monowitz and at Monowitz itself owned by various other companies that produced articles ranging from airplane parts and tank parts to anti-aircraft weapons and munitions. Alex has conflated these.

18. Ed. note: The usual estimate for the maximum population of Buna is 22,000, about 10,000 of whom were sent back to Auschwitz I or II where they were gassed or died.

19. Ed. note: *Muselman* (plural *Muselmänner*) is the term used for those who had given up. They walked around without any sense of life or purpose and died very quickly. Some modern thinkers have maintained that this term signifies a new form of *homo sapiens*, invented in our century by the nazis. The actual term means a Muslim and would today be viewed as discriminatory. In modern English one might call them "zombies." As a matter of ethics, this word is always capitalized.

20. Ed. note: This incident is not otherwise documented in Auschwitz and an ordinary SS officer would not be able to initiate such action, though Alex's memory of it is very vivid, as the reader can see. There was a female SS officer at Auschwitz named Maria Mandel who had a reputation of being very cruel, but she is not known to have ventured into the men's camp and committed any atrocities there. The evidence is that human skin was used to make lampshades and other goods at Buchenwald but not at Auschwitz. Nonetheless, Alex's memory is quite clear on this subject. Perhaps, the boys were selected and he had heard that their skin would be so used. On Ilse Koch, "the Bitch of Buchenwald," see below, note 24.

21. Ed. note: The Allies actually bombed the Auschwitz complex on August 20, 1944; on September 13, 1944; and again twice in December, 1944, though they flew many missions over Auschwitz on reconnaissance and to other targets.

22. Ed. note: This is a misremembered moment. The slogan on Buchenwald was "*Zu Jedem den Seinen*," "To each his own."

23. Ed note: Alex is correct that the ovens worked full time; the gas chambers were operated only as needed.

24. Ed. note: Ilse Koch had left Dachau in 1943. On the "Bitch of Auschwitz," see above, note 20.

25. Ed. note: Alex's village was on the linguistic border between Czech and Ukrainian. The village was under Hungarian rule, was settled by ethnic Germans (Schwaben), and populated by Yiddish speaking Jews. Alex, therefore, had a broad, if untrained, language background.

26. Ed. note: There are various reports of stashes of goods taken from concentration camp prisoners which were later discovered by the Allies. One such stash was reported by Maj. Howard McBee of the 1st Army JAG staff on April 29, 1945. Alex may be referring to this. The Property Division of the Office of the Military Governor, United States, would have taken charge of such finds in the American zone and it is unlikely that the goods were turned over to the "German people."

27. Ed. note: On the press, see D. Lipstadt, *Beyond Belief: The American Press and the Coming of the Holocaust* (New York, Free Press: 1986) and R. W. Ross, *So It Was True: The American Protestant Press and the Nazi Persecution of the Jews* (Minneapolis, MN, University of Minnesota Press: 1980). There are many books on American policy and the abandonment of the Jews.

28. Ed. note: See, for instance, B. Bellon, *Mercedes in Peace and War* (New York, Columbia University Press: 1990) and J. Borkin, *The Crime and Punishment of I. G. Farben* (New York, Free Press: 1978).

29. Ed. note: As noted above (note 1) it is my custom, for ethical reasons, never to capitalize the words "nazi," "holocaust," "anti-semitism," etc.